THE
HOUSEBUILDING
BOOK

THE HOUSEBUILDING BOOK

Dan Browne

McGRAW-HILL BOOK COMPANY

New York | San Francisco | St. Louis | Toronto

456789MUMU798765

Library of Congress Cataloging in Publication Data
Browne, Dan.
  The housebuilding book.

  1. House construction—Amateurs' manuals. I. Title.
TH4815.B76   690'.8   73-17076
ISBN 0-07-008486-6
ISBN 0-07-008487-4 (pbk.)

Acknowledgments to:

Bruce Davidson, who took most of the pictures.
Eric Andruseen, who took a few.
Kevin Larmee, who did most of the drawings.
and Debby, who gave me the encouragement I needed.

Contents

INTRODUCTION

My father was a carpenter and I grew up with saws and hammers as toys. At fifteen I worked for a summer on my first house and learned to carry lumber, sweep the site, and go to the store for beer. I resented this less than never being allowed to do anything "skilled," although I knew how to cut rafters and frame a wall. No one bothered to teach me, and the little I learned by watching and listening was a poor substitute for doing.

It wasn't until I was hanging doors and laying brick rather than mixing mortar that my frustration disappeared, but I didn't forget how I'd felt. On the first job I contracted, I showed my "helper" (who also happened to be my girl friend) how to replace rotted cedar shingles and acted as her helper part of the time.

Since that first contract I've built more than a hundred custom houses, two motels, renovated brownstones in Manhattan, a former monastery on Corsica, factories in Paris and San Francisco, and what purports to be the largest gay bar in the world. I have continued to do my share of carrying and cleaning and have always made the transmission of my skills to others an integral part of every job.

I was taught masonry by various masons, wiring by electricians, and similarly learned other building trades. It has been a continuous process—only a couple of months ago a young plumber showed me a way to install a cast-iron waste line that was superior to my way of doing it.

Teaching others has taught me that few people grip and swing a hammer correctly, a fact that takes on a new meaning when you consider that there is a quarter of a ton of nails in the average three-bedroom house. I've learned that the fundamental operation of cutting a board squarely and to length is difficult for most people until they absorb the simple technique of using a power saw and protractor in unison. Throughout the construction process difficulties arise in the course of doing the work. In this book these difficulties are anticipated and their solutions demonstrated.

Frequently these solutions eliminate "skill" from skilled operations. This approach is by no means original—its purpose is to assure quicker completions with more consistent quality and only incidentally to make the work easier. The construction industry itself has been evolving in this direction. A large part of the skills in skilled work has already been removed. The abysmally long apprenticeship programs are now more than ever a "protection" for the journeyman and a source of cheaper labor for the contractor.

When I say that I've built more than a hundred houses, I mean that I personally have done much of the work on all of them. I've never subcontracted any aspect of the carpentry. Except in a few cases, I've done all the foundations, usually alone. I've often subcontracted wiring and plumbing, though occasionally I've been obliged to do part or all of both. In several instances I was unable to hire a mason and built the fireplace myself. Only once did I buy kitchen cabinets. I've usually made them on the site and used the occasion to teach someone else to make them. Most often my crew consisted of two or three people, skilled or unskilled. Four custom houses I built entirely alone from start to finish.

Many times, the unskilled person who started a house with me felt secure enough after its completion to build on his or her own. I'm not implying that these people had learned *all* there was to know, but an adequate level of competence had been attained and they did in fact go on to build houses.

In the winter of 1971, I opened a free building school in the former American Can Company factory in San Francisco. During the following year students constructed a two-story house inside the factory as a means of learning the building trades. Many women were students. None found the work too difficult physically; when a situation that was too demanding did arise, something invariably was being done incorrectly. Performances varied with individuals rather than sex. Several women went on to form a carpenters' cooperative. At last word they were getting all the work they could handle.

My conviction is that anyone can build a house if the determination to do so is there and continues to be there throughout what is certainly a great deal of work. I would not recommend doing this work alone, but only because of the loneliness. Building a house should be a happy experience, and I don't know how that's possible without sharing it.

PRECONSTRUCTION

1

I usually enter the building process at the point when the prospective owner hands me a set of plans and asks me to give him a price. I've probably looked at a thousand plans, since I've examined ten for every house I've gone on to build.

I once made a tentative bid on a cabin without knowing where it was to be built. The owner had drawn the plans himself. He was delighted with my bid and drove me to the proposed area. His wife came along. For the next half hour we climbed a mountainside. The site to be occupied by the structure had a 270-degree view of mountains and valleys covered mainly with evergreens.

The man told me that they'd camped there several times just to see the sunsets. I suppose his wife must have seen my expression since she asked quickly, didn't I think it was a marvelous spot?

I said that I found the view sensational, but were they prepared to climb half an hour each time they came and pay for a helicopter to bring building materials? I didn't mean to be snide. My anger was directed at the real estate shark who had sold them the property.

She said that it was only a few hundred yards to the highway and couldn't I build a road? Any old thing would do since they intended to trade their car for a four-wheel-drive vehicle.

I told her that I didn't own a bulldozer, that the few hundred yards to the highway was a steep incline and any passable road would be several miles long. They later received an estimate of $10,000 from a road builder, more than the cost of the land and cabin combined. They were not able to afford it. Now, years later, the cabin still isn't built and they are still stuck with the land. A brief discussion of feasibility before they bought the land would have stopped the sale. This experience and similar ones have convinced me that builders enter the process later than they should.

I'm not suggesting that all real estate agents and land purchases should be approached with great suspicion. On the contrary, most land is suitable for building with no great hidden costs. However, unsuitable land is sold often enough for the prospective buyer to talk to a local builder about it. This is particularly true in acreage sales where frequently there are substantial additional costs.

◄ ►

The price of a road will vary with its length, obstructions to be removed, grading required, width, and surface. It may cost more than $10,000 or as little as $75, which is what I paid for an 800-foot unsurfaced road in Amagansett. Access is an integral part of building and its cost should be determined before the land is bought. (This should include snow removal. County roads will be plowed free of charge but not private ones.)

Water supply is another consideration that should be dealt with before buying land. The source may be a public or private utility, natural springs, shallow or deep wells, lakes, streams, and very occasionally a river.

Water supplied by a utility will usually be around $50 per year for ordinary household use plus a small initial connection fee.

If the source is natural springs, often found in mountainous areas, a base price of $300 for a gravity system is a reasonable estimate. The cost of the pipe, valves, and fittings needed to bring the water from the springs to the house should be added to this. The local Board of Health will usually analyze a sample for potability.

A stream is often an unreliable source of water since it may diminish to a trickle or dry out after spring runoffs. A stream that flows year-round can be treated similarly to natural springs. Otherwise, special water-storage provisions, such as basement cisterns, must be made. In Vermont, Yugoslavia, and Lesbos I've seen cisterns that were the entire basement of the house. In relatively arid areas, cisterns can be partially supplied by rainwater channeled from the roof.

Fresh water, particularly in coastal areas, is often not far below the ground. I recently installed a complete system for $450. The well was twenty-seven feet deep and the only piece of special equipment I needed was a five-foot length of two-inch pipe and cap, which I used as a jackhammer. However, there is a substantial danger of pollution with shallow wells, especially in populated areas, and the water should be analyzed whether local codes require it or not.

On Long Island, a well seventy feet deep with a brass submersible pump capable of supplying water all year round to four houses cost $2000. Price of identical installations in other areas may vary a great deal, however. Local well-diggers offer deals, sometimes with a guarantee of water and sometimes not. The matter is negotiable and the cost should be part of the decision in buying land.

Electricity is another consideration. If the land is in a populated area, the utility company will supply the necessary poles and make the hook-up for a modest charge.

There is a growing trend throughout the country to use what is called underground service, with the wire from the pole to the house buried in a trench. Some building departments have incorporated this into their codes and made its use mandatory.

I pay $5 per foot for the wire itself, but the added cost for underground service may be anywhere from five hundred to several thousand dollars.

If the area is sparsely populated but with adjacent land already subdivided and likely to be developed, the utility company may try to make the prospective owner pay for the poles initially, then reimburse him as other services are installed. It's negotiable. I've had as many as sixteen poles installed free and other times have been obliged to pay $35 for a single pole. In both instances I was dealing with the same utility company, but different employees were interpreting policy. It is necessary to speak to the person in charge at the local utility to determine what is involved, and this should be done before the land is bought.

In many undeveloped areas, negotiations for the cost of bringing electricity to your house are not possible; you will have to pay a set initial fee. Several thousand dollars is not unusual. Reimbursement plans based on future use by neighboring homeowners are almost always offered.

For remote areas, an alternative home electric-generating system is available. Sears, in particular, offers several, and can be relied upon to determine which system fills your needs best. But this alternative should be used only when the cost of getting electricity from a utility company is absolutely prohibitive.

Some land, such as sections of the Oakland hills, in California, is unstable and building on it precarious. Nevertheless, lots continue to be sold in these areas and houses constructed. If you are interested in building on an attractive site beside a cliff with an excellent view, talk to a local builder or architect. Building departments are notoriously slow to prohibit construction on this type of land and owners energetic about getting rid of their lots.

When the tide is very low on the Fire Island beach, now and then a piece of chimney will appear several hundred feet from the dunes. It marks a former row of houses and evidences the erosion that has occurred during the last fifty or so years. I suppose at least a hundred houses have washed away during this period, but only last summer I built one directly behind the present location of the dune. The owner was fully aware of the risk and had bought $35,000 of federal flood insurance for a premium of $80 per year. However, other people own land on Fire Island that the sea has claimed long ago, and many other beach areas have similar stories.

Some sites, such as the Santa Barbara hills, have a prolonged dry season and are prone to fires. Fire is a significant risk and also a factor to be considered before buying land.

In Florida, I had to go down nine feet through a mucky area before I found an adequate bed to build on. This added substantially to the cost of the house.

In Vermont, massive slabs of granite on the site made the price of excavation five times more than anywhere else I've built.

Land formerly used as a dump and covered lightly with earth creates difficulties and raises costs substantially.

I've heard about sites with underground streams which would require deflection but have never encountered this problem personally.

Other things may be "wrong" with the prospective land, but if it appeals to you the overwhelming odds are that none of these things will make it an impossible site.

The land you are thinking of buying most probably has a number of restrictions on it pertaining to use. These will have been specified by a governmental group called a Zoning Board. Its restrictions are incorporated into the local building codes and have the force of law.

It's not at all unusual to find that in some areas a minimum of two and a half acres of land is required before a building permit for a single-family dwelling will be issued. In an adjoining area, a 30 x 80-foot lot may be sufficient for a twenty-unit apartment building. Most often, the Zoning Board has demarcated all the land under its jurisdiction, established a zone for each segment, and specified the requirements each proposed structure in that zone must fulfill.

◄ ►

At the local Building Department is a map on which these demarcated zones are drawn. Each segment is usually labeled with a letter of the alphabet. If the prospective land lies in Zone A, you will find a description of how land in Zone A may be used in literature available at the Building Department.

The Building Department can only enforce the restrictions promulgated by the Zoning Board and has no authority to change any. It is obliged to refuse a building permit to any applicant whose plans for use do not conform. If, for example, in Zone A all buildings must be set back at least 25 feet from the front property line and you propose to build with a 20-foot set-back, the application for a permit will be denied.

This refusal is not final. You may present your reasons for wanting 20 feet rather than 25 to a Board of Appeals, which usually meets once a month and does have the authority to waive the restriction. The waiver of a restriction is called a variance, and if the Board of Appeals does grant you a variance to build 20 feet from the front property line, the Building Department must issue you a building permit.

Established zones are by no means fixed for all time, and the Zoning Board frequently changes designations—a procedure almost invariably called upgrading. Pressure on the Zoning Board from residents in a certain area may result in changing half-acre minimum building plots to two and a half acres, to keep "undesirables" from building in that area by making it too expensive. Pressure from town officials to rezone an area for commercial reasons is also frequent. Do not place much hope in having the land you buy rezoned, however, unless a significant number of homeowners in your zone also want its designation changed.

◀ ▶

Large numbers of young people have been moving to northern California, southern Oregon, Vermont, and other regions far from urban and populated areas. In southern Oregon alone, a recent estimate was 200,000 young people living on the land. Few have money and even the relatively modest price of land in these regions is too much for any individual. Often a group will pool their money and buy a tract of land with the intention of dividing the tract into lots and selling these lots to repay loans and the balance of purchase price due. At some point, before actual construction begins, the person who holds title to the land will come into contact with the town or county officials having jurisdiction over this land. He learns that the tract cannot be divided unless subdivision requirements are met. These requirements are paved roads to each building plot, a water-supply system, a sewage system, and other things which only a commercial developer with commercial goals can afford. Restrictions on intended use must be determined beforehand. A local lawyer or the town attorney can be relied on for answers.

Sooner or later in the building process, questions concerning zoning, subdividing, access, water, and power will arise—and all have to be answered. The time to answer them is before the land is bought. For the actual purchase, a local lawyer should represent you.

On the deed, the document that proves owner-ship of the land, there will be a description of that land which specifies its location as determined by a licensed surveyor. If the survey was done a long time ago, the corners of the property will probably have concrete markers. The property lines themselves may be delineated by a low mound of earth or stone walls. A sidewalk may have a cross inside a circle chiseled into it to indicate the corners of the property. More recent surveys use lath sticks with ends painted red to show property lines and oak stakes driven into the ground for corners. A nail is driven into the oak stake and this marks the actual corner. By the time you take possession, any or all of these markers may be gone.

A recent survey of a small building lot cost me $75. You will need two surveys, one before and one after the house is built. Hold off until you are ready to build before getting one. The possibility of the stakes being removed will be reduced, and for little or no extra charge the surveyor will also stake the corners of your house.

◀ ▶

After land is bought, the question of what kind of house to build is no longer academic. Most people take this question to an architect for solution. He will determine how many people will occupy the house, the amount of money you intend to spend, your needs in respect to privacy, your ideas about materials and shapes. He will visit the property with you and, with you, select the site. He will then draw plans based on the information you have supplied and these plans will conform to local building codes.

When you appear in the office of an architect, the chances are that you have never dealt with an architect before. You are likely to be unfamiliar with the building process and probably vague about your own needs. In this situation the architect's point of view will be dominant.

Since plans use the special language of architects and builders, the architect will usually construct a model of the proposed house. He will submit this to you for approval, make changes by mutual agreement, then draw the final plans and specifications.

This process often takes several months; at its conclusion, a house designed to your particular needs, desires and pocketbook—a custom house—is ready to be built.

A year ago I submitted a bid of $60,000 to build a house. The prospective owner showed me her contract with the architect. He had agreed that the house he would design would cost a maximum of $47,000. This is not an unusual discrepancy. In fact, I have never built a house where the final cost was even near the architect's estimate; it has always been substantially higher. Nor is my experience unique. Every builder I have ever talked to about this, and there have been many, has had the same experience.

I mention this not to put down architects but because I believe that architects should not be held to their estimates. Only the builder can be held responsible, and it is unfair and unrealistic to expect an architect to know exactly what the proposed house will cost.

The particular house I mention was located on a bay and a room to store a boat was drawn in the plans. However, the owner told me that she did not own a boat, hated them, and had explained this to her architect. This type of misunderstanding doesn't usually occur but what does happen is that the house is in the image of the architect, which may or may not coincide with what the owner had hoped.

I've rarely known an architect to accede to the wishes of the owner when their opinions differed, and have witnessed many confrontations between both sides. The formidable arguments of the architect invariably won, though many times I felt the architect was wrong. Even when it was simply a question of whether the doorknobs were to be brass-plated or brushed aluminum, the owner was rarely humored. I don't intrude into these arguments but have seen that the frustration of the owner was in direct proportion to his ignorance and only knowledge on his part could alter the unequal situation.

The term "custom house" means that the house has been tailored to suit you rather than built first, then offered for sale. In most instances, however, custom houses are almost identical to houses that haven't gone the "custom" route.

Recently I looked over plans for a two-story, four-bedroom custom house. A tapering ramp forty feet long which went from the ground to the front door on the second floor and a glass-enclosed stairwell were the only unique features. All the materials proposed were standard and used in standard ways. I've seen dozens of identical floor plans. Although the architect worked out these plans in the "custom" manner, everything both inside and out, except for the two unique features, was the same as many other "custom" houses.

Although most people are probably not aware of it when they first come to their architect, the plans they will receive from him already exist and essentially the same house has already been built. Since an architect's fee is normally 10 percent of the cost of the house, whereas detailed plans are available elsewhere for $35, I would explore this alternative if you are not interested in uniqueness.

To me, an architect's principal function is originality of design, which includes using available materials in innovative ways and developing new materials. If you wish to see and live in an environment you haven't experienced, by all means take the architect route. (I find it interesting that the two most original houses I've built were both conceived by a designer working for an architectural firm rather than by an architect.)

If you decide to work without an architect, you should be prepared for the fact that in planning a house you must choose between a variety of windows, doors, floors, etc. Making an intelligent choice presupposes a knowledge of your options. Acquiring this knowledge is time-consuming and often tedious. In choosing tile for the bathroom, for example, its size, color, etc., must be specified. Deciding on this one item will involve trips to places that display and sell tile, comparing costs, etc. Similar decisions will have to be made on hundreds of items.

One 2600-square-foot house I built was constructed from plans which were purchased for $35. The owners spent several weeks looking at renderings of different houses, floor plans, and elevations. They selected the one most closely suited to their needs. They were both well versed in construction and together we made all the changes they desired.

If you decide to design the house yourself, either by buying and altering existing plans or developing your own concept, you may still want to have an architect or engineer examine your work for omissions and mistakes and then do your final drawings. I have built a number of houses where the owners followed this route. In this sort of situation, the fee for examining and drawing the plans is usually under $500.

You will need at least four duplicate sets of complete plans. These will include a plot plan that shows the location of the house in respect to the property; a foundation plan, which specifies the manner in which the house will be supported; a floor plan, which shows how the interior will be divided and what the various rooms will be; four elevations, which are exterior views of the house from north, south, east, and west; a section, which is a portion of the exterior of the house stripped away to show the various structural members behind it and their dimensions; a plumbing schematic, which indicates the piping; and an electrical schematic showing the proposed wiring. The information conveyed by these drawings will by no means cover all the specific things that will be in the finished house, nor should total coverage be attempted. Any set of plans in which every detail is specified does not take into account availability of materials and this type of inflexibility invariably makes for a costlier house.

On the other hand, it is far easier to change something on a plan than redo it in the structure, and all major decisions should be made in terms of specific needs.

I have never built a house where the result was exactly as the plans had indicated. It is difficult to envision all the components from plans and inevitably, as construction proceeds, new improvements are indicated, although care should be taken about those which involve structural changes.

Once something is built, I would strongly advise that it be left as is. The cost of a house goes up or down not so much with any one particular item but with an accumulation of items, and redoing already-finished work raises costs substantially.

The best approach to any plan is one of flexibility—where the builder can say, for example, that the cost of cedar shingles is very high and what about using cedar siding instead? I did this one year when the price of cedar shingles was outrageous. The owner said, "Why not use shakes?" We did use shakes, and this one item for the exterior of the house meant a difference of four hundred dollars. Price of materials and availability is a very definite reality in construction, and plans should acknowledge that reality.

◄ ►

You must now prepare yourself for the nightmare of dealing with Building Departments. One of my typically frustrating experiences occurred on Long Island when I went to get a Certificate of Occupancy for a house I'd built. This document certifies that the house has passed all inspections, conformed to all codes, and is approved for occupancy. The bank will not release the final mortgage payment without it, and the owner must have it before moving in legally.

I inquired at the information desk where to find the clerk who handled this. I was directed to a large room near the end of a corridor; there I learned that the clerk had been moved from that room several weeks earlier. None of the people knew his new location.

I went back to the information desk. The receptionist said she had been on the job only a few days. She made two calls and redirected me.

The clerk was away on a coffee break. I waited about twenty minutes, then asked another employee when she expected him back. She looked at her watch and thanked me for reminding her that it was time for her own coffee break.

I went across the hall and asked if anyone knew where the clerk who handled Certificates of Occupancy had gone. I was told I was in the records section and to inquire at the information desk.

I explained that I had already been to the information desk twice and that the Certificate of Occupancy clerk was not at his desk.

I was told that, unless I had business with the records section, I could not be helped.

I heard voices in an adjoining room. A robust woman was teaching a rather reluctant building inspector how to do the samba. I waited in the doorway until a pause and asked where I could find the Certificate of Occupancy clerk. The woman said that she was the clerk.

I followed her to her desk and gave her the armload of papers I was carrying. She went into an adjoining room. Half an hour later I went into the room and asked her what had happened?

"Oh yes," she said, "you want a C.O." She returned my papers and told me I would first have to go to the main room and see the applications clerk. Since I had been waiting, she led me there.

The new clerk glanced through my papers and stopped at the survey which showed the location of the house on the property. He returned my papers and said that no certificate could be issued since the house was only five feet from the side property line and fifteen feet was the minimum set-back in that zone.

I handed the papers back to him and said a variance had been granted for the shorter set-back. He asked me for the number of the variance. I said I didn't know the number. He returned the papers and said in that case nothing could be done.

I said some rude things, which merely caused another delay. However, the disturbance brought the chief clerk to the counter. I told him about the variance and the name of the owner who had secured it. He looked into a file and found a paper from the Board of Appeals which corroborated what I'd said. However, the number of the variance was not on this paper. The chief clerk said he could not understand why there was no number on it. He phoned a superior, then telephoned the Board of Appeals. About fifteen minutes later, the number of the variance was found and transmitted by a clerk of the Board of Appeals.

The chief clerk and the applications clerk discussed whether they could accept information over the phone or must insist it be in writing. The chief clerk decided to accept the number that had been given by the Board of Appeals but requested the Board to write a covering letter.

No record of a final plumbing inspection could be found. Fortunately I had seen the man who had made the final plumbing inspection. I ran into another room and brought him back to the counter.

The clerk and inspector got into an argument about whether the inspection card was misplaced in the files or had never been turned in. The chief clerk said there was nothing to be done right then and I would have to wait until the files were searched and the missing card found. It had to be in the files, he said to me, since the inspector was certain he had turned it in.

The inspector said that I should not be made to wait if the fault lay with the department. He suggested that a duplicate card be filled out which he would sign and to hell with the missing one. This necessitated a phone call to the deputy chief of the Building Department. The deputy chief arrived with his assistant. After a prolonged discussion, the deputy chief agreed to the inspector's proposal.

The same sort of things went on and on. Needless to say, I did not get the Certificate of Occupancy that day since a new regulation prohibited giving this document to the builder in person. It would have to be mailed to me or given to the owner.

I was told to expect it the following day. Three weeks later, the owner got it in the mail.

My only suggestion in dealing with Building Departments is to resign yourself to the fact that getting a building permit will intentionally or unintentionally be made to seem as difficult as possible.

First go to the Building Department which has jurisdiction over the property and get a list of what it requires you to submit before issuing a building permit. Do not rely on one person's information, but question several. (Nonetheless, by the time you comply, there's no guarantee that there won't be new requirements.)

The following is what will *probably* be needed before a building permit will be issued and you can legally begin construction:

1. A survey of your property by a licensed surveyor; the surveyor to give all other necessary information on it.

2. A copy of an application for waste disposal approved by the local Board of Health.

3. The street name and number of the proposed house.

4. A copy of the deed to the land as proof of ownership.

5. Three copies of the Building Department's application for a permit that you have filled in, with your notarized signature. This application includes such items as the name and address of the owner, name of plumber, electrician, etc., plus information about the proposed house which is already specified on the plans.

6. Three sets of complete plans.

7. An approved application for the proposed plumbing work with name and license number of the plumber. (This is not always required, especially in less populated areas.)

8. An approved application for the proposed electrical work with name and license number of the electrican. (The plumbing and electrical applications are approved by the same Building Department.) A licensed electrician is frequently not a requirement. In some areas the Building Department does not make electrical inspections. This is done by an inspector from a Board of Underwriters, an insurance group. He will examine the work done and, if approved, issue an Underwriter's Certificate. The Building Department and bank will accept this certificate as proof that the electrical codes have been complied with.

9. Three blank checks to pay for fees. The total cost is likely to be under a hundred dollars.

When all requirements are met, a permit will be issued. This is a card or sheet of paper with a number stamped on it that corresponds to the number stamped on the application. It will also have a date on it, and construction can begin any time within six months. (Usually the permit can be renewed if work has not begun within that period.)

The permit must be displayed in a conspicuous place at the site. A set of plans will be stamped with the seal of the building department; this set must be presented to a building inspector on demand.

Along with the permit, several post cards will also be issued. These will have printed on them *rough carpentry completed, plumbing first inspection,* etc. Each card corresponds to the completion of a stage of construction. As these are completed, the card is mailed to the Building De-partment and an inspector will come to examine the completed work. If it is satisfactory, the work may continue. If not, a violation of the code will be posted and the unsatisfactory work must be corrected.

When a Building Department approves a set of plans, it does not assume responsibility for those plans. If there is a violation it must be removed, despite the original approval. In one house I built, plans were initially approved despite the fact that the windows in two bedrooms violated a section of the code which specified that these windows had to be no higher than 42 inches above the finished floor and of a minimum size in order to provide an alternate fire exit in rooms with only one door. I was aware of this, but it was a section of the code everyone had ignored for twenty years and there were at least a dozen houses nearby with the same violation. In this case, the Building Department later decided to enforce this particular item and I was obliged to make the windows conform to the code.

I've found it impossible to do renovation work in New York without bribing not only inspectors, but police, utility company employees, and many others in a position to enforce ridiculous items in the codes. However, in no other area of the country have I had even a hint that anyone was looking for a bribe, nor have I experienced any harassment that was due to any cause other than the idiocy of some of the building codes themselves.

For some reason, most of the building inspectors I've encountered have been retired plumbers. I've found them to be reasonable men with a derivative knowledge of construction and a point of view that regards a house merely as something that surrounds the plumbing. Being part of a bureaucracy as entrenched as any in our society, they have been easier to deal with than most officials.

◄ ►

The most common house in America is a rectangle with an inverted **V** roof, or gable. Each chapter of this book demonstrates a step in the construction of such a house; the order of the chapters is the actual sequence of construction.

The latter part of each chapter provides additional information relevant to the work covered, solutions to problems that arise in trying to master work techniques, and alternative means of building a particular item without the specific tools I use. My orientation is primarily toward inexperienced people who are likely to encounter difficulties and be without the more expensive tools.

The particular house in this book has been built everywhere in the country. It's neither the easiest nor the most difficult to construct. Absorbing the methods used will enable most people to build a good many other types of houses, since these methods are directly applicable to many designs.

The way in which the interior of the house has been divided is a common one. I have used it because it permits a wide exposure to many construction details; knowledge of these can be used in a large variety of interior designs.

The tools I recommend are those which have performed best for me. I don't mean to preclude other makes, which may very well be as good or better.

In the choice of materials I have been guided by considerations of economy and value rather than by aesthetics.

The prices of materials that I give are what I paid for them in late 1973 as a contractor. However, these prices are volatile in an upward direction—a 30 percent rise occurred during the course of writing this book. With this in mind, it's prudent to contract to buy all materials *before* construction begins.

The names of items in the house are those used on the job. Whenever more than one name is used for the same item, I try to give both. However, those used in this book will be understood by lumber companies, architects, and all others involved.

The methods and techniques that I demonstrate have evolved over the course of more than thirty years of building houses. Some differ from those used by other builders. Most of these differences are the result of my having deliberately changed an accepted practice in favor of one I believed to be better, and only those which have been verified in practice are retained in this book. If a competent professional offers an alternative to a practice I use, weigh the two and choose the more promising. Also, approach with extreme caution the advice and suggestions of well-meaning friends, truck drivers who deliver material, passersby, and above all of those with a little bit of knowledge and even less experience, who seem to be the most articulate.

I have been asked many times whether I consider it practical for a person with little or no experience to attempt to build a house. My answer has always been Yes, and this judgment has been confirmed many times.

None of the work involves a capacity greater than that of most people. Of course the more dextrous will complete the work more quickly. Those less so will take longer, but both have the means of achieving a good house. In either case, a great deal of work is involved. If this book illuminates that work and makes it easier to execute, its purpose is accomplished.

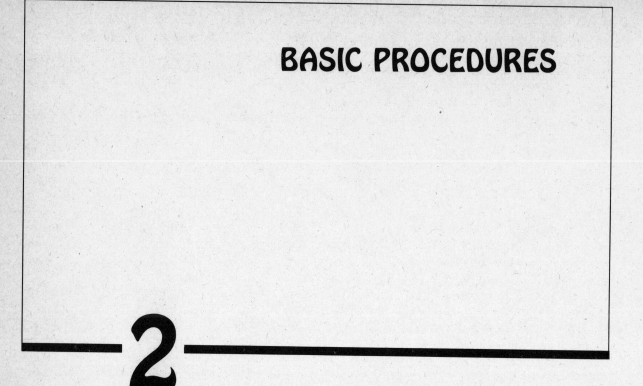

BASIC PROCEDURES

The bulk of the work in building a house involves measuring and marking various materials, cutting and then fastening them. Most of the material is wood in one form or another. The cutting is done mainly with power saws and the fastening with appropriate nails. These acts are performed over and over again from start to finish and the manner in which they are done is of fundamental importance, since the final appearance will depend on accuracy and the time required to complete the house will in large measure depend on the speed with which they are done.

A single cut with a power saw takes a few seconds but this act is performed thousands of times; the difference between a good technique and a bad one results in saving a good deal of time and effort. The same holds true for measuring, marking, and nailing.

Measuring

For measuring distances more than 16 feet, I use a Lufkin 100-foot white-faced tape. A metal arm at the end of the tape pivots at a right angle to hold the tape at one end so that it may be unwound and used by one person. When rewinding the tape, I press it between my left middle and index finger to remove dirt that would otherwise enter the tape's case.

For lengths shorter than 16 feet, I use a 16-inch Lufkin power-lock tape.

When a member (the general term used for any item in the building) is already in position and the tape measure cannot be hooked onto an end, I use a 6-foot Lufkin folding ruler with a brass extension. I also use it for measuring distances up from the floor, down from the ceiling, or laterally from fixed members. The extension is convenient for measuring inside over small distances between two fixed pieces.

For longer distances, such as between two walls, I use two long straight 1 x 2s. I extend their ends to each wall and mark the opposite end of one of the second piece. This is particularly convenient when installing moldings or determining the distance

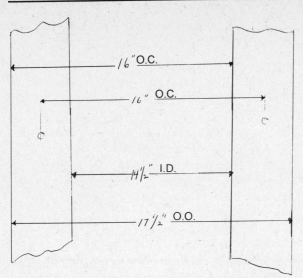

Standard measurements

between floors and ceiling.

Whenever practical, I do not use a ruler at all, but simply place the material to be cut in the position it is to be installed and mark. This eliminates a step and reduces the chances of error.

Marking

Flat carpenter's pencils are best for marking because they may be sharpened to a flat line and retain enough strength not to break easily.

I extend the appropriate ruler along the side of a board closest to me, place a mark on the material to be cut opposite the desired length as shown on the ruler, then turn this mark to the left or right to indicate the piece that will *not* be used.

When cutting material less than 12 inches wide it is not necessary to extend this mark across the width with a square. The mark itself need not be more than 1/4 inch long, but it shouldn't be smaller, which would make locating it difficult.

In the drawing above are several marking conventions used throughout the country.

The lines with arrow tips at their ends indicate where the measurement is being made. The number indicates what that measurement is and may be located at any convenient place along the line.

The abbreviation *o.c.* means on center. As used in the drawing, it signifies that the distance between the two members is 16 inches when measured from the center of one to the center of the other.

In practice it would be awkward and laborious to measure or mark various members by their centers; the same result is achieved if the marking is done from one side of the member to the corresponding side of the second member.

When two marks are made 16 inches apart, in order to avoid confusion about which side of the mark to place the member, an **X** is placed beside the mark for later reference. When the member is installed, it is placed at the mark and on the **X**. This convention is used throughout the country.

The abbreviation *o.o.* means from outside to outside.

The abbreviation *i.d.* means inside diameter. However, it rarely relates to circles and in carpentry has come to mean the distance between two members when the measurement is made between their inner sides.

The line inside the circle indicates the midpoint or center.

Sawing

For cutting wood less than 1-1/2 inches thick, I use a 6-1/2-inch (blade diameter) heavy-duty Skil electric portable saw. It costs $42.

For cutting wood 1-1/2 inches or thicker, I use an 8-1/4-inch Skil heavy-duty portable electric power saw. It is priced at $79.

I am naming these specific tools, and all others throughout the book, because they have performed well for me over long periods of time and for no other reason. Several manufacturers offer more expensive worm-driven saws that are better mechanically than the two I've mentioned, but I found them to be unbalanced, heavy, and clumsy and was obliged to use both hands while making most cuts. This last fact alone ruled out this type of saw for me since my left hand will be in use while I am making most cuts.

Manufacturers' cheap models should be avoided. They simply don't stand up to the hard use in building a house or doing a substantial renovation.

All saws are sold with adequate maintenance instructions and recommendations for types of blades to be used for cutting various materials.

I use a 28-tooth carbide-tipped blade in the 8-1/4-inch Skil saw for all rough work. The teeth of this blade are made of carbide steel and stay sharper many times longer than the chrome steel or other alloys used in ordinary blades. They are resharpened by grinding rather than filing, a service that costs about $8. The carbide-tipped blade costs $22 versus $3.50 for a chrome blade. A general practice is to throw the chrome blade away when it becomes dull or accidentally hits a nail. The blade needn't be thrown away, however, since it takes only ten minutes to resharpen by filing the teeth along the original shape until the metal is shiny again or the deformations caused by striking the nail are removed. A convenient vise for filing can be set up by placing the blade between the framework of the building and a scrap of wood and nailing the wood to the building through the center hole of the blade.

Carbide steel is brittle and will chip if struck against other metal. Occasionally a tooth is knocked loose from the blade and will cost several dollars to replace. Despite these drawbacks, I find this blade superior.

For fine work, I use a plywood blade in the 6-1/2-inch saw. I throw this blade away when it becomes dull because the teeth are too numerous and would take too long to resharpen.

Except for ripping (cutting lengthwise with the grain) and cross-cutting material wider than 12

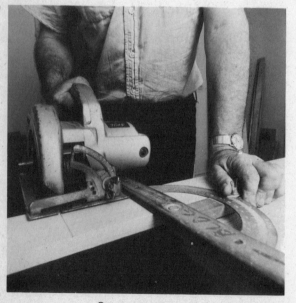

Saw, protractor, and board on horses

inches, I always use a protractor in conjunction with either saw.

The protractor has a long stationary arm which lies across the board that is to be cut. The short arm is adjustable from 0 to 45 degrees left or right and the degrees are marked on a semicircular scale. A wing nut on the short arm locks or unlocks the protractor. The end of the wing nut comes to a point and serves as an indicator on the scale. The short arm lies along the far side of the board.

Most often I will be cutting (*cutting* always means cross-cutting as opposed to ripping) the board at a right angle. I do this by first setting the protractor at 0 degrees. (When first purchasing a protractor and intermittently thereafter, it's a good idea to draw a line across the board with the protractor set at 0, then place a steel framing square along the line and side of the board to determine whether it is in fact a right angle across the board. If it is off, the protractor should be adjusted to the framing square and the position of the right angle marked on the scale.) When the long and short arms form a right angle, I place the protractor on the board, short arm against the far side, long arm across.

I hold the short arm firmly against the board by pressing toward my body. I place the table of the power saw on the board. The left side of the table lies against the long arm of the protractor. The blade is *back from the wood to rotate freely.* I press the trigger and start the saw.

With light foward pressure, I push the saw forward through the wood while sliding the base along the side of the long arm. Since the long arm is at a right angle to the board and I am making a parallel cut, the cut will be at a right angle.

For cutting during rough work, after marking the desired length, I shift the saw and protractor in unison until a tooth of the blade will bisect the mark while the rest of the thickness of the blade (kerf) lies on that side of the board which will not be used. I move the saw back so that the blade will rotate freely while maintaining the same location with the protractor and make my cut.

The power saw has torque (a pulling to the right) when first started, and this sometimes causes a slight alteration of position. For very fine work I start the saw first and establish the correct position by shifting the saw and protractor in unison and nicking the edge of the wood until the running blade is cutting exactly at the mark. I do this by moving the saw in and away from the wood, altering the position of saw and protractor together *only when the blade is away from the wood.*

When the power saw is rotating freely the sound is a high-pitched whine. As a cut is begun it rotates less quickly and the pitch will be lower, but if it is operating properly the characteristic whine will remain. This whine will be replaced by a flatter-pitched sound as greater stress is placed on the motor and the blade rotates at slower speeds. The optimum speed at which to make a cut is the most rapid possible without placing undue stress on the motor, something that is best identified by sound.

During any cut, the blade encounters resistance from the wood and heats up. If the cut is being made too slowly, more heat is created and this heat has a longer time to build up. Greater heat tends to warp a blade, and a warped blade encounters even greater resistance. Excessive heat builds up rapidly and creates greater warpage. If this circle isn't broken, it isn't at all unusual for a new blade to be "worn out" in half an hour of cutting.

This condition is also aggravated since the greater heat causes the resin in the wood to caramelize on the blade, which reduces the sharpness of the teeth and makes for even greater friction. I once discussed this with a student who told me that he was forced to make the cut very slowly since there was so much smoke it was hard for him to see what he was doing.

If smoke appears while cutting, stop immediately; you may be using a very dull blade or sometimes the smoke will be caused by the machine itself because of the wrapping on the armature. This has an acrid odor and if the machine is sniffed at the ventilating grill in the rear, the trouble may be located.

If the problem isn't the machine or a dull blade, check the blade with a wet forefinger. Do this quickly since the blade can heat up enough to fry an egg. If the blade isn't excessively hot, there is probably an unusual amount of resin in the particular piece of wood and the cut can be continued.

Toward the completion of a cut, I push the saw through quickly to prevent the nearly sawed piece from falling of its own weight and tearing a piece of the stock with it.

The blade rotates counterclockwise, so that the cut is made from the bottom of the board upward through it. This leaves a smoother surface on the underside. (The reverse is true with a table saw.) In the early stages of construction neither side of the wood will be exposed, but a good habit to develop is to mark the side that will eventually be hidden.

I mentioned earlier that when the power saw is started the blade should not be against the wood but should be rotating freely. Aside from safety, this is to allow the full power of the motor to develop, rotating the blade at the maximum revolutions per minute (r.p.m.) and with a resulting minimum strain on the machine. If the blade is held against the wood when starting, it will often jam and cause a short by overloading the circuit. Most probably, it will also buck backward toward the operator, and since the bucking action is violent it can cause injury.

Most of the cutting that is done will be with a board placed on horses. The portion to be cut off should be *free to fall beyond the horses.* When this isn't practical, as in cutting a long board in half, another long board should first be placed on the horses, with the board to be cut on top of it. To the bottom and left of the saw handle is a wing nut. When this is loosened, the saw's table can be raised or lowered and the wing nut tightened when the blade is at the desired depth below the table. I set this depth 1/8 inch deeper than the thickness of the board to be cut, then make the cut. This leaves a saw mark on the board below, but it is only 1/8 inch deep and doesn't prevent later use. I use the same board over and over again in these situations.

When this precaution is not taken and the board to be cut is laid on horses without another underneath, any cut that is made between the horses begins in the normal way but the board begins to drop into a **V** at the cut and the top of the **V** pinches the blade as the cutting proceeds. This causes the saw to buck back even more violently than starting with the blade against the wood. It is running on maximum power and this maximum power is now being transferred into the bucking action. It is also rapid and unexpected.

I have never had an accident with a power saw but have witnessed a carpenter cutting a board as I described. The saw bucked so quickly that the guard over the blade did not have time to drop and the man's thigh was ripped open.

The power saw is nevertheless *a safe tool* when the simple operating procedures described are followed. It is also a powerful tool and should be respected as such at all times.

When cutting materials such as a 4 x 8-foot sheet of plywood, I first place four 2 x 4s on the floor a foot or so apart and parallel to each other; 8-foot lengths are convenient. (A level patch of ground is an alternative to the floor.) The 2 x 4s serve as a cutting table.

I place the plywood on top of the 2 x 4s, measure along opposite sides, and mark for my intended cut. I pop a chalk line between the marks to indicate where I will cut the sheet. (A chalk line is a spool of string inside a chalk-filled case. It is stretched taut across the sheet on the marks, raised a few inches, then permitted to snap down. The type with a clip at the end of the string is handier than those without, since one person can use it alone.)

If I am making a cut that is parallel to the 2 x 4s underneath, I shift a 2 x 4 if it lies under the path of the cut. If I am making a cut that will be at roughly a right angle to the 2 x 4s, I don't move them.

I set the blade of the saw so that it will cut about 1/8 inch deeper than the thickness of the plywood. This can be done by lifting the guard, placing the blade against the side of the plywood, then raising or lowering the table as needed. The alternative is to measure down from the table to the lowest tooth of the blade.

I place the blade at the chalk line. Each tooth of the blade is flared out in an opposite direction. During a cut these teeth will remove what the width of that flare is: 3/16 inch is common. I therefore place the blade so that this 3/16 inch will be on the piece I don't intend using.

At the front of the saw is a **U**-shaped slot that corresponds roughly to the position of the blade.

When the blade is where I want it at the chalk line, I note the position of the slot and keep that same position throughout the cut, watching the slot in relationship to the chalk line and not the blade.

I begin my cut from a crouch. (Housemaid's knee is a common occupational hazard of carpenters; avoid kneeling whenever possible.) I check the cut I am making to see whether the slot is in fact in the correct relative position to the chalk line, adjust if it is not, and continue if it is. With this arrangement of 2 x 4s on the floor or ground, I can proceed in my crouch across the plywood. The cut portion is being supported, will not bounce about or pinch the blade throughout the cutting.

While cutting, I am pinching the left front corner of the saw's table with my left index finger and thumb. My index finger also is pressed against the plywood.

The pressure of my index finger against the plywood helps stabilize the forward path of the saw and keep it from drifting. The handle is much farther back from where the cutting is being done; control is more difficult from there. Even slight corrective movements from the handle result in much larger ones at the blade.

If neither side of the plywood will be seen, I use a combination blade in the 6-1/2-inch saw. If one side of the plywood will be seen, or both, I'll use a

Saw table being pinched

Saw in position for plunge cut

Two-pound hammer

plywood blade in the same saw. If the cuts I intend making all lie within the sheet, I start with what is known as a plunge cut.

I have the guard raised with my left hand. I start the saw, the blade *away* from the wood, lower it into the plywood until the table is flat on the sheet, then proceed as if it were the same cut made earlier.

Nailing

For a long time I paid no attention to the type of hammer I used or the way I swung it. This came to an end when I was nailing oak flooring with a 20-ounce hammer that had a solid steel shaft and rubber grip. In the same room a man I had recently hired was laying three pieces of flooring for every one I did. I knew that I was about average in speed but had never realized how slow that could be and was both a little embarrassed and miffed. I later studied his swing, but at the time I only noticed that he was using a two-pound hammer with an ordinary wooden handle and an oversized claw head. I asked to use his hammer. The greater weight and size made an extraordinary difference in power and accuracy and left me feeling that I had been previously tapping nails with a toy. I offered to buy the hammer. He laughed and gave

it to me. I still have that hammer and use it for all nailing.

I grip at the end of the handle. My thumb goes completely around and rests on my index finger. If the hammer handle is gripped too hard, undue strain is placed on the wrist and forearm. Gripped too loosely, the handle will slide in the palm and blisters will result. The force of the grip should be only what is necessary to keep the handle from sliding when the nail is struck.

A common error is to place the thumb on the handle in order to guide the head. The thumb cannot provide an adequate means of control and the head will rock to one side and cause the user to be inaccurate. To compensate for the incorrect grip and loss of control, the user shortens his swing to an ineffectual tapping.

I use my wrist only to raise the hammer at the beginning of the swing.

Another common error occurs at this point when the wrist continues to be used to guide the hammer and provide force for the blow. The wrist is located at the pivot point of the swing, at the center of the arc, and from this location can only deliver a minimum of force. The wrist also has a relatively weak joint and the person using it as a source of power will tire quickly.

Once the hammer has been started upward, no

15

further strain should be felt either by the wrist or forearm. Power in the swing should be provided first by the shoulder and later, when practice has created a facility, by the back—which is the best source of power. It is useful to regard the arm and shoulder as an extension of the hammer and the back as the source of power.

At the top of the swing the hammer head should be slightly behind the shoulder. As the hammer is brought down on the nail, the weight of the body is added to the force delivered from the back.

If nailing is done incorrectly, the wrist and forearm will tire in fifteen or twenty minutes and production will suffer through inaccuracy and ineffectiveness. Using the two-pound hammer and a correct swing, two or three blows are required to drive a tenpenny nail rather than seven or eight, and I, who am of average strength, can nail all day without tiring.

An incorrect swing also places undue strain on the elbow, which may result in tendonitis or tennis elbow, a not infrequent ailment of carpenters. This isn't alarmism if you consider that in this work one will drive more nails in a day than most people do in a lifetime.

Once the nail is started with a light tap, which embeds it into the wood only deeply enough to keep it from falling, the left hand should immediately be removed from the nailing area and placed in the nail apron for another nail. The presence of the left hand is gratuitous at this moment. The blackened fingernail of my left index finger supports this view. I missed the nail and hit the finger instead, which was doubly irritating since there was no reason at all for my left hand to be anywhere near the nail.

When nailing two pieces together, it is almost always useful to start the nails into one of the pieces at the appropriate location and drive them down till they are almost through the wood. This makes it easier to nail the piece in the proper position without having it bounce about.

Another good rule to follow wherever possible is to nail through the already-stationary member into the one that isn't. It is much easier to position a piece accurately if the nail is being driven through the stationary member.

Nails hold least well when driven absolutely

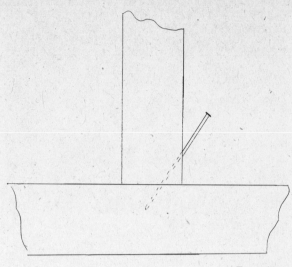

Toenailing

straight through one piece of wood into another. It is not only unnecessary to strive for this straightness, but it should be avoided.

A particularly useful type of angled nailing is called toenailing.

Especially during framing, this type of nailing occurs frequently. I start the nail about an inch up from the end at about a 60-degree angle and drive it down until the head is partially embedded.

The most common difficulty when doing toenailing of the kind shown is that the vertical member bounces about before the end of the nail has gone into the horizontal member and stabilized it. One way to reduce this is to lay the vertical member flat and drive the nails at the 60-degree angle until they are almost through, then position the vertical member on the horizontal member for fastening. However, this is time-consuming and should be used as a means of familiarizing oneself with toenailing, not as a regular practice.

By positioning a shoe against the opposite side of the vertical member from where the nailing is being done, the forward motion can usually be prevented. When this isn't effective the nail is probably being driven at too shallow an angle.

If the angle of the nail is too steep, most likely it will cause the wood to splinter. The 60-degree angle works for me, but it does vary for different people. It takes a fair amount of toenailing before a person finds the right angle for himself. The goal in all cases should be that angle which produces adequately fastened members with a minimum of movement while it is being done.

I've tried a variety of nail aprons and returned to the canvas type with two large pockets and a string which is tied around the waist.

When nailing below my waist I stoop or crouch and turn my apron so that the pockets are along my left side. This makes removing nails easier.

I wear two aprons when framing. One contains 8s and 10s, the other 16s. I keep my hammer at my right side when not in use. The wooden handle lies between my body and the string around my waist. It slides in and out freely without snagging on the string. (Handles with rubber grips frequently snag.)

The galvanized nails I recommended have a rough texture and as I reach into the pocket of the nail apron, my left fingertips hit this rough surface. If I repeat this often during a few days or a week, I may lose feeling in my left fingertips. They recover their feeling several weeks after I stop nailing.

I don't suppose there's any adult who hasn't nailed something together at one time or another and in the course of doing it adopted a "technique." Probably that technique is what's most comfortable and how that person feels most secure. If the technique I've described is tried, one has to be prepared to miss nails for a while, but perseverance will pay off in much greater effectiveness.

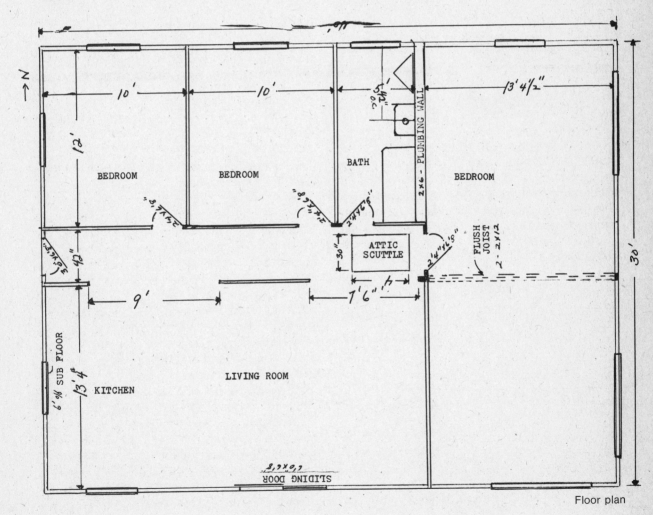

Floor plan

SITE PREPARATION AND FOUNDATION

3

The rectangular house with a gable roof that I'm going to build is 30 x 40 feet. This same house might be placed on several kinds of foundations. I am going to use a type of foundation called *continuous*. A continuous foundation supports the exterior walls continuously and the interior of the house intermittently.

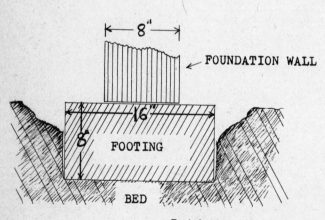

Bed, footing, foundation wall

Probably 90 percent of the houses built last year used this type of foundation.

It is composed of three parts: (1) the ground itself, called the bed; (2) the footing—a slab of concrete usually 8 inches thick and 16 inches wide on top of the bed that follows the perimeter of the house; (3) the foundation wall—a wall usually 8 inches wide made of concrete or concrete blocks that lies on the footing.

When the area between the foundation walls has been excavated deeply enough to provide head room, a basement is created. When it is only partially excavated, it is referred to as crawl space. This house will have crawl space.

The first step in building a continuous foundation with crawl space is to prepare the site. To do this, I must determine how deep below grade I will place the footing, grade being the ground level when the house is completed.

The depth below grade of the footing depends on a factor called frost line. This is how deep the ground will freeze. In New York, where I will build this house, the frost line is 32 inches. *The minimum depth* of the footing below grade is the same as the frost line.

The footing is placed at this minimum depth because the ground expands as it freezes and if the footing is located within the expanding area it may shift, with subsequent damage to the house.

The frost line of every locality is incorporated into the local building codes and the local Building Department will inform you what that frost line is.

Establishing the Area to Be Excavated

The site is on Long Island. Since the house has no basement, I will excavate to the frost line, which is 32 inches. In order to establish where on the lot this excavation is to be done, I refer to the plot plan, which specifies the location of the house.

I locate the two front surveyor's stakes. (They

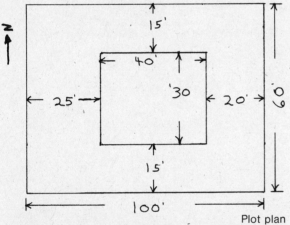

Plot plan

are small; if difficult to find, a reference line can be established from other houses, which usually have the same set-backs, or from the utility poles which are located on a right of way along the property line at back of the lot.) After locating the stakes, I measure in 10 feet from each side and drive my own stakes. I hammer a nail partially into the tops of these stakes. This is called tacking.

I hook a hundred-foot tape on each of these nails. I extend one tape into the property at roughly a right angle and the other on a diagonal. I shift the tapes so that the 30-foot mark on one intersects the 50-foot mark on the diagonal. At the intersection I am at an exact right angle from the front property line.

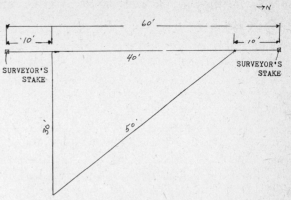

Using 3-4-5 triangle to establish excavating area

I am using what is known as a 3,4,5 triangle. The two legs or sides of this triangle may be 3 or 4 or any multiple of these. The longest side, or hypotenuse, is 5 or any multiple of 5. With these dimensions, the meeting of the shorter legs forms a right angle.

I drive a stake at 20 feet along the 30-foot leg. This stake is 5 feet from the front and side of the house. I extend the tape along this same line and drive another stake at 70 feet. Since the front set-back is 25 feet and the side of the house 40 feet, this new stake is also 5 feet beyond the house. I repeat this on the opposite side to arrive at four stakes, each 5 feet from the house.

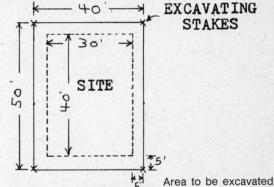

Area to be excavated

The stakes mark the area to be excavated. The allowance of the additional 5 feet beyond the perimeter of the house is for convenience while working on the foundation and because the soil removed will make surprisingly large mounds and some may fall back into the work area. If there are trees or bushes within this 5-foot band, I excavate around them or prune branches that fall within the site.

I have hired a bulldozer and operator to dig the "hole." The operator pushes dirt to three sides and leaves the area clear in front for the delivery of materials. The job takes four hours to do and costs approximately $200, the price per day for the operator and machine.

The earth that is excavated is known as "clean fill." I retain enough to refill the 5-foot band later. This is called back-filling. (A dump-truck owner will remove the balance for nothing. This fill is in demand and if anyone wants to make the effort to find a buyer and arrange for delivery, part of the excavation cost can be recovered.)

The soil on the excavated site is a mixture of loose, coarse sand and gravel. It makes an excellent bed capable of supporting three or four tons per square foot, although the total weight on each square foot of this bed will probably never exceed several hundred pounds.

Marking Front Property Line and Side Set-backs

I drive stakes beside each of the front corner stakes placed by the surveyor, and tack nails into each so that they are in line with the surveyor's nails.

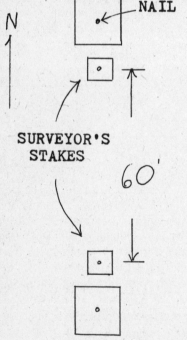

Stakes beside surveyor's stakes

I make a slip knot out of nylon mason's string, place it around one of the nails, then tighten the string around the second nail. To tighten, I pull the string with my left hand and wind the slack around the nail with my right. I use a half-hitch to secure the string to the second nail.

I tap the nails to shift the string so that it bisects the nail heads in the surveyor's stakes.

Slip knot

Half-hitch

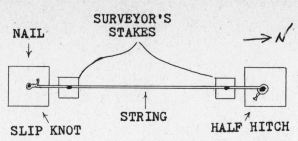

Four stakes, nails, and string

The string is the front property line.

From the nail in the surveyor's stake, I measure in 15 feet along the string. I mark this distance by knotting a smaller piece of string to the stretched string. I do the same on the opposite side.

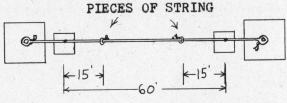

Marking side setbacks

Siting the House with the Builder's Level

The photo is of a builder's level. It's very similar to the more expensive transit level and is an extremely accurate instrument. Unlike the transit level, the telescope of the builder's level cannot be tilted up or down, and this makes siting the house a bit more involved and time-consuming. (This one was sold by Sears in 1973 for $92, which included wooden carrying case and a rod or ruler. The ruler is composed of two 4-foot sections graduated in quarter-inches. The two sections can be joined where more height is needed.)

I spread the legs of the tripod and push them into the ground while keeping the base plate roughly centered over the knotted piece of string. This approximation is done by eye.

I attach the level to the base plate by inserting the threaded bolt into the threaded hole in the level and turning clockwise till snug.

I lower all four leveling screws by turning clockwise until they rest against the plate.

I unscrew the head of the plumb bob, which has a hole in its center. I thread nylon string through the hole and knot it inside to keep the string from pulling through the hole. I cut the string to a length of 5 feet or so and make a slip knot. I place the loop of the slip knot inside the clip attachment on the bottom of the bolt. The plumb bob can now be raised or lowered by sliding the knot up or down. I place the plumb bob 8 inches or so above the knotted piece of string.

I press the tripod legs more deeply into the ground, maintaining an approximate level of the base plate and the plumb bob over the knot. When the tripod feels stable, I lower the plumb bob until it is an inch or so above the knot.

I bring the plumb bob within a quarter-inch over the knot by pressing down on those legs which are opposite the "off" position of the plumb bob. I make a small final adjustment by loosening the threaded bolt and shifting both the level and plumb bob so that the end of the plumb bob is directly over the knot. I tighten the attaching bolt.

I rotate the telescope so that it lies over two opposite screws. If the bubble is on my right, the right side is high. I grip *both* opposite screws with my thumbs and forefingers, turn the right one clockwise and the left counterclockwise. This keeps both screws snugly against the plate as I turn them simultaneously. As the bubble begins to move toward the center, I turn more slowly and

Builder's level

stop when the bubble lies between the marks on the glass.

There are two sets of marks on each side of the center. These are provided to make level readings easier since the bubble will contract in hot weather and expand in cold; the additional set is for convenience under different temperatures.

I rotate the telescope directly over the two other opposite screws and center the bubble again.

I return to the first position, recenter the bubble, and repeat in the second position. I keep adjusting the screws until the bubble remains centered when the telescope is rotated in a complete circle.

Establishing Front and Back Corners of House on South Side

I remain at the builder's level while my helper bisects the nail in the northwest surveyor's stake with the right side of the rod as I look at it. He places a 4-foot level against the side of the rod, its bottom also bisecting the nail, and plumbs both rod and level.

I rotate the telescope, sighting along the top until it is in line with the rod. I focus by turning the brass knob above the eyepiece, then shift the telescope so that its vertical crosshair lies on the right side of the rod.

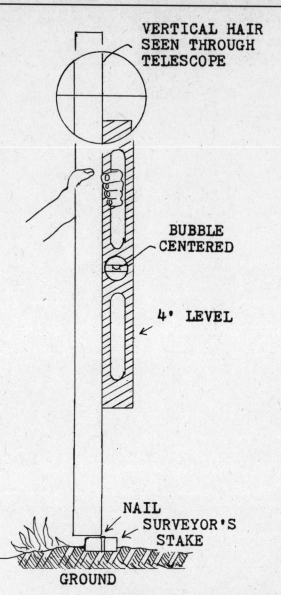

VERTICAL HAIR SEEN THROUGH TELESCOPE

BUBBLE CENTERED

4' LEVEL

NAIL
SURVEYOR'S STAKE

GROUND

Level against side of rod and plumb

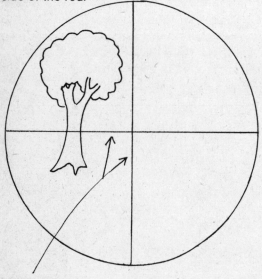

CROSSHAIRS

Vertical crosshair is the projected line of the side of the house

I cannot lower the telescope to see whether the vertical crosshair actually does bisect the nail in the surveyor's stake, but since the rod is plumb I can assume it. I turn the locking knob clockwise until snug to keep the telescope from moving.

I turn the inside scale under the eyepiece so that its indicator points to 0 degrees on the fixed outer 360-degree scale. I loosen the locking screw, turn the telescope toward the site until the indicator is at 90 degrees, and lock it.

As I look through the telescope now, the vertical

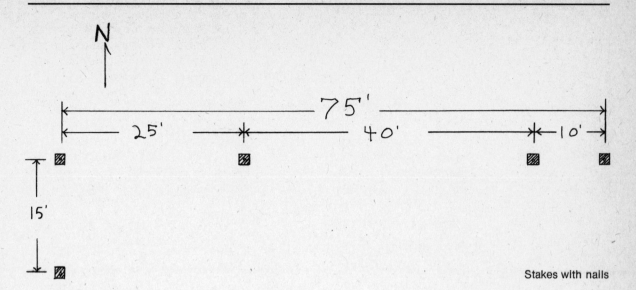

Stakes with nails

crosshair corresponds to the south side of the house.

The front set-back is 25 feet, the side of the house is 40 feet long—a total of 65 feet. My helper moves back 75 feet or so in line with the south side. I direct him left or right until the right side of the rod is approximately on the vertical crosshair. He marks the spot on the ground by digging in his heel, then drives a stake here.

He places the rod and 4-foot level on the stake and moves the top until it is aligned with the vertical crosshair. He then shifts the bottom of the rod until it reads plumb on the level. He drives a nail into the stake at that point.

I drive a stake under the knotted piece of string, place a level at the knot and on the stake, plumb it

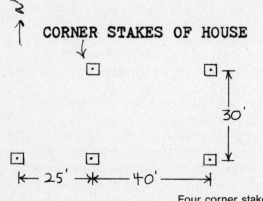

Four corner stakes

to the knot, and tack a nail into the stake.

I hook the hundred-foot tape on the nail and extend it across the nail my helper has tacked. I hold the tape tightly as he drives stakes and nails at 25 feet and 65 feet. These nails correspond to the corners of the house.

I repeat this process along the north side of the house and establish the two remaining corners, which are also represented by nails in stakes.

Transferring Position of Nails in Corner Stakes to Batter Boards and String

I have now sited the house by using the front property line as a reference. The nails in the stakes are in the position the corners of the house will actually occupy. My next step is to build forms for the footing. It is awkward and time-consuming to build these forms using the nails in the stakes as a reference and much quicker and easier to demarcate the corners and perimeter of the house with string and batter boards.

A couple of feet or so from each of the corners, I drive three stakes made of 2 x 4s (lumber with an actual dimension of 1-1/2 x 3-1/2 inches). These stakes are 4 feet long, their ends V-shaped, and I use a 20-pound sledge to drive them into the ground. I leave 18 inches or so above ground.

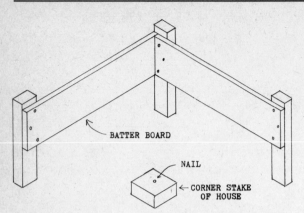

Batter boards nailed to stakes

To the stakes I nail 1 x 8 boards (actual dimension, 3/4 x 7-1/2 inches). These are called batter boards. I hold the side of my leg behind each stake to stiffen it while I nail the batter boards in place.

I place a 4-foot level (Sand's Level and Toll Co.; it is made of cast aluminum) so that it bisects the nail in a corner stake. The other end is against the batter board. I shift the level into plumb and mark it on the top edge of the batter board.

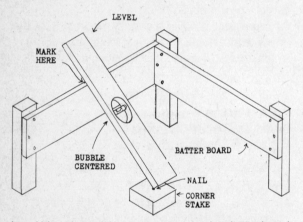

Level bisecting nail in corner stake, plumb to batter board

I mark the seven remaining batter boards in the same way. These marks are directional references.

I will also need a level reference to build the foundation. To accomplish this, I set up the builder's level near the center of the site and level it. No matter where I now look, the horizontal crosshair provides an accurate level frame of reference.

I sight along the top of the telescope and align it with any of the marks I have made on the batter boards. I focus the eyepiece.

My helper opens a yellow-faced Lufkin folding ruler and holds it beside the mark, an end in the air. I instruct him to raise or lower the ruler until the end is at the horizontal crosshair.

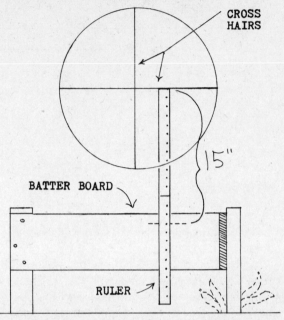

Ruler against batter board and end and at cross hair

My helper marks the side of the batter board at an inch mark that falls around the middle. It may be 15 or 17; the actual distance is irrelevant. However, once a specific measurement is taken, this same measurement is used throughout. Fractions should be avoided since they are harder to remember. Let us assume that from the end of the ruler to midway on the batter board was 15 inches.

My helper now holds the ruler against the seven remaining batter boards. At each one, I read the ruler and instruct him to mark the batter board 15 inches more than my reading. If it was 2-1/4 inches, he would mark the batter board at 17-1/4 inches, etc. The horizontal crosshair is level, and since the marks are all equidistant from it they will also be level with each other.

I now have a mark on the top edge and the side of each batter board. I tack a nail securely into the mark on the top edge and measure the distance between its head and the side mark. Say this is 5 inches. I now tack the seven remaining nails into the top marks so that their tops are also 5 inches from their respective side marks. The tops of the nails are all level with each other.

I now attach nylon string tightly between the eight nails.

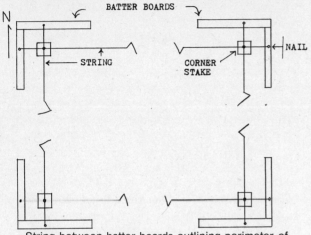

String between batter boards outlining perimeter of house

The perimeter of the house is outlined by the strings, and their intersections mark the corners. These intersections should form a right angle. I determine whether they do by measuring both diagonals. The lengths of these diagonals will be equal only when each intersection forms a right angle.

If the difference in diagonals is less than 3/4 inch I will remove the variation later. If it is more than 3/4 but less than 1-1/2 inches, I extend the shorter diagonal by tapping the nails outward and shorten the longer one by tapping the nails inward.

I now recheck the string level by having my helper hold the folding ruler on the head of any nail. Say it reads 10 inches to the horizontal crosshair. My helper proceeds from nail head to nail head and holds the folding ruler on it. If any vary from 10 inches, I tell him what the variation is, and he either taps down the nail that amount or raises it.

Preparing Forms for the Footing

Concrete is a mixture of Portland cement, aggregate or stone, sand, and water in specific amounts. When first mixed, it has no fixed shape, and doesn't assume any until it has dried sufficiently. In order to give it a definite shape, the plastic mass is poured into what is known as a form and

allowed to dry in that form, which has been built to the desired shape. I want a footing that is 16 inches wide and 8 inches thick. I intend to build an 8-inch-wide foundation wall on this footing. This leaves 4 inches of footing on each side of the foundation wall. I will therefore build the form so that it extends 4 inches beyond the perimeter of the house and use the string as a reference.

I drive a stake 4-3/4 inches i.d. (inside dimension) from the nail in the corner stake. This is made of 1 by 3 (3/4 x 2-5/8 inches). It is 16 inches or so long and I leave 5 inches or so above ground.

To make a form board, I lay a long length of 1 x 8 sheathing on its side against the stake. (Sheathing is the cheapest grade of wood and may be fir, cedar, or the commonest of common pine.) One end extends beyond the corner stake. The board is on the site side of the stake. I nail through the board into the stake.

At the other end, I drive another stake 4-3/4 inches from the string. The end of the form board lies midway across the stake, which later provides a nailing surface for a second form board.

I measure the distance between the top of the form board and the string at the nailed end. I then nail the second end to the second stake at the corresponding height.

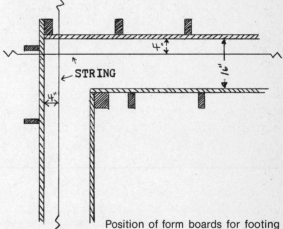

Position of form boards for footing

I butt the end of a second board against the end of the first, continuing around the entire perimeter in the same way until I have a continuous rectangle which lies 4 inches beyond the strings and is equidistant in height from the string.

As I finish nailing each board, I shovel dirt

against the outside of the board to within an inch of the top. I do this to prevent the form boards from bulging because of the side pressure exerted by the weight of the concrete. I place intermediate stakes every 4 to 6 feet for the same reason.

I make a rectangle of parallel interior form boards. I use 8 x 8 x 16-inch concrete blocks as spacers (the measurements of this size block are actually 7-5/8 x 7-5/8 x 15-5/8 inches).

I install an interior rectangle made of 1 x 8s in the same manner as I did the exterior form boards.

I level the tops of the interior boards with the exterior ones by laying a level across the two and adjusting the interior boards.

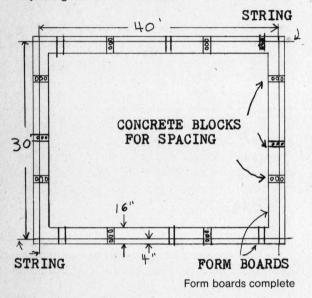

Form boards complete

Pouring the Footing

The ingredients of concrete may be mixed on the site or delivered in a plastic state by ready-mix trucks. It is almost always cheaper and easier to have it delivered already mixed and ready to pour.

Concrete is sold by the cubic yard. One cubic yard will fill 30 feet of an 8 x 16-inch footing. Since the footing is 140 feet, four and two-thirds cubic yards are required. I allow approximately 10 percent for waste and order five yards. I specify that the concrete is to be used for a footing. This means that the ready-mix company would use a minimum of five sacks of cement and a maximum of seven gallons of water in each cubic yard.

Before the truck arrives, I use a garden hose to wet down the bed. I remove soil above the bottom of the form board, then compact the bed by slapping it down with the back of a square shovel and wetting it again.

I remove the string at the front of the house. I lay two sheets of plyscore (the cheapest grade of plywood) on the ground just inside the form boards at about the center of the house. I station two wheelbarrows on the plyscore. I then make a path to the rear forms by laying sheets of plyscore end to end over which to roll the wheelbarrows to transport concrete.

At one house on which I worked, I had the ready-mix driver back up to within a couple of feet of the wheelbarrows. The driver attached his chute. Before I could stop him he filled one wheelbarrow to the brim. One of the people working with me raised the rear end of the wheelbarrow and pushed forward. The load of concrete shifted in the wheelbarrow and it tipped over.

I mention this incident because I have seen it happen many times. Whenever concrete work is being done, a needless pressure to do things extremely rapidly occurs. One expression of this is filling the wheelbarrow completely. This makes a very heavy load that is difficult to maneuver. The wheelbarrow shouldn't be more than half-filled, and there is no need to rush this into the form as if it were going to harden at any moment. It will not harden to the touch until after a couple of hours.

Ready-mix companies demand a surcharge if the truck and driver are obliged to wait more than a specified amount of time proportionate to their load. An hour or so is usual. In any case, the amount of the surcharge is small. The important consideration when working with a material as heavy as concrete is not to place undue physical strain on yourself. Rather than the speeding up which usually occurs, working at a slower-than-ordinary pace is called for.

Three people to pour the footing is an ideal number. Two should move the concrete in wheelbarrows to places that can't be reached by the truck's chute. The third will wipe level, or screed, by moving a piece of 2 x 4 on a slight diagonal back and forth across the tops of the form boards.

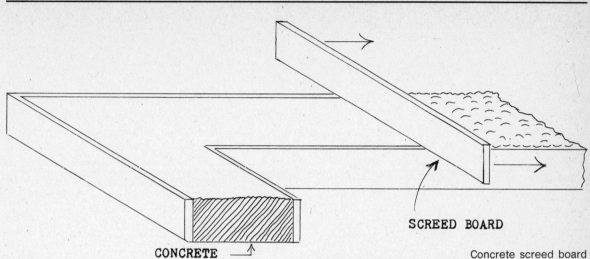

CONCRETE ⟶

SCREED BOARD

Concrete screed board

The three people should rotate jobs.

I fill the rear form first. In addition to the 2 x 4 for screeding, I use a 10-inch pointed trowel to move the concrete about, filling depressions and removing the excess. Occasionally I hit the side of the form sharply with a hammer. This helps the concrete to flow into the gaps and compact itself.

Once the rear form and half of two sides are filled, the driver swings his chute over the front form and pours concrete directly into it. The concrete is then moved by hoes where it is needed.

Three men working at a slower-than-ordinary pace should complete pouring the footing within an hour.

If the weather is hot and dry or it looks like rain, I cover the footing with sheets of 4-mil plastic.

Late Friday afternoon is a good time to do this work. It will allow the concrete to set during the weekend and permit the people who have poured it to rest.

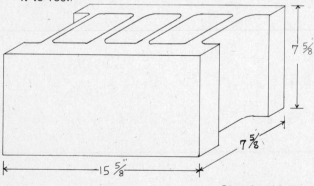

Stretcher block

Building the Foundation Wall

The footing has been allowed to cure during the weekend and, although this process has not been completed, more than enough time has passed to construct the foundation wall on it.

This wall is often made of concrete which has been reinforced with #4 bars of steel which have a half-inch diameter. Large tract developments use this method. I prefer a block wall, which is cheaper, takes less time to build, and is equally strong. The choice of the concrete wall in tract construction is a result of the fact that masons to lay the block are hard to come by and notoriously unreliable in appearing at the times they say they will. This doesn't lend itself to a smooth operation in mass construction and block foundation walls are therefore avoided.

Mortar

The material which lies between joints of blocks is called mortar. It is made of masonry cement, fine sand, and water. In place of the masonry cement, a mixture of 10 percent hydrated lime and 90 percent Portland cement may be substituted.

I put a quart of water into a gasoline-driven half-bag mixer. I cut a bag of masonry cement in half by slicing through the paper with the end of a shovel and dump one of the halves into the mixer. I add a bag and a half of fine sand or its equivalent, which for me is twelve shovelfuls. I start the mixer, then stop to estimate the water content of the

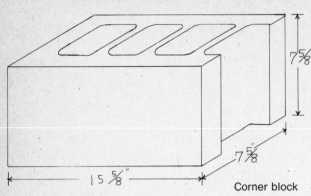

Corner block

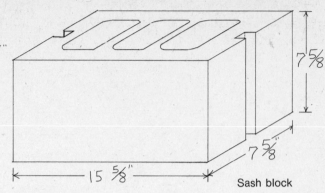

Sash block

sand. I add eleven more quarts of water if the sand is dry, nine if very wet, and ten if wet or damp.

I estimate the water content in the sand by picking up a handful and squeezing it. If water runs out or remains in my palm, it is very wet. If it remains in a ball, it is wet. If small clumps are left, it is damp; if it doesn't retain shape, it is dry.

I allow the mixer to run until all lumps in the mortar have disappeared and none of it clings to the sides, a matter of a few minutes. If some of the mortar mixture does cling to the sides of the mixer, I rap a hammer against the outside to knock it loose. I dump about half the contents into a wheelbarrow.

I wheel it to the front corner of the house. I place two concrete blocks on end and lay a 2 x 2-foot plywood piece over them to be my mortar board. The board is simply a convenient place to keep mortar. I place several shovelfuls on it.

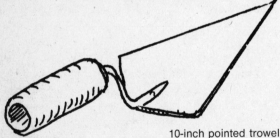

10-inch pointed trowel

If water runs out of the mortar, I sprinkle masonry cement and sand over it in a 1-to-3 proportion and mix it thoroughly with the trowel.

I tilt the right side of the trowel down at a slight angle and swing it toward me in an arc while pressing down lightly on the mortar. If the troweling action has left a smooth unbroken surface on which a small amount of water appears, I sprinkle a little masonry cement upon it and remix.

If the surface isn't continuously smooth and has pulled apart, I sprinkle water on it in addition to masonry cement, remix, trowel it again for a continuous unbroken surface.

The consistency of the mortar should be that of butter which is stiff enough to retain its shape and soft enough to spread easily. It should leave an unbroken swath after the trowel is pressed across it and no water should run out of its edges or collect in hollows.

Laying Mortar

I smooth the mortar, slice into it at approximately 45 degrees to a depth of an inch, turn the trowel flat, and lift.

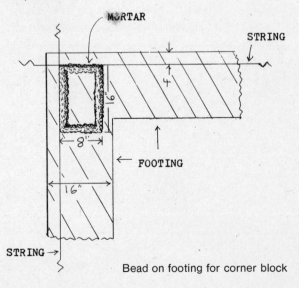

Bead on footing for corner block

An inch or so of mortar lies along the left side of the trowel. I swing the trowel in a horizontal position slightly beyond the intersection of strings. I turn the trowel on its side and the mortar slides off. In place, the mortar is referred to as a "bead." I lay on the footing a rectangular bead which corresponds to the outline of a block.

Erecting Corners of Foundation Wall

I stand a corner block on end. I insert my four left fingers into the bottom hole and my thumb in the middle hole. I place my four right fingers in the hole at the opposite end and my thumb inside the top hole.

I push the top of the block sideways, lift the bottom, *position the block in a horizontal attitude,* and set it down into the mortar.

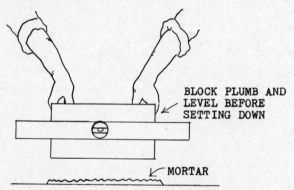

BLOCK PLUMB AND LEVEL BEFORE SETTING DOWN

MORTAR

Attitude of block prior to laying

I tap the high end of the block with the end of the trowel handle to achieve a rough level. I lay a level on the middle of the block along the length and tap the block until the bubble is centered.

I place the level on the middle of the block across the width and tap lightly on the high side until the bubble is centered.

I lay the bottom of the trowel against the block, slide it down through excess mortar, and remove it with an up-and-out movement. I return the excess to the mortar board by flicking the trowel at it and stopping the forward motion abruptly.

I can now see the thickness of the mortar joint. It should be 3/8 inch.

I stand my level at the intersection of the strings and plumb it. I shift the block so that its corner butts the side of the level.

I lay a corner block in the second front corner. The o.o. measurement should be exactly 30 feet.

I lay a third corner block at the rear of the house, and another in the fourth corner. I measure both sides, which should be 40 feet, then the rear, which should be 30 feet.

I measure both diagonals.

If the diagonals are equidistant, the blocks are the corners of a rectangle.

If the diagonals are not the same, since I have already adjusted the intersection of strings, the variation will be slight and I make the minor adjustment. This will usually be to reposition a block which is not directly under the intersection of strings.

I lay a bead, the outline of a block, adjacent to the corner block. I stand a stretcher block on end, cut an inch roll of mortar, and swing the trowel in a flat position to the block. The pointed end of the trowel is slightly beyond the block and its side slightly below the top.

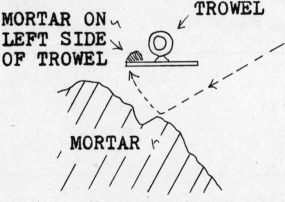

MORTAR ON LEFT SIDE OF TROWEL

TROWEL

MORTAR

Movement to transfer mortar to trowel

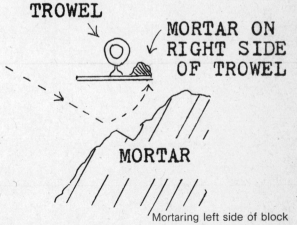

TROWEL

MORTAR ON RIGHT SIDE OF TROWEL

MORTAR

Mortaring left side of block

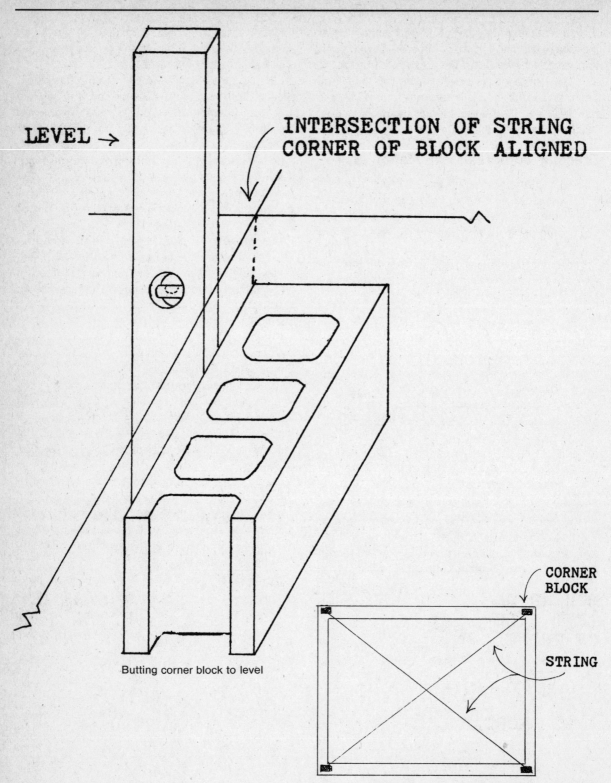

LEVEL →

INTERSECTION OF STRING
CORNER OF BLOCK ALIGNED

Butting corner block to level

CORNER
BLOCK

STRING

Establishing square through equal diagonals

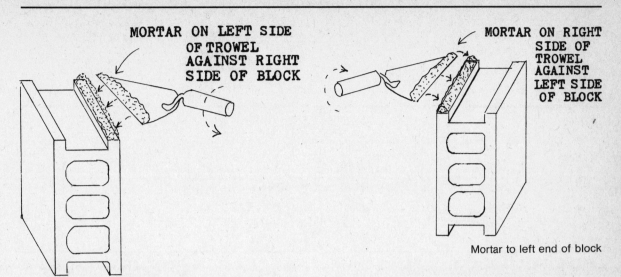

MORTAR ON LEFT SIDE OF TROWEL AGAINST RIGHT SIDE OF BLOCK

MORTAR ON RIGHT SIDE OF TROWEL AGAINST LEFT SIDE OF BLOCK

Mortar to left end of block

Transferring mortar from trowel to right end of block

I roll the trowel over, which causes the mortar to fall along the end of the block. Then, with a small but *definite downward pressure,* I press the mortar against the block. I continue the motion by sliding the trowel down and across the block, which completes the transfer of mortar.

I have been standing slightly to the right of the block and have mortared the right end. I pick up a roll of mortar on the right side of my trowel. I shift to the left of the block and transfer the mortar to the left end with the same technique.

I raise the block to a horizontal attitude, set it down on the bead while pressing the mortared end against the corner block. My lateral pressure is sufficient to reduce the mortar in the joint to 3/8 inch but not enough to shift the position of the corner block. The side of my index finger is about 3/8 inch thick and is a quick reference.

I establish a rough level by eye for the stretcher block by tapping with the handle of the trowel. I lay my 4-foot level on the middle of both blocks along the lengths and tap down the stretcher block until its height is the same as that of the corner block.

I level the stretcher block across the width.

I stand the level with a side against the string and plumb. I shift the stretcher block to butt the side of the level.

I lay a bead, the outline of a block, half on the corner block and half on the stretcher block. I lay a second corner block, smooth end outside. I level

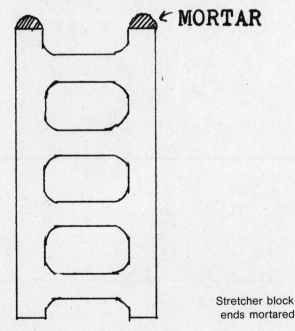

← MORTAR

Stretcher block ends mortared

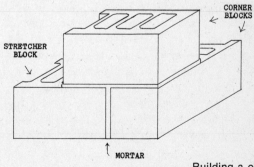

CORNER BLOCKS

STRETCHER BLOCK

MORTAR

Building a corner

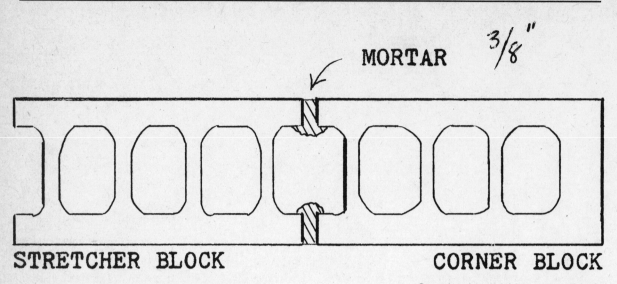

MORTAR ³⁄₈"

STRETCHER BLOCK

CORNER BLOCK

Stretcher block laid to corner block

it across the length and width.

I stand the 4-foot level beside the bottom corner block. I shift the top block against the side of the level and align it with the bottom block. I align the other exterior side of the top block in the same way to form a plumb corner.

I duplicate this at the other three corners.

Laying Courses of Block between Corners

I knot the end of a nylon string and lay the string into the groove of a plastic device called a clip. The knot lies to the outside.

I place the clip against the bottom corner block. While maintaining tension on the string to keep the clip from moving, I unwind string from a ball till it is a foot or so beyond the opposite corner. I lay the string in the groove of a second clip and wind it around the clip until the stretched string is about 3 inches shorter than the o.o. distance of the corners. I pull the string taut and clip it to the bottom block so that it lies exactly at the top of the block. I raise the string to the top of the first block.

On my knees, I sight down the string. If it has sagged, I shorten the string with a few more turns around the clip and reposition the clip. (Most companies who supply blocks will send these clips along at no charge.)

Trucks that deliver concrete blocks are frequently equipped with a hydraulic lift and extension boom. The blocks are stacked and this equipment permits the driver to remove many at a time and place them at various parts of the site. I position the blocks at 3-foot intervals inside the footing all around the perimeter to eliminate needless handling.

I lay a bead with its center directly under the string. Its length is 4 feet or so, the width an inch

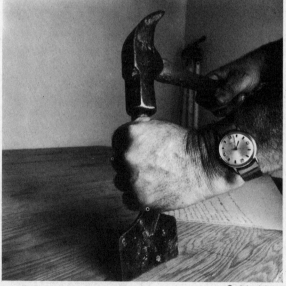

Cold chisel

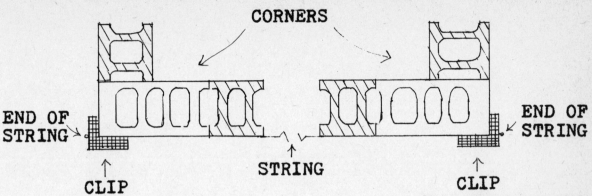

CORNERS

END OF STRING

END OF STRING

CLIP

STRING

CLIP

Clips and string between corners

or so. I lay a parallel bead 8 inches to the inside.

I stand up stretcher blocks in a row and mortar their ends.

I position myself inside the site so that the string will be on the outside of the block.

I place a block on the mortar so that its side is a quarter-inch away from the string. I tap it with the end of the trowel along the length to bring it down to the height of the string.

I level it across the width by eye.

I tap the block forward so that it lies against the string *but does not move the string.*

I continue to lay blocks in this way until less than the length of a block is needed to complete the row from corner to corner.

Cutting Block

I measure the i.d. between the blocks. Say that it is 12 inches. I allow 3/8 inch for a mortar joint at each end and therefore want a block 11-1/4 inches long.

I mark both smooth sides of a stretcher block at 11-1/4 inches. I lay the cold chisel upright on one of the marks, tap lightly, and slide the chisel forward. The force of my taps is only strong enough to score the block not much deeper than a scratch.

I turn the block over and repeat, then tap with increasing force along the scored line. If the block doesn't split when moderate force is used, I turn it over and hammer moderately on the first line until it does.

I mortar both ends and set the block.

The completed row of blocks laid end to end is called a course.

I lay the first course on the three remaining sides.

I build up each of the corners by laying another two blocks on them.

I raise the clips to the tops of the second corner blocks. I start with a full block, which will automatically stagger the vertical joints of successive courses.

I check the elevations for an access door to the crawl space. This is usually along the rear wall and a 2 x 2-foot opening is common. I mark its position and do not lay blocks within this area. I place the smooth ends of corner blocks along the sides of the opening.

On completion of the second course, I set up the builder's level near the center of the site and check the heights of the corners. If they vary, I will make the mortar joints thinner at a high corner and thicker at a low one to eliminate the difference.

I begin the third course with a full block to maintain an aligned joint with the first course.

For the fourth and final course, I place an additional block on top of each corner only for the purpose of securing the plastic clip properly. If the string is still not taut, I may need still another block on top of the additional one to keep the taut string from pulling the unmortared block out of position and becoming slack.

Ventilating the Crawl Space

Circulation of air should be provided in the crawl space in order to avoid the build-up of excessive humidity, which is conducive to rot. This is usually done by means of 8 x 16-inch metal grilles set into

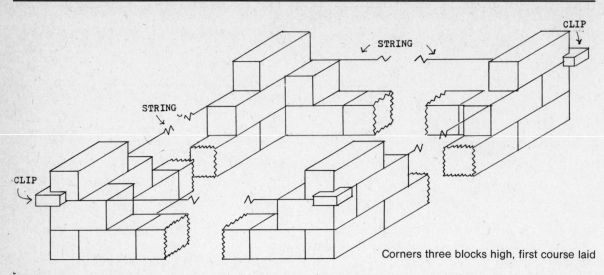

Corners three blocks high, first course laid

the fourth course of the foundation wall. A knob on the outside opens and closes metal bands. Behind these bands is screening to keep out insects and small animals. A common practice is to space three along the 40-foot sides and two on the 30-foot sides.

As I lay the fourth course and arrive at the location of a grille, I lay a sash block. I place the grille so that its metal side lies in the slot of the sash block. I lay a second sash block so that the other side of the grille also lies in its slot.

The slots in the sash block are wider than the thin metal sides of the grille, and to keep the grille from rattling I fill the gap behind the metal with mortar.

The structure above the completed foundation wall will be made of wood, and I need to provide a means of attaching that wood to the block wall. This is usually done with bolts.

I tear up the empty bags of mortar and stuff the paper into holes in the block 1 foot from the corners. I leave at least 6 inches between the paper and the top of the block. I stuff holes at 6-foot intervals along the rest of the entire foundation wall.

I place 9-inch-long 1/2-inch J bolts in these holes. I fill the holes with mortar and the paper keeps the mortar from falling farther down the wall. By eye, I plumb the bolt and leave about 3 inches of the threaded end above the top of the block.

Foundation for Interior

An arrangement must now be made to support the structure which will lie above the crawl space. The foundation in this area is intermittently spaced and made of masonry and wood.

Positioning of Piers

The masonry of this part of the foundation is called a pier and is composed of a footing and concrete blocks stacked on each other.

I mark 9 feet 4 inches, 19 feet 4 inches, and 29 feet 4 inches along both 40-foot sides of the footing and stretch strings across corresponding

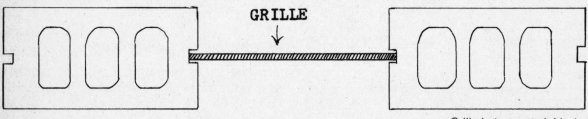

Grille between sash blocks

MORTAR "J" BOLT

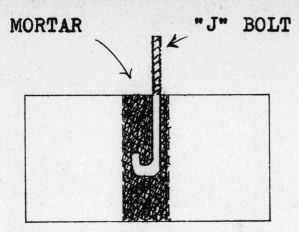

J bolt lagged in block

marks. I wind the string around a block at each end to keep it taut.

I measure 9 feet 4 inches from the foundation wall along the string and knot a piece of string to the stretched string to mark this distance. I place another knot at 19 feet 4 inches. I mark the same distances along the remaining two strings.

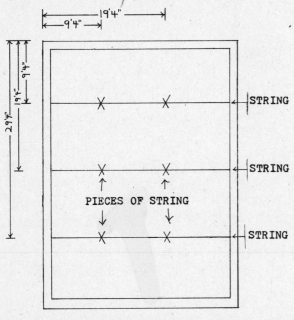

Marking position of footings for piers

Footings for Piers

Out of 1 x 8 sheathing I make six rectangular forms with inside dimensions of 16 x 24 inches. I place each of these forms so that a corner is

under the knot and its side parallel to the string. The top of the form is 2 inches above the string and is level.

I will have positioned these forms for the pier footings before the arrival of the ready-mix-concrete truck and filled them at the same time the footings for the exterior walls were poured. The bed is wetted and compacted before pouring.

On each of these six footings, I lay three blocks vertically (this is called stacking). The height from the top of the footing to the top of the stack is exactly 24 inches. The long side of the blocks are parallel to the 40-foot footing.

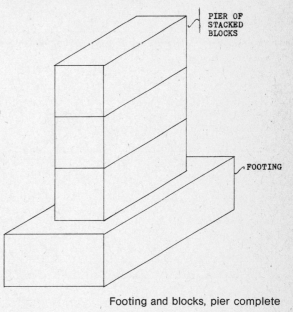

Footing and blocks, pier complete

Installing Girders

On top of these piers will be wooden members called girders or sills. They will run east and west and their ends will be supported by the foundation wall. The tops of these girders will be 1-1/2 inches higher than the foundation wall. I have done this because the next member which lies flat on the foundation wall is 1-1/2 inches thick, which will make both members flush.

To support the ends of these girders, I remove a portion of block in the foundation wall that corresponds to the shape of the girder. The result is called a pocket.

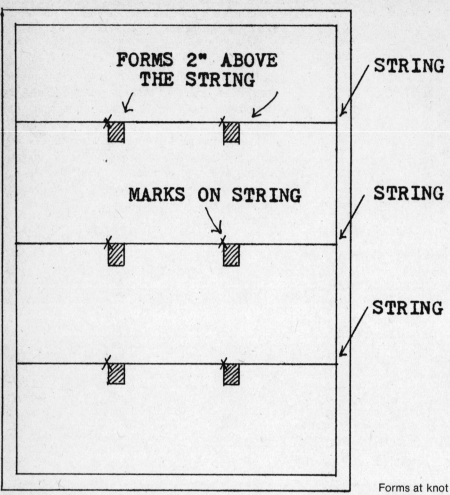

FORMS 2" ABOVE THE STRING

STRING

MARKS ON STRING

STRING

STRING

Forms at knot and 2 inches above string

Making Pockets for Ends of Girders

I mark 10 feet from the outside of the foundation wall on the 30-foot side. I use a small adjustable square called a T square to mark a **U** shape on the block, 2-1/4 inches from each side of the 10-foot mark. The **U** is 4-1/2 inches across, which is the thickness of the three 2 x 8s that make up the girder. It is 6 inches down, which leaves 1-1/2 inches of the girder above the height of the foundation wall.

The process of removing this **U** from the block is called notching; to do it, I place a composition blade in my 8-1/4-inch power saw. This blade has no teeth and cuts by abrasive action. It will cut through most masonry almost as easily as a

toothed blade cuts through wood. I cut down each side. A slight tap will cause the **U** to fall out. I use a cold chisel to clean out a "pocket" that extends 4 inches into the block.

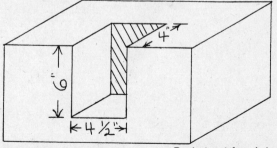

Pocket cut for girder

I make another pocket at 20 feet and two more corresponding ones in the opposite 30-foot wall.

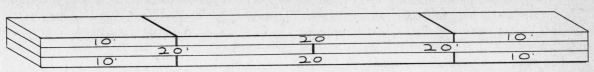

Girder with assembled 2x8s

Making Girders

I assemble a 6 x 8 girder by nailing together 10-foot and 20-foot 2 x 8 members in the following sequence:

I use 10d common galvanized nails when nailing together two 2 x 8s and 16d common galvanized nails when nailing three 2 x 8s together. The 2 x 8s are nailed from both sides and the nails are staggered at about a foot from each other.

I measure the o.o. of the corresponding pockets, trim the girder to that length, wrap each end in tar paper (15-pound felt), and install it in pockets and on the piers. (Blocks become wet during rain and the tar paper acts as a moisture barrier to inhibit rot.)

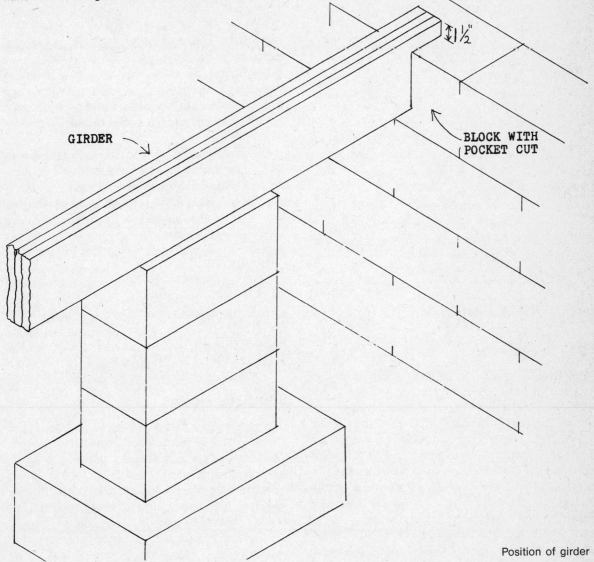

GIRDER

BLOCK WITH POCKET CUT

$1\frac{1}{2}''$

Position of girder

This girder or sill has been "built up"—meaning that it has been formed by fastening components together rather than being one solid piece. A built-up girder is stronger than a solid 6 x 8, since the grain is not continuous—the opposing grains of the components reinforce each other.

If I am working alone, I assemble both girders directly on the piers, since their final weight and length make it difficult for one person to place them into position.

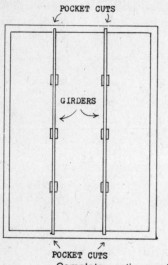

Complete continuous foundation

The continuous foundation for a house with crawl space is complete.

ADDITIONAL INFORMATION

Site Preparation

Providing a source of electricity should be included in the site-preparation stage since it will be useful right from the start to cut stakes and batter boards. If another house is within 500 feet or so of the property, I would make an arrangement with the owner for the use of an outlet. The cost of electricity for building a house is under $15.

I use a roll of #12 wire with a male and a female end as an extension cord. I will use the same wire later for appliance circuits in the house.

If power is unavailable from a house but there are power poles nearby, I arrange with the utility company for temporary service. The fee for a temporary hook-up is likely to be in the neighborhood of $50.

If there are no poles, I will make every attempt to have the utility company install them before I begin so that I can have the temporary hook-up.

If no electricity from a utility is possible, I use my 1500-watt generator. It supplies all the power I need, is light enough to handle myself, and is small enough to fit into the trunk of a car. It is gasoline-driven and makes a terrible din, but the noise is less irritating than working without power tools. The cost of this generator in 1973 was around $300.

Another item in the preparation of the site is access. If a road is required, it should be made at this time since delivery of building materials will begin shortly. In many instances, the bulldozer that digs the hole can do the road at the same time. If the road is to be surfaced, that should be held off until construction has been completed to avoid wear and tear.

Arrangements should also be made at this time to have the bulldozer return as soon as the foundation walls have been completed for the purpose of back-filling. Raising the ground level around the perimeter of the house will make heights more easily accessible, simplify handling materials, and provide a more convenient platform to walk and work on.

During back-filling the land should be sloped away from the house to keep water from running toward the house. Normal practice is to cover three courses of block and leave the fourth exposed. Mortar joints along the fourth course should be cleaned with an S-tool.

Siting the House

Using the builder's level in the manner I described should result in siting the house within an inch of the specified set-backs. However, if a minor error occurs and the house is 24 feet 9 inches from the front property line instead of the 25 feet specified, there is no cause for alarm. Most houses are not located exactly on their designated sites, and neither a bank nor a building department is likely to create difficulties because of this. I don't mean that one is free to place the house wherever he chooses nor am I advocating sloppiness in siting, but I am stating that there is a tolerance in respect to siting a house and that exactitude should be reserved for those operations where it is needed.

If the site is in a city, most probably exactness would be essential. This was brought home to me unpleasantly in San Francisco. In the course of renovating a house, I placed the mast for a new electric service on the side of the house nearest the old main. (The mast is a metal pipe in which the wire from the power source is brought into the house. The main is the box into which this wire enters and from which electricity is distributed throughout the house.) I was later obliged to move the mast when a neighbor objected that it was on his property. This was true. There were no side set-backs at all and the house I was renovating was located exactly on the side property line.

If a transit level rather than the builder's level is used in siting the house, the procedure is very similar. However, once the transit is leveled (this is done exactly as with a builder's level), the vertical screws are unlocked and the telescope lowered so that stakes and nails in them can be viewed. This elimates the need of plumbing the rod. In all other respects, the procedure is identical.

If either the builder's or transit level has been set up and anyone bumps into it, the operation must be started again from scratch. I've been the offender most of the time when this occurred by tripping over a leg of the tripod while moving away from it. I've cut down these accidents by looking at the legs of the tripod as soon as I stop looking through the telescope.

When setting up the builder's level, the leveling screws should never be tighter than snug since the base plate will be damaged if the screws are tightened too much.

The first few times either instrument is used, one should expect the bubble to keep moving off center while the telescope is rotated and not be discouraged. These are precise instruments and need fine adjusting. After fifteen minutes or so of practice, the leveling operation will not take more than a few minutes.

If neither a builder's nor a transit level is available, the house can be sited with reasonable accuracy by two hundred-foot tapes and the use of the 3, 4, 5 triangle.

The string across the front property line is set up as if the builder's level were going to be used and the 15-foot side set-backs established on it. From that point, the four corners of the house are laid out with stakes and nails in them using exactly the same procedure I described for establishing the area to be excavated.

Batter boards are erected in the way described when using the builder's level.

It now becomes necessary to establish reference marks on each of the eight batter boards that are level with each other.

I fill a garden hose with water and place an end against the side of a batter board; my helper does the same in another corner. We each place a mark on the batter board that corresponds to the height of the water in the hose. Since water finds its own level, these marks are level with each other.

I keep my end of the hose and water at my mark. My helper takes his end to a third corner, holds it against a batter board, and marks the height of the water on it. In this manner we establish four level marks on four batter boards in each corner.

I place my 4-foot level at a mark and level it across to the second batter board in the same corner to get the same corresponding height. I do this in the four corners and have eight marks level with each other.

The balance of siting the house is done in the manner already described.

A less reliable alternative to the use of a garden hose is to establish an arbitrary height in one corner and level boards in succession to a second corner and around the house to the third and fourth. This method is prone to error since over lengths of 30 feet and 40 feet even a small error in the position of the bubble in the 4-foot level will mean several inches at the far end. If the errors are cumulative (all up or down), the variation in height from one corner to another can easily be several inches.

While it is true that the location of the house on the property has a relatively high tolerance, the siting of the house itself with respect to being level (and square) should be precise. Not that a variation in height of an inch from corner to corner will ever be noticed by anyone walking on the finished floor, but successive members between these corners will require different cuts in order to fit. Throughout the construction of the house there will be needless additional work in fitting various materials. (A similar situation will exist if the house isn't square.)

Every effort should be made for exactness, since this will make things easier later and contribute to a neat final appearance.

Batter Boards and String

Batter boards should all be set at roughly the same height when they are first nailed into position. If they vary more than a few inches, the same size nail often cannot be used to establish the same height; if they vary even more, nails alone won't do. If this occurs, a plumb line is drawn from the directional mark on a high batter board, then a handsaw is used to cut down the line to make it equal in height to the other marks.

If one batter board is too low in relation to the others and a longer nail won't make up the difference, a second batter board is nailed on top of the first to provide additional height and a surface for a level mark.

When the diagonals between the intersection of strings in the corners vary more than 1-1/2 inches, the entire process by which they have been established should be repeated until the error is found. This variation is too much to correct by simply repositioning the strings.

Bed

The type of soil that will be found on the site after excavation will of course vary in different parts of the country and even in the same locality. Soft clay is the least suitable for a bed, but even soft clay will support a ton per square foot and the total weight per square foot on the clay will rarely exceed a few hundred pounds. It is therefore perfectly safe to build the footing on this type of soil.

After excavation, if the bed is found to be muck or has significant amounts of rubble, garbage, or other foreign material mixed into it, it is unsuitable and excavation will have to continue to a depth where these elements aren't a factor.

An alternative to deeper excavation is to switch to another type of foundation—pier or noncontinuous type. This kind of foundation is similar to the arrangement made for supporting the interior of the house in the continuous foundation. Further excavation would be necessary only at the location of the piers rather than throughout the entire site.

An alternative to excavation if the bed is unsuitable is the use of telephone poles which have been pressure-treated with creosote. They may be water-jetted down to an adequate bed or driven down with a jackhammer.

In many coastal areas, the bed may very well fill up with water after excavation. It will have to be pumped out of the forms and the bed exposed before footing is poured.

If these or any other unusual conditions appear in connection with the bed, seek the advice of a local builder or engineer on how to deal with it. None of these conditions is likely to be insurmountable or involve a great expense, but many options are open on how to proceed and these should be known before a choice is made.

Footing

The 8 x 16-foot footing is more than sufficient for most houses unless unusual weights and stresses are anticipated. A convenient guide for determining the size of the footing is to make it twice as wide as the intended wall and of equal thickness. A garden wall 4 inches wide, as an example, would have a footing 8 inches wide and 4 inches thick.

Of the five types of Portland cement, type 1 is most commonly used in footings. However, if the weather is very cold, "high-early strength" type 3 is used instead. It will cure more quickly and attain high strength in a week or less.

If the temperature is below freezing when the footing is being poured, special precautions *must* be taken (use of anti-freeze in the water, heating the concrete, etc.). I would not attempt pouring concrete in freezing weather without thorough consultation with a mason, engineer, or local builder.

If the weather is hot and dry when the footing is being poured, an admixture of Pozolith is helpful. Pozolith is a hydration retardant and delays water in the concrete from evaporating too quickly and thereby weakening it. I would also cover the footing with white plastic sheets for the same purpose, white reflecting heat rather than absorbing it.

If for some reason ready-mix concrete is not used for the footing, a good mixture may be prepared on the site from one bag of Portland cement, 47 shovelfuls of "bank run" gravel, and 6 gallons of water. Bank run is a mixture of sand and pebbles quarried at river banks and makes an excellent aggregate in concrete.

Erecting the Foundation Wall

When laying the first corner block, a bead of mortar having its outline is placed on the footing. This is done by eye, but the outline of the block in its correct position can be drawn on the footing first and then the bead of mortar placed on the outline. Doing this should no longer be necessary after one has laid a couple of blocks.

When laying blocks, as the block is raised into a horizontal position, the mortar on the ends occasionally falls off. One should expect this to happen often when block-laying is first attempted. It is caused by the mortar being too dry or not pressed onto the block or both. I have taught many people how to lay blocks and, on an average, the mortar ceased to fall off the ends after they laid twenty or so.

If more than a light tap with the handle end of the trowel is necessary to lower the block into position when building the wall, the mortar contains too much sand and should be remixed with additional cement and water.

If the block sinks below the string of its own weight, too much water is present. Cement and sand should be added to thicken the mortar.

Some people find it awkward to lay mortar on the left side of the block. If one turns around to do this, the application becomes the same for both sides.

Concrete-block walls have relatively little lateral strength and in building the foundation wall, in order to increase this lateral strength, the use of a metal grid 6 inches wide, 3/16 inches thick, and usually 10 feet long is sometimes specified. It is laid directly on the blocks of every third or fourth course, mortar placed on it and the next course of blocks laid as if it weren't there. The grid is called Durowall. I do not use it unless specified.

The last block to be laid in each course will usually have to be cut and laid between two already in position. Both ends need to be mortared, which doubles the chances of mortar falling off. The block may also split irregularly and leave a rather large joint. I place my palm behind the joint on the inside of the block and press mortar into the larger-than-normal joint. My palm keeps the mortar from falling through.

Before weight has been placed on the foundation wall, or any masonry wall for that matter, it has little lateral strength. If some serious error has been made, an entire course can be removed quickly. Any weight on top of the wall should first be removed. Work should proceed from the top course down. The blocks are easily removed by butting a length of 2 by 4 against them. Dried mortar is cleaned off by tapping or scraping and the block can be reused.

During the construction of the foundation and also later on, the mixing of small amounts of masonry materials will be required. A handy thing for doing this in is a wheelbarrow. "Tubs" are also available for this purpose. The tub is a one-piece metal container; one 2 by 3 feet is a convenient size and costs about $14. Avoid making wooden tubs. They are heavy, unwieldy, and wind up being more expensive. A hoe with two large holes is used to do the mixing.

Girders

The individual pieces of lumber which make up the members of a girder are rarely straight. In order to provide a level surface for the finished floor, it is necessary to make a straight girder out of variously curved members. I do this by first sighting down the side of each board and lay one on the other so that their curves are opposite. I nail them together at one end and proceed down their lengths from that end, drawing one in or the other out to align them. At first this is easy, but it becomes more difficult as the non-nailed portion becomes shorter. When it becomes too difficult to align them manually, I turn the girder on its side and toenail through the high member to drive it down into alignment with the low one.

Usually this will suffice, but if the curves are very great and toenailing won't do it, I use an I-bar furniture clamp which will draw the two members into alignment. I then nail them together (A good deal of lumber today is badly warped. Furniture clamps are very useful in dealing with this. They will also be needed for cabinet work, etc., and are necessary tools. Three or four clamps are sufficient for the entire construction process.)

In assembling the girders (and all the rough carpentry that will follow) I use mainly three kinds of nails: eight-penny, ten-penny, and sixteen-penny common (sometimes written 8d, 10d, and 16d; the d refers to the English penny, a designation that is being used less and less). The common nail has a large head and is made of galvanized steel; it is resistant to rust and holds much better than a plain steel nail. An 8 is 2-1/2 inches long, a 10, 3 inches, and a 16, 3-1/2 inches.

I use the following in selecting the size of the nail: An 8 for 3/4-inch stock nailed to 1-1/2-inch stock, a 10 when nailing two 1-1/2-inch pieces together and a 16 when nailing 1-1/2-inch to material thicker than 1-1/2 inches.

General

A contractor's price for building the 30-by-40-foot continuous foundation is likely to be around $3000. It may be a great deal more but certainly not much less. It will not include the girders.

The cost of excavation and materials will be around $500. This leaves $2500, an amount that might encourage you to do the foundation yourself.

BUILDING THE PLATFORM

4

A number of new members are now to be built on top of the girders and foundation walls, the last of which will be the subfloor. This substructure is known as the platform or deck.

Termites

If anything is to be done about termites, the time to do it is at this point in the housebuilding process.

I have never seen any termites in a house I built, have never heard of any appearing later, nor have I ever known of a house infested by them—although once in central Florida I saw a colony eating a log in a marshy area.

I have been asked several times to look at houses when the owner suspected termites were present. I found none, despite the fact that exterminating companies had asserted that they were present and submitted bids of several hundred to several thousand dollars for removing them.

In one house I found a patch of dry rot, and that was all.

In California a state law makes it obligatory for an owner to have a termite inspection prior to sale. I'm sure there were good intentions behind this law, but the effect has been to lend credibility to the existence of myriad termites eating their way through a multitude of houses. Termites have damaged homes, but their danger has been vastly exaggerated. I would approach any termite-exterminating work with caution and suspicion.

The most common termites in our country are white ants of the subterranean and nonsubterranean types. The subterranean ants are most prevalent in the South. They live underground, come out to feed, then return to the soil for moisture. They build tunnels over materials they cannot burrow through and use them to travel back and forth between the soil and wood.

If a house is being built in an area where their existence is definitely a factor, some architects specify that the wooden substructure be pressure-treated with chemicals toxic to termites. A cheaper alternative measure is to poison the soil under the house. This should be done by someone versed in the toxic chemicals required.

A simple, excellent measure is to leave the crawl space clean and free of wood scraps. The most common structural precaution taken is a flat band of sheet metal that lies directly on the foundation wall. It is called a termite shield. I do not know what value it has, nor did two entomologists I spoke to about it.

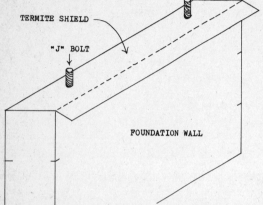

Termite shield on foundation wall

I use 11-inch-wide thin-gauge aluminum for the shield and Wiss hole-cutting shears to cut holes and slit the aluminum so that it will lie flat around the J bolts that have been lagged into the top of the foundation wall. (An alternative is to bore holes.)

Attaching the Mud Sill

On top of the termite shield I place a long 2 x 8. An end is flush with the corner block and its side butts against the J bolts. I lay a framing square against each side of a J bolt and mark parallel

corresponding lines on the 2 x 8. I measure the distance between the center of each bolt and the outside of the block and mark this distance between the parallel lines.

I place the threaded tip of a 1-inch Greenlee auger-type bit on the mark and use a heavy-duty half-inch Black & Decker drill to bore the hole. (The drill revolves at 375 r.p.m. and costs about $80.)

I mark and bore holes for each of the protruding J bolts, lay the 2 x 8 over the termite shield, place washers over the bolts, and begin to tighten nuts on the bolts to fasten the 2 x 8 to the foundation wall.

I have purposely used a 1-inch bit, although the bolt is only 3/8 inch in diameter, in order to be able to shift the 2 x 8 and align it easily with the outside of the foundation wall.

This member is called a mud sill. It covers the top of the foundation wall continuously around the entire house and lies flush with the wall's outside.

(The use of a 2 x 8 rather than a 2 x 6 for this member is for cosmetic reasons. A 2 x 6 will leave exposed part of the holes in the block of the foundation wall. However, using a 2 x 6 will save the equivalent of 140 feet of 2 x 2 lumber.)

After the mud sill has been fastened, I place a 3-foot scrap of 2 x 4 on top of the portion of the termite shield that extends beyond the foundation wall. I clasp the metal and wood together and bend the metal down to approximately a 45-degree angle.

(From time to time it will be necessary to bend thin-gauge metal. A similar technique is always used. A straight 2 x 4 is clamped on top of the metal along the line of the desired bend. The metal

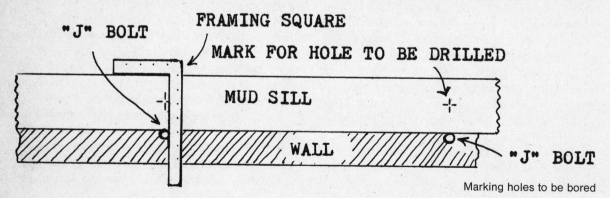

Marking holes to be bored

is then lifted partially up against the side of the 2 x 4. Another 2 x 4 scrap is then placed so that the partially bent metal lies between both 2 x 4s; the bend is completed by hammering the scrap and metal against the side of the clamped 2 x 4.)

Fastening the End Joist or Boxing Board

When a board is positioned on its side, it is referred to as being on edge. I place a 2 x 8 on edge on top of the mud sill. I shift the end so that it is flush with the end of the mud sill and outside of the foundation wall. I toenail an 8d nail through the end of the 2 x 8 into the mud sill. I then proceed down the length of the 2 x 8 and toenail it every 4 feet or so to the mud sill, keeping its outer side aligned with the outer edge of the mud sill.

I lean my body weight on top of the 2 x 8 while nailing it to minimize its shifting around. I am also driving the toenails at about a 60-degree angle. This reduces the movement of the 2 x 8 while I am nailing and makes aligning it easier.

Since I am standing outside the site and nailing toward it, the tendency is for the board to move inside the mud sill. If difficulty is encountered, scraps can be tacked (not nailed completely, having 1/2 inch or so of the nail head up from the scrap) to the mud sill 1-1/2 inches back from the outer side. This will provide backing while nailing and ensure alignment.

I proceed around the perimeter of the house, butting 2 x 8s, nailing them to the mud sill until

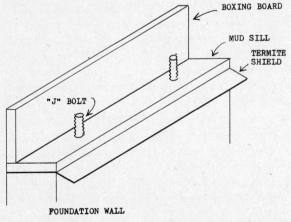

BOXING BOARD

MUD SILL

TERMITE SHIELD

"J" BOLT

FOUNDATION WALL

End joist nailed to mud sill

I have completed the rectangle. I space the nails along the 30-foot side 16-inches or so apart. Unlike the boxing boards along the 40-foot sides, which will later be nailed to another member and can be attached with nails every 4 feet or so, the end joists on the 30-foot sides will not be secured along their bottom edges except by these nails every 16 inches.

Here again, nailing should proceed from one end to the other of the 2 x 8 rather than fastening both ends first, in order to make alignment with the mud sill easier.

Floor Joists

The member which is attached to the top of the girders and crosses them at right angles is called a floor joist. An end will rest on the mud sill and butt the boxing board.

The size of a joist is a function of the span or unsupported distance it will have to cover.

SPAN	SIZE OF JOIST
6'–8'	2 x 6
8'–10'	2 x 8
10'–12'	2 x 10
12'–14'	2 x 12

The girders of this foundation have been placed 10 feet apart; using the table above, a 2 x 8 as the size of the joist would be appropriate. Had the girders been spaced closer or further apart, the size of the joist would change accordingly.

The same holds true for the girders themselves. In this case the piers were spaced 10 feet apart and a 6 x 8 was used across this 10-foot span. Other combinations may be used in this way:

SPAN	SIZE OF GIRDER
6'–8'	4 x 6
8'–10'	4 x 8
10'–12'	4 x 10
12'–14'	4 x 12

In this table I have omitted the third member of the girder. I believe a 4 x 8, for example, is strong enough to cover a span of 8 feet and that a 6 x 8 is excessive. My belief is based on the fact that I have always used the above modules in houses I have built with no subsequent structural problems whatsoever; and on firsthand knowledge of many houses built in the last century, where even greater spans were used with equivalent members and no structural problems resulted. (I have used the 6 x 8 as a girder in the house described in this book only because it was part of the code where the house was being built.)

My own preference is to use 4 x 6 girders spaced 6 feet apart, and 2 x 6 floor joists. It is a strictly pragmatic preference since, of all the combinations, this module results in the most "solid"-feeling floor. Costs work out about the same for any module.

Marking the Position of the Floor Joists

How far apart the floor joists will be spaced depends on what material will be used for the subfloor which will later be nailed on top of them.

In the vast majority of houses, the subfloor will be a type of half-inch-thick plywood called plyscore. This material should be supported every 16 inches and I will therefore space the floor joists every 16 inches.

Not only plyscore, but a great number of other materials that will go into the house are designed to be supported at 16-inch intervals. On blueprints this designation will read *16-inch o.c.*

I hook my hundred-foot tape to the end of the boxing board in the southwest corner. I unwind it so that the tape lies on the board and place a mark on the inside edge of board at 16 inches. Each 16-inch multiple is marked in white rather than black for quicker identification.

I place an **X** to the right of the mark to indicate that the joist will be positioned on this side of the mark. This marking convention is used throughout the country.

I continue to mark off multiples of 16 inches with **X**s to the right. However, instead of marking 96 inches, I make the mark at 95 1/4 inches. The reason for this is that I later intend to lay the plyscore sheets (which are 4 x 8 feet) on these joists. One end of the 8 foot side of the plyscore sheet will be flush with the boxing board. The other end will fall midway along this joist spaced at 95 1/4 inches and provide a nailing surface for the next sheet which butts to it.

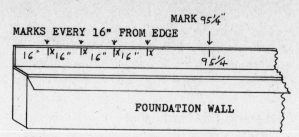

16-inch o.c. spacing of joists and at 95-1/4-inch mark

I tack a nail through the 95-1/4-inch mark, hook the tape on it, and continue to mark 16-inch multiples along the south 40-foot side.

I make corresponding marks on the girders.

Along the opposite 40-foot north side, I begin marking from the northwest corner and also place the **X** to my right. In doing this, the distance between the first two joists will be 14-1/2 inches rather than 16 inches. I do this because I want the joists from the north side to lie beside the joists from the south side rather than butt them, which would require that all the joists be cut. With the exception of the first two joists and the one at 95 1/4 inches, all will maintain the 16-inch o.c. module.

Installing Floor Joists

Standard lumber is sold in 2-foot multiples which begin at 8 feet and end at 24 feet. Lumber yards have begun to place a surcharge on lengths longer than 16 feet. Lengths longer than 24 feet can be secured but are very expensive.

The 2 x 8 joists will have a total length of 30 feet less the thickness of the two boxing boards, which total 3 inches. For reasons of economy, I will use two lengths of 2 x 8 to cover this 29 feet 9 inches rather than purchasing 30-foot lengths and trimming them.

I select 20-foot lengths and 10-foot lengths since their ends will rest on a girder. An 18-foot and 12-foot combination, or 14 feet and 16 feet, would leave the ends between girders and create a structural weakness that would have to be rectified with additional work and material. (Another 10-foot length would have to be placed across the girders beside each of these and the ends nailed to the 10-foot piece.)

I sight down the side of a 20-foot 2 x 8 to deter-

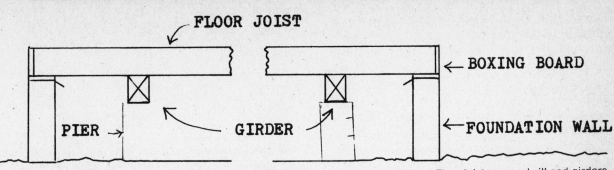

FLOOR JOIST

BOXING BOARD

PIER → GIRDER

← FOUNDATION WALL

Floor joists on mud sill and girders

mine if it has a curve. Most likely it will have one. The high side is called the crown. In installing all the floor joists, I will sight down each one and place the crown up.

I place the 2 x 8 on edge, crown up, and use three eight-penny nails to toenail it into the mud sill, two from one side and one from the other. I use three 10d nails in the same manner to toenail the joist to the girder. The side of the joist lies at the mark and over the **X**. I use 2 10d nails to nail through the boxing boards into the end of the the joist.

If the crown is minor, I lean my body down on it before nailing in order to bring the bottom edge down to the girder. If the crown is moderate, I sit on it. This is usually enough to bring the bottom edge down to the girder. If the weight of my body is not enough to accomplish this, I use the furniture clamp.

If I come across a 2 x 8 that is terribly warped, I cut it at the highest point of the crown and use the two pieces elsewhere. If a joist is twisted to one side or the other, I let it go and straighten the twist when I install the plyscore.

Since the joists are 16 inches o.c., I will need three for every 4 feet plus one for the end, a total of thirty-one. I already have two installed, the boxing boards or end joists. I therefore need twenty-nine floor joists. I install the twenty-eight remaining ones in the same manner as the first.

I move to the north side of the house and place a 2 x 8 on edge. One end butts the boxing board, a side is at the mark and over the **X**. The other end lies beside the 20-foot joist. (Most often boards are an inch or two longer than the length at which they were sold.) By placing them side by side, I have avoided cutting any of the joists.

I install the remaining 10-foot joists in the same manner.

Bridging

Along the top of both 30-foot boxing boards, I mark 5, 15, and 25 feet from either 40-foot side. These are the centers of the three spans of the joists. I stretch a chalk line over the corresponding marks, tighten the string, raise it a few inches, and let it snap down. On top of each joist there should be a chalk mark at each of these distances.

I nail a piece of metal bridging beside a chalk mark using six common nails. The bridging has predrilled holes. I allow the other end of the bridging to lie between the joists. On the joist nearest to it, I nail another piece of bridging on the side opposite the mark that I nailed first. I install all the bridging in this manner, all ends lying in the area between joists. The area is called a bay. Sometime after the roof is on I will go under the house and attach these ends to the bottoms of successive joists. The ends of the bridging are flat and are bent so that they lie flat on the joist.

The purpose of bridging is to stiffen the joists and diminish their lateral movement. Hopefully this will lessen the possibility of creaking in the

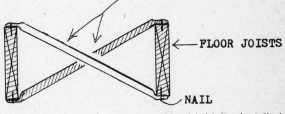

METAL BRIDGING

FLOOR JOISTS

NAIL

Metal bridging installed

47

finished floor. I find the value of bridging dubious, but it is frequently specified in plans for spans greater than 8 feet. It is omitted in spans under 8 feet.

The Subfloor

The 4 x 8 sheets of half-inch plyscore that will be installed over the floor joists make up the subfloor, which will be covered later by the finished floor.

Plyscore is the cheapest grade of plywood and sells at about $7 for a 4 x 8-foot sheet. It is made in either five thin layers or three thicker ones. The five-ply sheets are stronger and are usually bound together with a better grade of glue. Both kinds use exterior glue, but several times in building houses the three-ply sheets came apart before I had completed the framework—a matter of less than a week. Since plyscore may be exposed to the weather for an even longer period, avoid using the three-ply. I've had best results using the five-ply sheet made by Weyerhauser.

Installing Plyscore

I begin at the southwest corner and lay a sheet over the 20-foot joists. The 4-foot side lies along the west boxing board and the 8-foot side along the south boxing board. I tack a 7 common nail near the corner and another at the end of the 4-foot side. I push the boxing board in or out so that it will be aligned with the plyscore and nail.

I do the same with the 4-foot side. The plyscore can be relied upon to be square and have straight edges; by aligning the top of the boxing board with it, I am removing variations.

I move to the opposite 8-foot side and if necessary twist the joists by hand to straighten them before nailing. If more force is needed I use my heel to do this; if that isn't enough, I clamp the furniture clamp to the joists and use the leverage provided by the bar to twist them to an upright position, then nail.

I nail down the rest of the sheet, spacing the 7s every 10 inches or so along each joist.

I install five sheets along the 40-foot south side to form a row.

I mark 4 feet along both 8-foot sides and pop a chalk line between the marks.

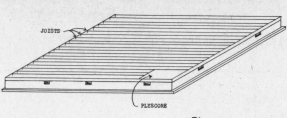

Plyscore on joists

I loosen the wing nut of the saw, pull back the guard, place the blade against the side of the plyscore, and adjust the table so that the teeth of the blade are slightly below the plyscore. I tighten the wing nut with the teeth set at that depth—slightly more than the thickness of the plyscore. I make my cut and have two 4 x 4-foot pieces less the width of the flare of the blade's teeth (about 3/16 inch, the kerf).

I start the adjoining row with a 4-foot piece. This staggers the joints between rows of plyscore and is done to avoid having all the ends fall on the same joists and creating a structural weakness.

I nail five rows.

On the sixth row, I trim 1 1/2 inches from the 8-foot side of the sheet so that this end will fall midway along the 10-foot joist. The remaining sheets needn't be trimmed and will all fall along the centers of their respective joists.

I complete two rows. A strip 2 feet wide remains to be covered along the north side. I rip five 2 x 8-foot pieces and nail them to complete the subfloor.

The structure as it now stands, the deck or platform, is complete.

ADDITIONAL INFORMATION

When the word *lumber* is used, it means wood that has been milled from logs to various thicknesses and lengths as delivered to a lumber yard. After this lumber has been installed it is referred to most often by the structural function it serves. The 2 x 8s were lumber when I received them and floor joists when in place.

Structural lumber today is mainly Douglas fir, an evergreen that grows chiefly in the Northwest. It is strong and well suited for structural purposes. Another evergreen, hemlock fir, is also widely used. Many consider it inferior since it is softer, not as strong, and supposedly shrinks more. I prefer hemlock. It has the distinct advantage of being lighter, easier to handle, splits less easily when nailing, and—most important—is usually far straighter over longer lengths than Douglas fir.

It's true that Douglas fir is stronger than hemlock but any stress placed on a structural member of the house will be borne perfectly adequately by hemlock, so the fact that a house of Douglas fir is stronger has no real practical significance.

It's true that hemlock is softer, but hemlock is hard enough to fulfill any hardness requirements placed on it and so I can see no disadvantage in that respect.

As far as shrinking is concerned, this used to be a real problem when lumber was often delivered "green" or very wet and did shrink considerably, but lumber today is delivered fairly dry and shrinkage is no longer a factor of great importance.

My preference for hemlock is personal. I think the two woods are fairly interchangeable and, in fact, when fir is ordered today either hemlock or Douglas or both will be delivered at the same price.

Lumber is sold by the board foot: 1 x 12 1 foot long or its equivalent. One lineal foot of 2 x 6 equals one board foot. A 2 x 4 is two-thirds of a board foot, etc.

The price of lumber today is so variable that no figure I could give would be meaningful. In the past year it has risen from $220 per thousand board feet to $320.

I mentioned a surcharge earlier in the chapter on lengths longer than 16 feet. This has been 10 percent for lengths to 20 feet and 15 percent for lengths to 24 feet. Lengths longer than 24 feet can be secured from companies who specialize in them. As an example of their prices, a 6 x 16 30 feet long costs in the neighborhood of $350. This does not include a delivery charge of $40.

Nails

Nails were formerly sold in hundred-pound kegs; they now come in 50-pound cardboard cartons. Galvanized steel nails and steel nails are most often used. Steel nails are $17 per 100 pounds, galvanized $30.

Steel nails hold least well and also rust badly and quickly. I never use them in beach areas or where there is a high content of salt in the air. In fact, I rarely use them at all.

Galvanized nails are satisfactory except when the head will be exposed to the weather, as in nailing an exterior finish of cedar siding. The head will decompose slightly; rain washing over it will leave a streak on the wood. The nail is said to "bleed." (I use aluminum nails in this particular situation.)

Subfloors

Subfloors are a sound structural feature but not an indispensable one; many houses have been built without them. A little more than $300 can be saved by eliminating one. This may not be a staggering amount in itself, but where economy is the primary factor the subfloor should be eliminated.

If the subfloor is eliminated, framing (which is the next step) can begin.

A builder friend once put up one house several blocks from where I was working on another. The subfloor had been eliminated. The architect had specified that the single finished floor was to be 1 x 3-inch oak. The flooring was to be laid and left exposed to the weather for as long as it took to complete the exterior. Some delays were encountered and it was several months before the exterior was completed. During this period the raw oak floor was rained on and dried out a number of times. My builder friend and I had both been flabbergasted at first and smirking later, but we were both obliged to eat our smirks when surprisingly there was almost no warpage or buckling and a rather attractive patina resulted.

If the subfloor is eliminated, the finished floor is laid directly on the joists. This can be done immediately after the joists are installed or later, when the exterior of the house has been completed.

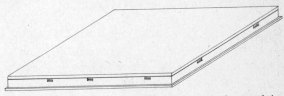

Platform or deck complete

WALL FRAMING

5

The cutting, assembling, and installation of those members which form the skeleton of the house is known as framing. The most widely used type of framing is platform (sometimes called Western).

Another type, balloon framing, was formerly common but has been disappearing because of its greater complexity without compensating advantages.

The 30 x 40-foot house has this floor plan (see p. 17) and north elevation. Those features not relevant to framing have been omitted from the drawings. Since I have also omitted the three other elevations which would ordinarily be included, I must note on the floor plan that the kitchen window has been placed at 6 feet in height, a detail that would appear on the west elevation.

Shoe

I place a 2 x 4 on the flat, an end even with a corner. I nail it with 16s at the corner and continue down its length while aligning it with the boxing board. At each 16 inches I drive a nail through the 2 x 4 and plyscore into successive joists and the boxing board. I drive an additional nail into the boxing board midway between joists. I nail 2 x 4s end to end until they form a continuous rectangle around the perimeter of the platform. This member is the bottom of the wall and called the sole or shoe.

Shoe; 2x4 around perimeter of completed platform

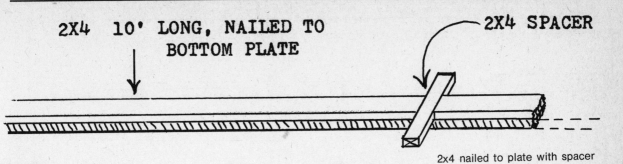

2X4 10' LONG, NAILED TO BOTTOM PLATE

2X4 SPACER

2x4 nailed to plate with spacer

Plate

The top of the wall is called the plate and is composed of a double layer of 2 x 4s which run horizontally on the flat. The bottom half of the plate is a duplicate of the shoe, and I lay 2 x 4s end to end on top of the shoe.

I begin the top half of the plate 3-1/2 inches from the northwest corner. I don't measure this but use a 2 x 4 as a spacer to mark it. I leave this gap because wherever walls intersect one another at right angles, as they do in all exterior corners, the top half of the plate of the intersecting wall will extend into this gap and tie the two walls together. It is called a lap joint.

I have started at the northwest corner, and as I look at the floor plan I see that the first partition to intersect the north wall is at 10 feet i.d. I cut a 2 x 4 to that length and nail it to the bottom half of the plate with 10s spaced every 12 inches.

I place the spacer at the end of the 10-foot 2 x 4. The plan indicates that the second partition is also at 10 feet i.d. I cut a 2 x 4 to that length, butt it to the spacer, and nail. I lay the spacer against the end of the 10-foot 2 x 4.

The third partition lies at 5 feet i.d. I cut a 2 x 4 at 5 feet and nail it.

The third partition is a plumbing wall and is made of 2 x 6s. This wall is wider, to accommodate pipes which will later be installed inside it. I lay a 2 x 6 spacer against the end of the 5-foot 2 x 4. The distance to the east wall is 13 feet 4-1/2

inches. I cut a 2 x 4 to that length and nail it.

Plate for North Wall

I align the completed plate with the shoe and tack it to the shoe by toenailing. This is to keep the plate from shifting when I mark the position of other members on both the plate and shoe.

The plan indicates that there are no partitions along the east wall. I cut 2 x 4s for the bottom half of the plate so that 3-1/2 inches are omitted at each end. I cut the top half so that the butted 2 x 4s are exactly 30 feet, which leaves each end extending 3-1/2 inches beyond the bottom half. When I erect the walls, these 3-1/2-inch extensions will fit over the bottom half of the plate of the intersecting walls.

One partition at 13 feet 4-1/2 inches i.d. is indicated along the south wall. The bottom half of the plate is flush with the corner. I cut the top half to length and nail it 3-1/2 inches back from the corner. I place a 2 x 4 spacer against the other end of the piece and continue the plate to the southwest corner, where the top half of the plate is 3-1/2 inches back from that corner.

Two partitions of the hallway intersect the west wall. I assemble the plate for this wall in the same way as the others, leaving a 3-1/2-inch gap where both walls intersect. The top half of the plate extends 3-1/2 inches beyong the bottom half at each end.

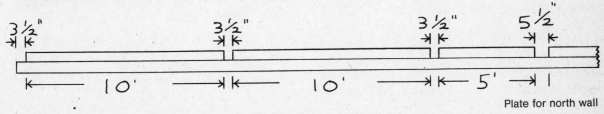

3½"   3½"   3½"   5½"

10'   10'   5'

Plate for north wall

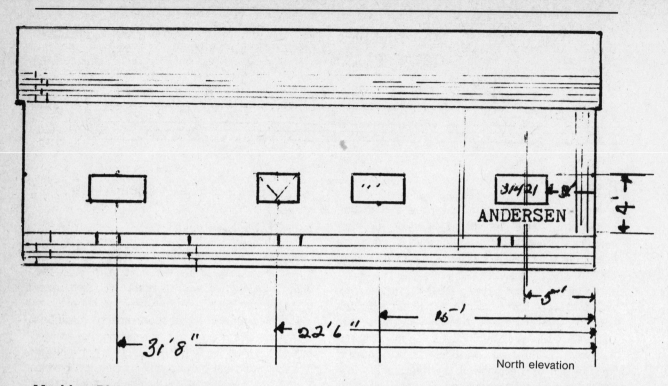

North elevation

Marking Plates and Shoes Simultaneously

The north elevation is the north side of the house as seen from the outside while facing south. A window is indicated 5 feet o.c. from the northwest corner.

The number on the window refers to a specific window which the manufacturer details in a catalogue supplied at no charge by the lumber company. For framing purposes, the detail I am interested in is the r.o. (rough opening). This is the area in the wall which I will leave open in order to install the window later. This particular window is manufactured by the Andersen Co. In their catalogue, under r.o. for the number on the window, 42 x 23 inches is given. By convention, width is always given first.

I mark 5 feet o.c. on the side of the plate. I measure outward 11-1/2 inches from the center mark and draw squared lines down and across the shoe and plate. I place a **J** to the outside of each line, the **J** standing for jack. I place the 1-1/2-inch side of a 2 x 4 spacer over the J and adjacent to the lines and mark an **X** outward from both Js. The **X** stands for stud.

The continuous vertical members between the shoe and plate in a wall are called studs. The vertical members which go only part of the way from the shoe to the plate and are used as a support for other members are called jacks.

The three remaining windows along the north wall are marked out in the same way as the first. In each case, the distance between jacks is equal to the width of the r.o.

Two windows are indicated along the east wall. The r.o. of these windows is given in the catalogue as 84 x 30 inches.

The width of these windows is established in the same way as the narrower ones, but instead of one jack and one stud at each side of the opening, a double jack is used and is marked **JJX**. When the width of an opening is 6 feet or greater, many building departments require the double jack.

The windows along the south wall are marked off in a similar manner.

Width of window marked **J** and **X** on shoe and plate

The sliding door along the south wall is treated the same as a window. It has a r.o. of 72 x 82 inches. I use a double jack on either side of the opening and also a double stud. This is indicated **JJXX**. The additional stud serves to strengthen the doorway opening.

A 36-inch-wide door is indicated on the west wall. The width of the r.o. of all exterior doors is 3 inches greater than the door size. I have already marked out the partitions intersecting this wall. They have a measurement of 42 inches i.d. I mark 21 inches on the plate between these partitions. I place a circle around this mark, which indicates by convention that this is a center mark. I measure outward 19-1/2 inches on either side of the center mark, draw lines over the plate and shoe, and place a **J** outward from each line. I then mark lines for a double stud and label **JXX** on each side. The i.d. width between jacks is 39 inches. The double stud is used to help keep the house from shaking when the door is slammed.

The windows on the west wall are marked in the same way as the other windows.

Making Corner Posts for Walls

I fasten three scraps of 2 x 4 to a stud with tenpenny nails. Each scrap is at least 1 foot long. Two are flush with the ends and the third is centered.

I nail a second stud on top of the blocks with 16s spaced every 10 inches or so. I turn it over and nail from the other side.

Marking Studs

I return to the northwest corner, hook my tape on the plate, and mark off multiples of 16 inches on the plate and shoe with the **X** to my left. This is to position studs and I ignore my other marks while doing it. I stop at 95-1/4 inches and begin 16-inch multiples again from that point.

I repeat this on the three remaining plates and shoes.

When marking the position of studs of the exterior walls, the 16-inch module should be kept throughout the length of the wall despite the fact that around openings and partitions there will be clusters of 2 x 4s. These studs will provide a nailing surface for the next member to go on the exterior of the wall.

I remove the nails which have tacked the plate to the shoe and drag the plate back so that it lies parallel to the shoe and about 8 feet away. I turn the plate on edge so that the marks I made are up.

The height of the walls are specified as 8 feet, a frequent dimension. Lumber yards sell what is known as a precut stud which is a 2 x 4, 7 feet 8 inches long. The thickness of the shoe and plate total 4-1/2 inches, and when added to the precut stud will make a wall that is 96-1/2 inches high. (The precut stud is sold at the same price as the 8-foot stud. All studs I refer to now are precut.)

I lay the stud-block-stud on edge and nail a third stud with 16s so that a side is flush. This last stud is called a return and provides an interior nailing surface in the southwest corner.

The three studs and block nailed together in this fashion are the member in each corner of the house, called the corner post.

I place the corner post between the plate and shoe and push the plate forward until the end of the post lies against the shoe. The return stud is on the subfloor and is flush on the outside. I toenail a 16 through the bottom half of the plate into the outer stud, then into the inner stud. I toenail 16s through the post into the plate from three sides.

The north elevation indicates that the tops of all windows are 4 feet. This framing measurement is always from the subfloor unless otherwise specified.

Two jacks are required for each of the four windows. Since they will be positioned on the

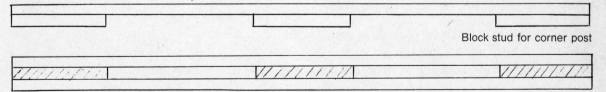

Block stud for corner post

Stud, block, stud for corner post

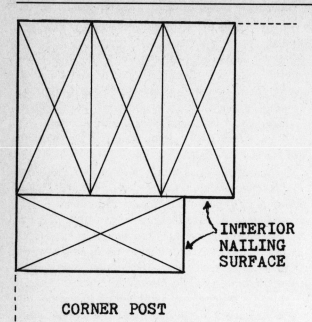

CORNER POST

Stud, block, stud, return stud complete corner post—end view

shoe, I cut eight 2 x 4s to a length of 46-1/2 inches, which will give me the 4-foot height specified when the thickness of the shoe is added. Jacks for all openings are 1-1/2 inches less than the specified height.

I nail a jack to a stud. I toenail a 16 through the bottom half of the plate into the stud then two 10s through the stud from either side into the plate. Three nails are adequate for attaching vertical members to the shoe and plate. The jack and stud lie over the **JX**.

I repeat this on the other side of the opening.

Headers

The member which will lie on top of the jacks across the r.o. is called a header. In bearing walls it is always placed on edge for greater strength. Bearing walls are those which support additional weight. Conversely, nonbearing walls only support their own weight. All exterior walls are considered load-bearing.

Headers are almost always made of two pieces of 1-1/2-inch stock that are nailed together. Since they are installed on edge, their thickness will be 3 inches while the width of the wall is 3-1/2 inches. This leaves a half-inch difference. This

difference is placed at the interior side of the wall.

The size of the 1-1/2-inch stock to be used is directly related to the span of the opening.

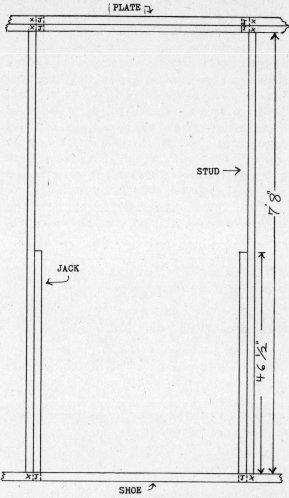

Jacks and studs for window opening

SPAN	SIZE OF HEADER
4'	4 x 4
6'	4 x 6
8'	4 x 8
10'	4 x 10
12'	4 x 12

These figures given for header sizes as related to spans are the lower range for each, so I would not hesitate to use a 4 x 12 across a 13-foot span or even 14 feet.

Between 14 and 16 feet I would use two 2 x 12s with a piece of 1/2 x 12-inch plyscore sandwiched between them. Plywood has a great deal of strength when placed on edge this way and will support much more weight than the fir which is three times as thick. This built-up header is stronger than a 4 x 16. It should be heavily nailed, every 8 inches or so, and the nails staggered so that they do not follow the grain of the fir.

The width of this r.o. is 42 inches. The o.o. of the jacks is 45 inches. I cut two pieces of 2 x 4 to a length of 45 inches and nail them together.

I place the header beside the plate and transfer the marks for the studs to the header.

I place the header on edge on top of the jacks.

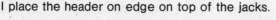

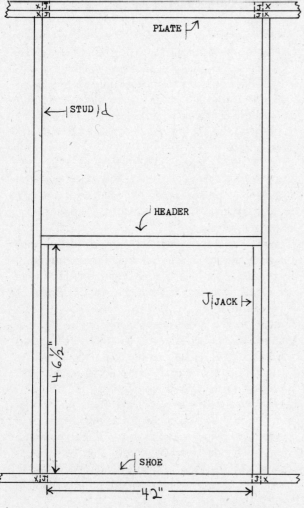

Header installed

I nail through the studs into the header, then toenail through the top of the header at each end into the studs. When I raise the wall, what is now up will become the outside and I therefore make the header in the same plane as the other members.

The final member which completes the r.o. lies parallel to the header and is called the subsill. It is a single 2 x 4 on the flat and is always the same length as the width of the r.o.

I cut a 2 x 4 42 inches long. I place it beside the shoe, each end at the line for the jacks. I transfer the stud marks on the shoe to the subsill.

The height of the r.o. is 23 inches. I mark this on each jack, measuring down from the underside of the header, and nail to each jack.

I measure up from the bottom of the jack to the underside of the subsill. It is 22 inches. I count the number of **X**s on the shoe that lie under the subsill and cut that many pieces of 2 x 4 22 inches long. I nail them to the subsill. They are called legs.

I measure the distance between the top of the header and the plate, which is 42 inches. I count the **X**s on the plate, cut that number of 2 x 4s 42 inches long, and nail them between the top of the header and the plate. They are called top legs or nailers.

In framing the r.o. for windows, if the opening is 1/2 inch or so larger than specified, it falls within the tolerance. However, care should be taken that the r.o. isn't *smaller* than specified. The window will usually be half an inch smaller than the r.o., but if the opening isn't square this half inch will be needed to level and plumb the window.

Except for the doorway on the west wall, the rest of the openings are all framed in this manner.

I nail a stud to the plate on all the remaining **X**s.

Wherever an interior partition intersects an exterior wall I have left a gap of 3-1/2 inches in the top plate. I place an **X** on each side of this gap.

I nail three scrap pieces of 2 x 4 on the flat between two studs. These scraps are flush on the interior side of the wall.

This member is called a partition return. I nail it to the plate so that the studs are on each side of the gap. These studs provide a nailing surface for the interior wall.

At the plumbing wall I use 2 x 6 scraps as blocking.

(For reasons of brevity in describing this procedure, I cut one header at first, one jack, one leg, etc. In actual practice I would cut all of these and position all studs so that all the members of the wall were in place before I began assembling them.)

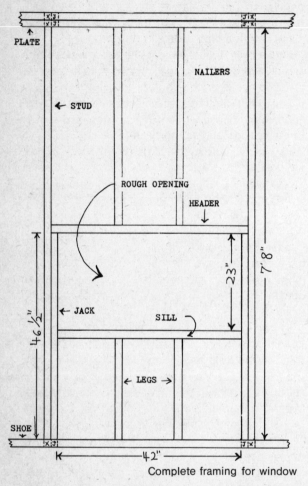

Complete framing for window

Raising Framed Walls

The north wall has been assembled and is ready to be raised and nailed to the shoe. It is 40 feet long, too heavy and unwieldy for one person to handle. I would use five helpers to raise the wall, then four to hold it upright while the fifth person nails and braces it. In general, one person is needed for each 10 feet of wall to be raised and a second to nail. If only three people were available, I would build the wall in 20-foot sections and nail the plates together after they were in position. All the walls

of this house can be raised without difficulty in less than an hour. No skill or great strength is needed, but an adequate number of hands is essential.

The people who help raise the wall must be instructed to remain at their position and hold the wall erect until it is braced. I once neglected to do this, and after the wall was raised one person let go of it and then a second. The wall fell off the platform. No one was hurt, but the entire wall had to be dismantled and reassembled.

If fewer people are present than was anticipated, I would separate the wall into proportionate sections by sawing through the bottom half of the plate, then the top half 16 inches away. I can renail them once the sections are raised, leaving the gap of the kerf.

If there is a high wind, I would use an extra person for the 40-foot wall; if the day is calm, use four.

I place a 10-foot 2 x 4 on edge against the outside of the corner post. One end lies a foot or so below the plate, the other toward the south wall. I nail it to the post with a 16. It will act as a temporary brace after the wall is raised. I repeat this in the other corner.

I lift the plate and slide a 10-foot 2 x 4 on edge under it for a foot or so. It lies against a stud; the other end is toward the south wall. I tack it with a 16. I repeat this every 6 feet or so. These will be intermediate braces.

I nail 1- or 2-foot-long 2 x 4 scraps to the floor joists so that they are in line with these intermediate braces and roughly 9 feet from the shoe. These are cleats, and the bottom end of the brace is nailed to them.

Each person positions himself about 10 feet from the next along the wall. They grip the underside of the plate and lift. As the wall rises, the vertical members press against the shoe. As the wall continues to be raised, some or all of the vertical members will lie on top of the shoe. As the wall is raised higher, the plate no longer becomes a convenient place to hold and lift. Each person shifts his hands to a convenient stud without releasing the forward pressure and continues to lower his hands and push forward until the wall is erect.

When the wall is nearly vertical very little forward

pressure is needed, and care must be taken not to push too hard or the wall will go over.

As soon as the wall is erect, one person toenails six 16s through the corner post into the shoe from all four sides. He then lifts the bottom of the brace, holds the end against the boxing board, and starts a 16 into the brace.

A second person holds a 4-foot level on the south side of the post. He taps the post north or south until the bubble in the level is centered and the post plumb in respect to north and south. The first person nails a 16 into the boxing board and then tacks a second. The same thing is done to plumb and brace the opposite corner and then all the intermediate braces.

A long 2 x 4 is laid against the inside of the wall in an east–west direction. One end is nailed to the corner post a foot or so below the plate. The corner is plumbed in relation to east–west, then the bottom of the 2 x 4 is nailed to the shoe and stud midway along its length. Since the corner post is plumb and all the vertical members are equidistant from it top and bottom, all vertical members are also plumb. A second brace is placed in the opposite corner for increased rigidity.

After walls are raised, the studs dangle. To nail their bottom ends, I place my instep against the end on the opposite side of the stud from where I intend to nail it. This acts as backing and leaves my hands free to position the nail and tack it. Once the nail is through the stud and into the shoe, I hammer the nail and stud forward together. If I go beyond the mark, I tack a second nail and drive both the stud and nail to the correct position.

If by error a stud is nailed less than 1 inch from its correct position, it needn't be removed and renailed. I start a nail into the stud, then drive the nail and stud to its mark. I then add two more nails when it is correctly positioned.

Raising and plumbing walls tends to be a hurried operation. I make a point of rechecking them at a later time in an unhurried way.

The 4-foot level is an adequate tool to plumb a wall. However, the best way to determine whether a wall is straight is to get up on a stepladder at a corner and sight down the plate. Variations are apparent and braces can be adjusted to remove them by tapping the brace forward or backward at the

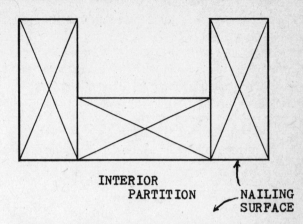

INTERIOR PARTITION   NAILING SURFACE

Partition return to provide a nailing surface in corners for interior walls

bottom end, then driving another nail through it into the cleat.

In assembling the east and west walls, the last stud at both ends is omitted, since each has already been nailed on the corner post as a return.

A double jack is used in framing the r.o. for the windows in the east wall, since the span is greater than 6 feet. The header will therefore be 6 inches longer than the width, or 90 inches.

Similarly, a double jack was used for framing the sliding door on the south wall; its header will be 78 inches.

On the west wall is the doorway. The r.o. height is 7 feet. This is constant for all exterior doors unless the door itself is specified to be other than 80 inches, which is standard. It will then be 4 inches higher than the height of the door.

I will also use a 4 x 6 header over this doorway, although the span is only 39 inches. This is to make

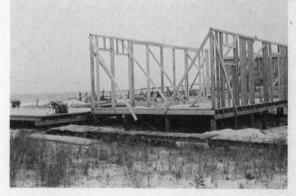

Walls erect and braced

the opening stronger since I anticipate frequent and hard use.

My first step in framing walls was to nail the shoe. An alternate technique is to position the shoe without nailing it, mark the shoe and bottom half of the plate, then assemble the wall by nailing 16s through the bottom of the shoe and top of the plate. The top half of the plate is now nailed, the wall raised, and the shoe nailed to joists and boxing board.

I have framed walls in this way and have found it equal to the one demonstrated.

Interior Walls

Almost always, the load-bearing walls in a house will run at right angles to the floor joists. They are constructed exactly the same as exterior walls.

The walls which run parallel to the floor joists will almost always be non-load-bearing. They may be constructed with a single plate and a single header on the flat. However, I construct all the interior walls with a double plate, since this eliminates cutting studs, but will use a single header on the flat.

In this house, the bearing partitions run east and west.

A useful technique is to butt successive members wherever possible rather than fitting each member between two others that have already been installed. Working in this way, I establish the following sequence in erecting the interior walls:

I mark 10 feet i.d. beside the north shoe, measuring from the west shoe, and tack a nail through the mark. I move back along the west wall to about 12 feet. At that point, I measure east again 10 feet i.d. and mark. I place an **X** on the far side of the mark. I pop a chalk line between the two marks. The north–south dimension of this room is given as 12 feet i.d. on the floor plan. I cut a 12-foot 2 by 4 and nail it on the **X**.

I mark 16-inch multiples on the shoe, stopping at 47-1/4 inches, then continue the 16-inch multiples from that measurement.

I place an **X** at the end of the shoe even if the distance between it and the last stud is less than 16 inches. If it is less than 1 inch from the stud next to it, I will omit the last stud.

The bottom half of the plate is identical to the

shoe; the top half extends 3-1/2 inches on each end.

An interior wall is assembled and raised exactly the same as an exterior wall. After it is erect, I slide the wall into the gap left in the top half of the exterior wall to fit the extension on the plate. I plumb the opposite end and brace it.

The second partition, which separates the bedroom from the bathroom, is built exactly the same as the first.

Plumbing Wall

The members of this wall will all be 2 x 6s. I cut and nail the 10-foot shoe first.

The center of the basin is given as 42 inches. I mark 42 inches on the shoe, measuring from the inside of the north wall.

Basins are available in a variety of sizes. The basin to be used here will be found in a supplementary sheet attached to the plans called the list of specifications. An 18 x 16-inch basin is a rather

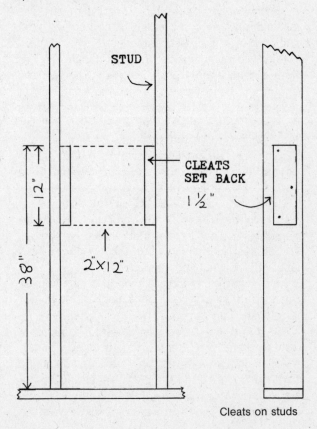

Cleats on studs

large one that is frequently used. I mark 7-1/4 inches outward from each side of the 42-inch center mark and place an **X** outward from each mark. These two studs will be 16 inches o.c. but also centered on the sink.

I mark 16-inch multiples on the shoe, beginning at the north wall, and begin again at 47-1/4 inches for the remainder. I don't have precut 2 x 6 studs and will therefore use a single plate. The plate itself will be 7 inches longer than the shoe and extend 3-1/2 inches on either end. I transfer the marks on the shoe to the plate, first positioning the plate with its ends extending 3-1/2 inches. I cut the studs, 7 feet 9-1/2 inches, assemble them, and erect this wall just as the other partitions.

I mark 38 inches up from the subfloor on the inside of the two studs positioned for the sink. I nail a 12-inch length of 2 x 4 to the inside of each stud; an end is at the 38-inch mark, the other end down. This cleat lies 1-1/2 inches back from the edge of the studs as measured from the bathroom side.

I cut two pieces of 2 x 6 14-1/2 inches long and nail them flat against the cleats. This is backing. The purpose of this backing is to provide a surface behind the finished wall in which screws will hold. The screws are used to attach a heavy metal bracket on which a wall sink is mounted.

I mark 5 feet up from the subfloor on the inside of both studs. This is to be the bottom height of a medicine chest. An ordinary medicine chest will have a r.o. of 14 x 18 inches. I cut two 2 x 6s 14-1/2 inches long. I nail the first at the 5-foot mark. I mark 18 inches up from this piece on both studs and nail the second piece above the marks. This is all that is needed at this time on the plumbing wall.

Three partitions are now erect along the north side of the house.

I nail the first shoe for the corridor partitions so that it butts the ends of these partitions. The shoe begins at the west wall and extends to the outside of the plumbing-wall shoe.

Three doorways are indicated along this wall.

The r.o. of all interior doorways is 2 inches wider than the width of the door to be used and 2-1/2 inches higher.

The exact location of the door is rarely given on a plan. A good practice is to locate it adjacent to intersecting partition walls and have the door swing toward that wall. Beginning at the intersecting partition wall, I mark a stud and jack on the shoe for the doorway, then complete the marking for the r.o.

I place the headers on edge since this is a bearing wall.

The rest of the wall is marked, assembled, and erected as the previous walls.

On the floor plan two openings are indicated along the second corridor wall. They are simple openings; no door is indicated. If there were some unusual feature about these openings, such as an arch or a special height, this would be given on a separate drawing titled "detail of corridor wall."

The heights would be 82-1/2 inches for both, the same as the r.o. height of a doorway.

The header for the 9-foot opening would be a double 2 x 10 on edge and the 7-foot-6-inch opening would have a double 2 x 8 on edge.

The final partition extends from the plumbing wall to the south wall. In making the r.o. for the door on this wall, I first mark the center of the corridor at 21 inches, then mark outward from both sides to frame the opening. This is to center the door in the corridor. The balance of the wall is the same as other walls.

If any of the interior walls are to be covered with individual boards installed vertically, such as 1 x 6 pine, a provision should now be made to provide a nailing surface midway along the length of the board.

I pop a chalk line at 4 feet along those walls to be covered with this type of material. I nail horizontal pieces along the chalk line between studs. These members are called cats.

ADDITIONAL INFORMATION

The 16-inch o.c. module for studs and double plate is a combination which will support weights far greater than any likely to be placed on them. In fact, this is another instance of overbuilding, since the studs could be placed 24 inches o.c. and still support weight on the wall adequately. Many houses have been built with this module and with no subsequent structural problems.

Not long ago I renovated a seventy-year-old

house in which there were no studs at all. The 2 x 4s were framed horizontally with boards nailed vertically to both sides. Over the years a bulge developed but certainly no danger of collapse. I don't recommend this type of framing, but it does affirm the fact that the present design of walls makes for overbuilding them.

The reason this module has evolved and been retained has little to do with the structural function of the wall and much more to do with modular development in the construction industry. Many materials now used to cover the walls, such as quarter-inch 4 x 8 sheets and insulation in bays, are manufactured with the 16-inch o.c. module in mind. These materials would not work well with wider spacing of studs.

My opinion is that we are lightyears ahead of other countries in construction. An important element in this is certainly the standardization that has been developed which supplies the builder with a flow of uniform materials. However, there are vices accompanying this virtue; the excessive use of material is one.

When framing lumber is delivered, it should be stacked according to size and length about 3 feet from the platform. It should be kept off the ground with scraps placed intermittently at right angles under the pile and covered with a canvas tarpaulin when not being used. Four-mil plastic sheets are a cheaper but inferior covering, since plastic tears easily and water condenses on the bottom side and wets the material.

During framing, most of the cutting is done on saw horses and a clutter of ends builds up quickly. I always take time to sort and stack these pieces for ease of use and to avoid tripping over them. Ends shorter than 1 foot I toss off the platform about 10 feet away. This area is to be my dump, and by situating it that far away I allow for its growth. I sweep the site at the end of each day. I'm far from being compulsively clean, but clutter on the platform is a hazard and walking over it becomes a needless obstacle course.

Flat bar and cat's claw

In general, I never remove a nail with a hammer. If two pieces have been nailed together in error, I use the following technique:

I insert the flat bar between the two pieces at an end and pry up the top piece by raising the flat bar. The top piece can then usually be removed by continuing to lift by hand, a foot holding down the bottom piece. I hammer the nails back partially and remove them by laying the hole in the flat bar around the head. The end of the flat bar lies against the wood, the rim of the hole under the head of the nail; I pull up to remove the nail.

If, for example, a stud has been nailed more than an inch in an incorrect position, the flat bar cannot be used to remove it since the nail heads are tight against the wood. In this case I place the cat's claw so that the nail to be removed is centered between its **V** end and the **V** placed down and back from the nail so that when the cat's claw is hammered down into the wood it will drive forward to the nail. When it hits the nail, I pull back on the handle and the nail comes partially out of the wood. I then place a scrap under the cat's claw, the claw below and against the nail head, and remove the nail completely with the same movement.

Both the flat bar and cat's claw are essential tools. Each sells for about $2.

In the course of building a house, invariably I have been asked by the owner, his friends, and passers-by to do things such as place a fourth nail into the stud rather than three, support non-bearing partitions by nailing a block between the floor joists under it, creosote the girders, and a variety of other things that are at best superfluous. The suggestions about how to build a "better house" have been extraordinarily numerous. At times when I've had the patience to explain why doing these things is wasteful and needless, the person has countered, "Well, it certainly can't do any harm."

The cliché of a little knowledge being a dangerous thing operates vigorously in construction. The tendency to overbuild because it can't do any harm is strong. The only reasonable attitude is to weigh carefully suggestions from people who have done the work themselves and refuse those from people who haven't.

CEILING FRAMING

6

On top of the bearing walls, on edge and crossing them at a right angle, will be members called ceiling joists. Their undersides will provide the surface to which the finished ceiling is attached.

They are required to carry only the weight of the ceiling in contrast to floor joists, which not only support the weight of the flooring, but also furniture, people, etc., and are therefore relatively lighter. Almost always I use 2 x 6 stock.

I avoid using 2 x 4s even when there is no structural reason because they bounce around a great deal when material is nailed to them, especially when the span is great; this makes the operation more difficult. They are also more likely to be warped and present an uneven surface. In addition, the area above the joists, the attic, is used to store things, and even a small amount of weight will cause them to sag.

The same ceiling joists have an additional function of maintaining the walls in a perpendicular position and as such are referred to as tie beams.

As tie beams they are made of two or more lengths of 2 x 6s and *must* form a continuous length of 30 feet from one exterior wall to the other.

As ceiling joists they are usually placed 16 inches o.c., an appropriate spacing for the ceiling material.

As tie beams they may be spaced 6 feet apart, which is adequate for maintaining the walls in a perpendicular position when stress is placed on them. This would be done if no ceiling was planned and the upper framework left exposed.

Marking the Position of Ceiling Joists

I start in the northwest corner and mark 16-inch multiples on the north wall plate measuring from the *inside* of the west wall. I stop at 47-1/4 inches and begin the multiples again from that point to the first partition. I omit joists less than 16 inches from the partition. I mark 16-inch multiples in the same way in the second bedroom, measuring from the inside of the partition.

I complete marking the north plate in the same way.

I mark both corridor plates and the south plate in an *identical* way.

Flush Joists

In the east bedroom, the floor plan shows three parallel lines which are noted as "flush joist." The word flush signifies that the bottom of this member is in the same plane as all the other joists.

A double 2 x 12 is also specified.

The span for joists in this area that has no bearing walls is 30 feet. This is much too long for an unsupported 2 x 6, and the flush joist is the means by which this span will be cut in half.

I nail two 2 x 12s together and trim to a length of 13 feet 11-1/2 inches, which is the o.o. distance between the partition and east wall. I place it 15 feet o.c. on top of both walls and nail it to the plates. This is the flush joist.

I mark both sides of the flush joists to correspond to the marks I have made on the north and south plates.

Joist Hangers

When a structural member butts another at a right angle as the joists will here, toenailing as a means

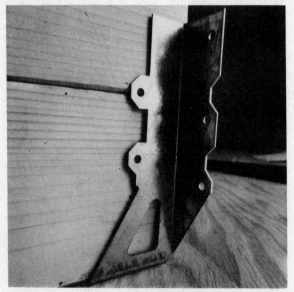

Flush joist on joist hanger

of tying the two together is insufficient. The simplest way of strengthening the joint adequately is by means of a metal device known as a joist hanger. They are sold in various sizes that correspond to the size of the member.

I nail joist hangers at each **X,** so that the bottom of each joist will be in the same plane as the flush joist.

It is structurally essential that the joist acting as a tie beam form a continuous unit across the 30-foot width of the house. I will use 14-foot lengths that begin in the same line from each exterior wall. Their ends will hang over the hallway walls. I will join these ends by nailing a third piece to each. This third piece will lie on top of the partition walls and be nailed to their plates as well as the 14-foot joists. This will form a continuous 30-foot length from the north to the south wall.

Trimming the Ends of the Joists

The width of a 2 x 6 is 5-1/2 inches, and this is the height they will be above the exterior wall. The rafter, as will be seen later, will be 1-1/2 inches or so below this at the exterior walls. The corner of the joist would therefore be higher than the rafter for a short distance. It would cause bumps 1-1/2 inches high at the ends of all the rafters unless the corner was trimmed.

I cut this triangular piece off the end of all joists. This cut end will be up and on the exterior walls. An alternative is to remove it with a hatchet after the rafters have been installed.

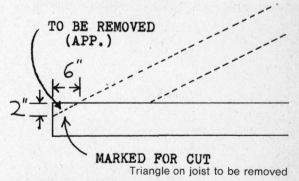

TO BE REMOVED (APP.)

6"

2"

MARKED FOR CUT

Triangle on joist to be removed

Installing Ceiling Joists

I stand each joist on end and lean the cut end against the north wall. The bottom end is near the hallway wall. I space joists down the length of the north wall at approximately the location in which they will be installed.

I stand on a stepladder so that my waist is about even with the plate. If only one ladder is available, I straddle the plate.

A helper climbs another stepladder while carrying the other end of the joist and lays it on the hallway plate. I turn it on edge and nail my end *first*. My end should be flush with the outside of the wall. The position of the other end is irrelevant. I toenail two 16s through both ends of the joist into the plate. The first joist lies so that its outside edge is flush with the inside edge of the west-wall plate. I nail the successive joists in the same way to the partition.

On top of the partition, I nail 2 x 8 scraps on the flat with 16s. They are centered over the plate and extend on each side of the partition for 2 inches. This provides a nailing surface for the ceiling in both bedrooms and eliminates a joist in each.

We continue to install ceiling joists until the next joist would intrude into the area in which the r.o. for the attic is to be framed.

Framing for Attic Access

The r.o. is given in the plan as 30 x 18 inches.

I omit temporarily the joists that lie along the 3-foot length and install the first one beyond it.

On the inside of each of these joists, I mark 21 inches, which is the center of the hallway. I measure outward 15 inches from each side of the center mark and place two **X**s to the outside. I nail joist hangers for 4 x 6s on the **X**s.

I cut two pieces of 2 x 6 to the i.d. length between the joists, nail them together, and install on the joist hangers.

I trim 14-foot 2 x 6s to the length between the outside of the north wall and the inside of the member on the joist hangers, and install.

At the plumbing wall, I use scrap 2 x 10s or 12s on top of the plate as nailers.

For the joists that lie along the flush joist, I cut lengths of 14 feet 10-1/2 inches. It is 15 feet to the center of the flush joist from the outside of the north wall. From this I deduct 1-1/2 inches, the thickness of a 2 x 12, to arrive at that dimension. I install these joists.

I duplicate this to install the joists between the south wall and the second corridor wall and flush joist.

I cut 4-foot lengths of 2 x 6 for as many joists as lie between the west wall and the beginning of the attic access.

I position these pieces on the corridor walls and against the joists. I want each piece to lap at least 16 inches over the ends of each joist. I nail each piece to the plates and then to the joists. I then nail through the joists into the piece and position the nails so that there is one every 8 inches or so, much closer than ordinarily, for greater holding stength.

I complete framing the attic access by cutting two pieces of 2 x 6 30 inches long and toenailing them into the double pieces on the sides of the opening to leave 3 feet.

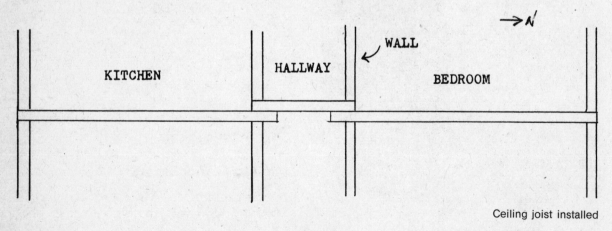

Ceiling joist installed

ADDITIONAL INFORMATION

Maintaining perpendicular walls through the use of tie beams limits the ceiling height to the height of the walls—8 feet in this instance. The ceiling height may be increased with no change in the height of the walls by installing the tie beam to the rafters and not to the plate. In this position, they are referred to as collar beams and form a triangle with the rafters.

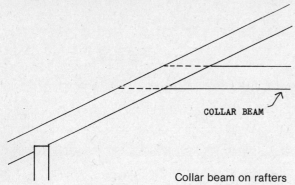

COLLAR BEAM

Collar beam on rafters

Collar beams, when also used as ceiling joists, are treated as if they were nailed to the plate. However, as the means of holding the walls perpendicular, their effectiveness decreases in proportion to the height along the rafter at which they are installed.

The lower they are to the wall, the greater their holding power. Once they are higher than one-third up the rafter, their ability to maintain walls in a perpendicular position decreases rapidly and becomes ineffective. I would not recommend their use more than a quarter of the way up the rafter.

The use of joist hangers in framing the ceiling was not to support any downward weight placed on the joists. Nails alone would do this. I use them because the weight of the roof will later tend to pull these joints apart, and the use of metal strengthens these joints and resists this force adequately. For this reason it is good to use nails in all the holes of the joist hanger.

WALL SHEATHING

7

The wall and ceiling framework is a rickety struc-ture. Before continuing to build higher I prefer to make it relatively rigid by nailing a "skin" over the entire outer surface of the exterior walls and linking all individual members together into a con-tinuous whole. The material and the act itself are called sheathing. Half-inch plyscore is a common covering.

Installing Plyscore Sheathing

The studs of the north wall were positioned starting from the northwest corner and I begin sheathing from that point.

One foot from the corner, I tack a 10 between the bottom of the mud sill and foundation wall and another at 7 feet.

I lay a 4 x 8 sheet of plyscore on the nails and shift a 4-foot side to be flush with the corner post. The opposite 4-foot side falls in the center of the stud placed at 95-1/4 inches. The nails position the lower 8-foot side to be flush with the bottom

of the mud sill. I use 7s to nail the sheet to *all* mem-bers of the wall and space the nails 10 to 12 inches apart.

I nail four more sheets in the same way along the 40-foot wall to form a row to the northeast corner.

The top of the plywood is a little over my head, and for convenience in installing the next row I assemble a scaffold at the northwest corner. It is composed of two end sections of tubular steel and two tubular **X**s which pivot on a centered rivet. The ends of the **X**s have holes which fit over threaded bolts welded to the side sections. I spread the **X**s and attach them to the side sections with four wing nuts. I use 2 x 10 rough-sawn spruce as scaffold boards, rough-sawn because they are thicker and stronger than planed boards and spruce because it is lighter, tough, and resists sagging and rotting better than fir.

After constructing the scaffold, I place a second sheet on top of the first and nail to start the second row.

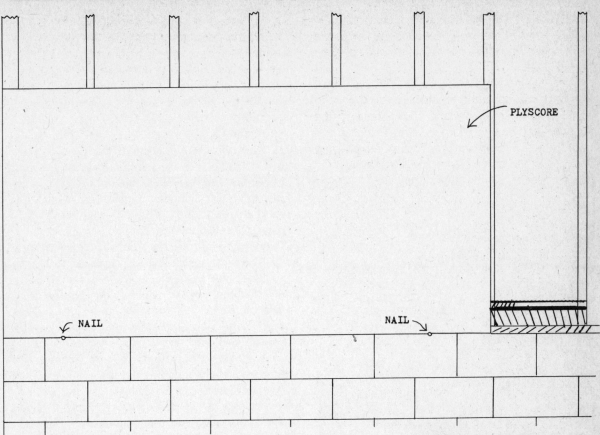

Sheet of plyscore at corner on nails

This sheet covers the r.o. for the window. I go inside and drill a hole in each corner of the opening. I come out and pop chalk lines between the four holes, which outlines the r.o.

I raise the guard of the 6-1/2-inch power saw and align the blade with the chalk line. I keep the guard raised and lift the back of the saw so that the *blade is above the wood and free to rotate.* The front end of the table is against the plyscore. The depth of the blade has been set to cut at 5/8 inch. I press the trigger and ease the spinning blade down into a line and continue down until the table is flat against the plyscore. 1 then cut on each line in the same way.

I do not cut all the way to the holes and keep 1 inch or so back. Because the blade is circular I would have to go beyond the corners to complete the cut and probably hit nails that attach the header. I use a 6-point handsaw (or sabre saw) to complete the cuts and remove the rectangle of plyscore that is the size of the r.o.

I measure the distance between the top of the second sheet and the middle of the plate and rip plyscore 1/4 inch less than that measurement. This will leave 1-3/4 inches of the plate exposed. The reason for this is that, when the rafters are cut, their bottom edges will be at the center of the plate and the additional quarter-inch is insurance against errors of a kind that would cause the rafter to butt the sheathing rather than the side of the plate.

I nail the ripped piece of plyscore, move the scaffold, and continue down the 40-foot wall and sheath it in this manner.

To sheath the east wall, I begin at the northeast corner since the 95 1/4-inch stud was positioned from there.

I sheath only two rows. Additional framing will be done above this wall and the rest of the plyscore will be nailed after it has been done.

Sheathing the south wall is an operation identical to sheathing the north wall with the exception that the plyscore under the sliding doors extends only to the bottom of the shoe. The shoe in the r.o. will be removed since the door frame is placed directly on the subfloor.

I also sheath only two rows on the west wall. I omit the plyscore entirely under the r.o. for the door. I will later remove the shoe, some of the subfloor, and boxing board in order to install the door frame at a height appropriate to the finished floor. After the frame is set, I will add a plywood piece under it to cover that area.

Wall sheathed

Sheathing Alternatives

Sheathing is an essential structural element which must be provided in one form or another. Half-inch plyscore fulfills this requirement but is hardly suitable as an exterior finish and must be covered with another material. This dual application is relatively costly if an exposed exterior wallcovering is used. It is competitive with single "skins" if a cheap exterior finish is used.

There are two types of materials mainly used for single "skins," both of which fulfill the requirement for sheathing and finished exterior simultaneously.

One is a plywood sheet with a ply on one side that presents a "finished" surface. This is usually cedar or fir with vertical indentations spaced to simulate boards. They are available in 4 x 8-foot and 10-foot and 12-foot sheets and in 1/8-inch multiples from 3/8 to 3/4 inches. The better types are manufactured with a high grade of exterior glue and the plies will not separate even after long exposure to the weather. They range in cost from 40¢ to 47¢ per square foot. Texture III is an example of this.

In regions where harsh climate is not a factor, this type of plywood is an adequate substitute for the double skin and results in saving the cost of plyscore and its installation, about $500. However, this saving applies only when the exterior material used as the second skin is wood or its equivalent in cost. Using half-inch plyscore as the sheathing, then an exterior of asbestos shingles, one of the cheapest exterior finishes, will cost about the same as the single plywood skin. Despite the additional labor involved, the double skin, however, is a far better arrangement since it gives a much better house for the same money. Leakage of air around openings is far less, greater insulation is achieved, outside noises are reduced, and wetness in the walls is minimized.

An alternative to the finished plywood exterior is an exterior composed of various types of wood nailed horizontally to the members of the wall. This is siding and the most common kinds are milled with a joint that is ship-lapped or beveled. These sidings are often redwood, cedar, or pine. As sheathing these sidings are adequate, though less strong than plywood.

When a single covering is used, I finish the roof framing first, then staple 15-pound felt on the outside of the exterior walls.

I install the finished plywood vertically and use the 47-1/4-inch measurement for placing the first stud from a corner. I use 8d aluminum nails and space them 10 to 12 inches apart in each member of the wall.

I place the bottom of each sheet slightly below the mud sill to cover the joint that it makes with the foundation wall. The top of the sheet may lie anywhere along the plate.

Where the total height of the wall is greater than 12 feet, as in the east and west walls, after installing the first sheet I nail a piece of aluminum edging over it. This edging is thin metal, 1-5/8 x 1-5/8 inches square, bent into a right angle. One side is nailed to studs, the other lies on the edge of the

Edging between vertical sheets of plywood exterior

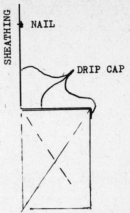

Drip cap over head of window casing

plywood and extends outward. I nail the second piece of plywood over it, then bend the edging down so that it lies over the bottom sheet. This makes a waterproof joint between the two stacked pieces of plywood.

While installing the plywood, I *omit* nails for 6 inches or so above each opening.

I place a window frame in the opening and mark its top on the plywood. I then set the blade of the saw to cut 1/8 inch deeper than the thickness of the plywood and remove this piece.

I pry the plywood away from the wall and insert a drip cap between the wall and plywood. A drip cap is a molded piece of metal or plastic with a right-angle shape. One side is nailed to the wall, the second sits on top of the frame and covers its top, then makes a second right angle that goes down over the front of the frame.

Drip caps must be placed above all frames to keep water from entering through the joint between the back of the frame and the plywood. Caulking will *not* seal the joint adequately.

I plumb the frame and nail it to the wall with three aluminum 16s through the casing (trim) into the studs. I use no nails on the head (top) piece of casing. After the window is installed, I nail a couple of 8s through the plywood above the window, which will then secure the drip cap.

If I am using siding, after stapling the tar paper

(Bostitch stapler, 3/8″ staples) I install all the window frames by inserting them into the r.o.s, plumbing, then nailing as described in the preceding paragraph. (The door frames are treated differently and their method of installation will be found in the chapter on finishing the exterior, page 84. They must also be installed before the siding is begun.)

On top of each frame, I nail the drip cap.

On each corner post, I tack two 5/4 x 3-inch pieces (1-1/8 x 2-3/4 inches) of the same material as the siding.

Each board of siding will butt these corner boards. The ends of each board will lie in the center of a wall member. Before another board is butted to it, the end is caulked with butyl rubber, then pushed against the end of the board that has been nailed to make a tight joint.

If the width of the board is 6 inches or less, two nails are used, three if 8 or 10 inches, and four if 12 inches. No. 8 common nails are used throughout.

One toenail is driven through the rabbeted top of the ship-lap into members.

I stop nailing the siding a foot or so from the top of the wall and will complete it after completing the necessary work on that portion of the roof which hangs over the wall. At that time I will also cut the corner boards appropriately and nail them, and then caulk all joints with butyl rubber.

ROOF FRAMING

8

The gable roof, with its inverted **V** shape, is probably the most prevalent type of roof. It rises from low points on two exterior walls to a high point, the ridge, usually at the center of the house. The shape, however, is not the only factor which determines the type.

The other element is the slope; this is given in the plans. Here it is 4 inches to 1 foot. The 4 inches refers to the increase in height or rise from the exterior wall and the 1 foot to the horizontal distance or run from the exterior wall. In this house, the height of the roof will rise 4 inches for each

foot as measured from the exterior wall to the center. The structural member which supports the roof and where this rise occurs is called the rafter.

When the rise is less than 4 inches to a foot, the roof is called a shed roof. With this type of roof, the weight of the roof and snow or ice upon it create a force which is mainly downward. The shallower the slope, the greater is this downward force. The flat roof, which has no slope at all, has a force that is completely downward.

When the rise is 4 inches per foot or steeper, the weight on the roof creates not only a downward force but an outward one as well. As the slope becomes steeper, the downward force decreases and the outward one increases. In practice, the steepest gable roof becomes an A frame.

The outward force of a gable roof will spread the exterior walls. This is the structural reason behind tie beams, which are omitted in shed roofs, rafters alone being sufficient to keep walls perpendicular.

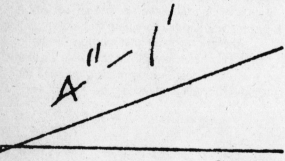

Slope of roof

Since the rafter of a gable roof is not required to support all the weight of the roof, it is made of lighter stock than the rafter of a shed roof, and as the slope becomes steeper and the weight proportionately less, the rafter stock may be less.

In general, where snow and ice is not a factor, 2 by 4s are used for rafters of gable roofs. Where snow and ice is a factor, 2 x 6s are usually sufficient. When the slope is 7 inches per foot or steeper, 2 x 4s are adequate even in northerly climates.

If the span of the rafter is 14 feet or more, the 2 x 6 rafter is likely to sag; either a 2 x 8 should be used or the span of the 2 x 6 reduced. This reduction of span is more economical than the heavier rafter and I use it for that reason.

Marking the Rafter

This method is applicable to practically all rafters for all types of roofs.

I pop a chalk line across the west wall that lies at the bottom of the north and south shoes. On this line I mark 15 feet, the center of the house.

I lay my 4-foot level on the center mark, plumb it, and draw a line up from the mark. I extend the line with a straightedge so that it is at least 5 feet.

The rise is 4 inches to 1 foot. Since the run is 15 feet, at the center of the house the rafter will be 60 inches higher than the wall. I tack a tenpenny nail through the vertical line at 60 inches.

I tack a second nail through the chalk line 1/2 inch from the end, which allows for the thickness of the sheathing and is in line with the exterior wall.

I lay a 2 x 6 on the nails. An end of the rafter should extend a few inches beyond the center nail and the lower end 16 inches or so.

I transfer the center vertical line to the rafter by marking the top and bottom edges, then setting the protractor to those marks. The angle should read about 18-1/2 degrees.

I mark the rafter where it passes the exterior wall, measure back 1/2 inch and, using the protractor, mark the same angle on the rafter.

The elevation drawing indicated that the roof extended 1 foot past the exterior wall. This overhang is called the eave. I measure 11-1/2 inches horizontally from the sheathing and, with the protractor, draw a line at that mark.

I now have three parallel lines on the rafter, each forming an 18-1/2-degree angle.

At the ridge, between opposing rafters, will be a member called the ridgeboard, to which the

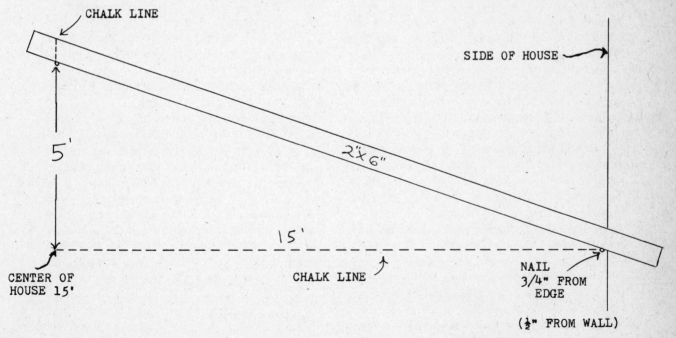

Marking cable wall for model rafter

CENTER MARK

ACTUAL CUT 3/4" BACK TO
ALLOW FOR THICKNESS OF
RIDGE BOARD

SIDE OF HOUSE

PLUMB CUT
FOR EAVE
Parallel lines for rafter cuts

rafters will be nailed. The ridgeboard will go continuously from the outside of the east wall to the outside of the west wall. Since I am using 2 x 6s for rafters, I will use a 2 x 6 ridgeboard as a convenience. The rafters will therefore not extend to the center of the house but will end at a point that is half the thickness of the ridgeboard, or 3/4 inch less than the line I drew. I therefore re-mark the center cut of the rafter 3/4 inch back from the line.

At the line which corresponds to the exterior wall, I measure up 1-1/2 inches. The rafter at this point will drop to the center of the plate, and this measurement equals the thickness of the plate. I place the framing square so that one arm lies along the line and a right angle is formed at the mark of 1-1/2 inches. I draw the right-angle line from the mark. The purpose of this cut is to have the rafter sit flat on top of the plate.

The two lines form a small right angle and when cut out are referred to as the bird's mouth. The vertical cut will butt the exterior side of the plate, its bottom at the center of the plate. The horizontal cut will lie flat on top of the plate.

The overhang may be dealt with in several ways. The drawing indicates a particular one, called boxing in the eaves. The member which lies between the exterior wall and the end of the rafter on the underside of the overhang is called the soffit. The outermost edge of this soffit must be provided with a nailing surface.

I measure up and mark 2 inches along the end cut, lay the framing square along the line and top at the mark. I draw a right angle at the 2-inch mark.

I make the five cuts drawn on the rafter, using the initial center line. I mark and cut four rafters with this first one as a model and label these hanging rafters. I set them aside to install later.

I cut 3/4 inch from the first rafter. I will use this as a model rafter. Since the house is 40 feet long and I will space the rafters 16 inches o.c., I will need thirty-one on each side, for a total of sixty-two. I use the model rafter to mark all of these and cut them.

At the bird's mouth, in order to saw out the piece, I must extend the cut beyond the right-angle mark. It doesn't weaken the rafter appreciably and saves the time of completing the cut with another tool.

The traditional way of cutting a rafter is to mark it out first with a framing square.

The framing square clip is set on the tongue (shorter arm) at 4 inches, which is the rise, and 12 inches on the longer arm (blade), which is the run. The total run is 15 feet and I simply step off this same measurement fifteen times, which gives me the length of the rafter from the center of the ridge to the outside of the exterior wall. Given the line for the plumb cut at the ridge and the plumb cut for the bird's mouth, the adjustment for the thickness of the ridgeboard and eave can be made in the same way described earlier.

Installing Rafters

I begin at the northwest corner and mark 16-inch multiples on top of the plate along the entire

PLUMB CUT

MODEL RAFTER

PLUMB CUT

BIRD'S MOUTH
3½" X 1½"

LEVEL CUT
Rafter cut

length. I do *not* use either the 47-1/4-inch or 95-1/4-inch since the roof has an overhang and these placements are not appropriate. I make corresponding marks along the south plate and the top edge of a 20-foot 2 x 6 which I will use for a ridgeboard. I use a second 2 x 6 to make a ridge whose length is 40 feet and continue the 16-inch multiples.

I place the scaffolding along the outside of the north wall for ease in nailing ends of rafters. I tack sheets of plyscore on top of the ceiling joists along the center of the house to serve as a working platform in nailing the other end of the rafters.

I cut two 2 x 4s 60 inches long and nail each to a stud. I tack the first into the plywood platform 1 foot from the west wall. I tack the second a foot or so short of the length of the ridgeboard. Both are centered by eye along the middle of the house.

Framing square with clips set at 4 inches and 12 inches

I lay the ridgeboard on the 60-inch piece of 2 x 4 and tack it to the stud as a means of holding the ridgeboard temporarily close to its proper location.

I stand on the platform on the ceiling joists. My helper hands me my end of the rafter. He then lifts his end and I slide it forward onto the plate. (If the helper happens to be short, a piece of 2 x 4 on the bottom of the rafter is used to raise it high enough.) We lay all the rafters flat between the platform and exterior wall at roughly 16-inch intervals.

My helper gets on the scaffold. The rafter is placed so that the bird's mouth is tight against the plate and three 16s are used to nail it to the plate. I nail my end so that it is flush with the end of the ridgeboard. The other end is flush with the northwest corner. I attach my end by nailing through the ridgeboard into the rafter with two 16s and then a 10 toenailed from the rafter into the ridgeboard. The top of the rafter is flush with the top of the ridgeboard.

We nail a second rafter at the farthest mark on the ridgeboard and the corresponding mark on the plate.

We then nail two opposing rafters on the south wall. The four rafters are sufficient to hold the ridgeboard in place, and I remove the 2 x 4s that held it temporarily.

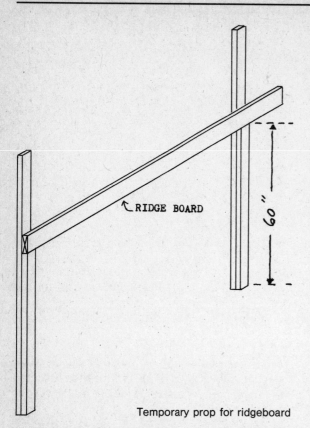

<-RIDGE BOARD

60"

Temporary prop for ridgeboard

I butt the second length of ridgeboard to the first and install four rafters. I then nail into place all the intermediate rafters.

The east and west sides of the house are now referred to as the gable ends. These gable ends should tilt neither in or out and be in the same plane as the gable walls.

I nail a brace to the ridge just behind the end rafters. I nail a cleat through the platform into the ceiling joists. The cleat lies parallel to the ridge. One person holds a 4-foot level and straight 1 x 3 on edge from the gable wall to the rafter. The rafter framework is pushed in or out so that it lies in the same plane as the gable wall as evidenced by the centered bubble in the level. The bottom of the brace is then nailed to the cleat temporarily. The opposite gable end is then braced also.

The inverted **V**-shaped area between the top of the plates and the bottom of the rafters is treated as a wall and framed with 2 x 4s, 16 inches o.c. These members are gable studs, and they will be located directly above each wall stud.

I mark this position by laying the 1 x 3 adjacent to each wall stud with the top end on the rafter.

The line of the wall stud is extended in this way and I simply mark the position of the gable stud on the side of the plate and rafter to correspond.

I stand a 2 x 4 on the plate, its sides against the mark on the plate and rafter. I draw a line on the 2 x 4 that corresponds to the bottom of the rafter.

I set the 6-1/2-inch saw to cut at an angle of 18-1/2 degrees and a depth of 1-1/2 inches and cut along this line. I measure up 5 inches from the cut and, with the protractor set at 18-1/2 degrees, make a parallel cut on edge with the 8-1/4-inch saw. I finish the cut by hand, since the saw will only cut to a depth slightly deeper than three inches.

I draw a line between the two cuts and rip 1-1/2 inches for the 5-inch length. I install this gable stud by toenailing into the plate and rafter and through the top of the gable stud into the rafter. This same gable stud is used in three other locations, and I mark three others before nailing the first.

I frame the rest of the area in a similar fashion.

The area between the ceiling joists and rafters is the attic, and ventilation for this area should be provided. This is usually done by means of a louvre, a series of slanted boards in a frame. They are made in metal or wood and in a multitude of shapes and sizes. They are almost always centered below the ridge. Each particular one has its own r.o. and this is framed simply in the same way as the medicine chest (see page 59) without jacks and one flat header and sill.

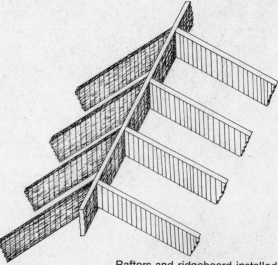

Rafters and ridgeboard installed

I will now complete the sheathing on the gable ends. In this connection, the ends of the plyscore are nailed to the rafters and can be a couple of inches below them but should not extend above the rafters where they would interfere with the plane of the roof.

Gable studs

ADDITIONAL INFORMATION

I have built several houses in which two sections with shed roofs were butted to each other and presented an inverted **V** shape that rose from a low on exterior walls to a high point in the center.

In spite of this shape, they were shed roofs and this was not simply a semantic consideration. Not only were tie beams omitted, but the rafters were heavier and followed this schedule:

SPAN	SIZE
10'	2 x 8
12'	2 x 10
14'	2 x 12

The spans given are the lower range and I have used 2 x 12s for 16-foot spans of rafters with shed roofs.

In the introduction, I mentioned building a house from plans which cost $35. These plans had a structural defect in the roof design. The roof slope was also 4 inches to 1 foot and incorporated a flush joist similar to the one in the house we have been building. Half the ceiling joists–tie beams were installed as the ones I have described, but the other half were specified to run east and west between the interior wall and the east gable wall. This meant structurally that a continuous tie-beam effect was not present, and consequently there was nothing to counteract the outward force of the roof. I didn't notice this while looking over the plans.

It was a two-story house, and while the roof was being framed I was busy building the fireplace on the first floor. A student came down and told me something was happening and I'd better come.

All the joists were in place and most of the rafters. The weight of the rafters alone, 2 x 6s, had already spread out the walls in what would correspond to the easterly area of the house we had been building. The corners were still plumb since the gable wall acts as a tie beam, but at each 16-inch multiple the wall tilted outward more and more and was almost 3 inches out at the centers of this section.

To correct it, we placed a double 2 x 4 under the ridge, placed a six-ton hydraulic jack under a post, and jacked up the ridge until the walls came back into plumb.

We then nailed sheathing to the top of the ceiling joists, making the entire area a continuous tie beam by attaching it one entire side to the flush joist and the other to the equivalent of the south exterior wall. The point of relating this is that when the slope is 4 inches per foot or steeper, it is *essential* to tie the exterior walls together in some manner to counteract the outward thrust placed on them.

The force of this thrust can be relieved somewhat through the use of posts which would lie between the top of the bearing wall and the bottom of the ridge. The weight on the ridge would be reduced and, as a consequence, the outward force as well.

Collar beams are somewhat effective in preventing outward movement of the walls, but not nearly as much as a tie-beam arrangement.

The rafters have a span of 15 feet and are likely to sag. Two by eights can be used instead of 2 x 6s, but this will be more expensive and not as effective as reducing the span by nailing 2 by 4s from

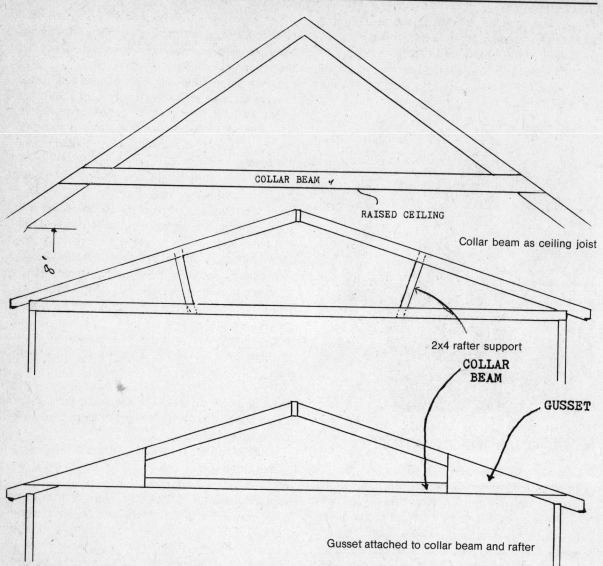

COLLAR BEAM

RAISED CEILING

Collar beam as ceiling joist

8'

2x4 rafter support

COLLAR BEAM

GUSSET

Gusset attached to collar beam and rafter

each joist to each rafter.

If the rafter span is more than 16 feet, I would use a 2 x 8.

When increased ceiling heights are desired without the additional expense of higher walls, collar beams have a particular value. Here the underside of the collar beam serves as a joist and nailing surface for the ceiling.

An excellent practice when using collar beams is to furr out the rafter with an additional length of 1-1/2-inch material, then nail a triangular piece of 1/2-inch plyscore to the collar beam and rafter. This member is called a gusset and will increase the holding power of the collar beam enormously.

The lower the collar beam is along the rafter, the greater its effectiveness. I would not use collar beams higher than a third of the distance up the rafter since they become relatively ineffective after this point.

When the ridge, the highest point of the house, has been installed, tradition has it that a bush be nailed there and that everyone quit work for the day and have a party. I'm not certain, but I believe that this tradition has a Scandinavian origin, and it is the focus of a scene in Ibsen's *The Master Builder*. Whatever its origin, I like it and never fail to put up the bush.

ROOFING

9

Roof Deck

The material nailed on top of the rafters is roof decking. Its function is to join the rafters into a structural whole and provide a surface for the roofing material.

The roof deck of this house will be 1/2-inch plyscore, the same material used for the subfloor and wall sheathing.

The rafters are placed 16 inches o.c., since this spacing is appropriate for 1/2-inch plyscore. If the spacing were wider the plyscore would sag from the weight of the roofing; at 24 inches o.c., it will dip appreciably when walked on.

However, if the roof decking was a material stronger than half-inch plyscore, the rafters could be spaced on wider centers corresponding to the strength of the roof decking.

An example of this is the use of 2 x 6 tongue-and-groove Douglas-fir boards. Construction lumber milled this way would permit the rafters to be spaced 4 feet o.c. since this decking will adequate-ly support roof weight at this width. The material cost $270 per thousand board feet in 1973. Allow-ing for waste, plus the fact that being tongue-and-grooved only 5-1/4 inches of each board is actually exposed, the cost of 2 x 6 roof decking will be about 70 cents a square foot. Compared to ply-score, which is 22 cents per square foot, it be-comes fairly expensive even when the omitted rafters are taken into consideration. It makes a very strong roof, but unless the bottom side of the roof decking is to be exposed, I would not recom-mend its use because it is too costly.

Douglas-fir roof decking is 1-1/2 inches thick and, since wood is a poor conductor of heat, makes a pretty good insulating material. Normal fiberglass insulation runs around six cents per square foot, so this amount can also be deducted since the 2 x 6 deck would eliminate the need for insulation.

One side of the 2 x 6 is milled so that the joint between boards forms a small **V**. This is a decora-tive touch which also reduces the unsightliness of imperfectly aligned boards.

2 x 6 tongue-and-groove fir decking

Blocking between rafters

If no interior ceiling was contemplated in a house, accompanied by 2 x 6 roof decking, I would space all the tie beams 6 feet o.c.; the rafters would be 4 feet o.c. and I would double them at the tie beams, which would be sandwiched between the two rafters to give a truss effect and greater strength.

An alternative roof decking material is Insulite. This is a composition material with a high degree of insulating quality. It is usually sold in 2 x 8-foot sheets which are 2 inches or more thick and also tongue and grooved and V-jointed. One side is "finished"; this finish is either white paint or white with a vinyl film over it. These finished sheets cost 40 and 47 cents respectively.

Two-inch Insulite will adequately support the roof when the rafters are spaced 30 inches o.c. Thicker Insulite will support wider centers.

This has the advantage of not only joining the rafters into a structural whole and providing a surface for the roofing, but it also insulates the roof well and makes a finished interior ceiling all in the same operation.

Its total cost will be about the same as plyscore plus the additional material and labor involved in using it.

Aside from aesthetic considerations, Insulite is a viable alternative, and the only practical difficulty I ever had using it was that it rotted on one occasion. This was limited to an exposed portion under the eave and happened only once.

When using 2 x 6 or Insulite decking, a "finished" surface is provided under the eaves and boxing them in becomes redundant.

For economy, the rafters should remain exposed along the overhang. The area between rafters is closed with blocks nailed between them. The blocks are installed along with the rafters and caulked from the inside. They should be placed 1-1/2 inches beyond the line of the wall, their bottoms flush with the bottom of the rafters.

The gable ends are more than 16 feet long on each side. It is difficult to align them to form a straight line and this should not be attempted. The same situation occurs when narrower pieces are used; this happens often. An efficient way of handling this is to allow the ends to extend beyond the contemplated line, then popping a chalk line and trimming along that line. This technique is always quicker and gives better results than trying to align individual members as they are installed.

Installing the Roof Deck

I begin at the northwest corner and lay a sheet of plyscore over the rafters while standing on the scaffold. I position the plyscore so that a 4-foot side lies midway on a rafter and the other side extends at least a foot beyond the gable wall. The lower 8-foot side is flush with the end of the rafters.

I nail the sheet to the rafters with 7s spaced every 10 to 12 inches. I butt a second sheet to the first and continue a row along the 40-foot side in the same manner. The last sheet in this row should extend at least a foot beyond the east gable wall.

I begin a second row with a 4-foot side midway on the rafter adjacent to the one from which I started the first row. This rafter is nearer the end rafter, and this sheet will hang over 16 inches more than the first. I complete the second row.

I start the third on the same rafter as the first.

The purpose of staggering the joints is to avoid having them fall on the same rafters and creating a weakness.

I rip the fourth row so that it lies midway on the ridgeboard.

I duplicate this on the opposite half of the roof.

On the roof deck, I mark 12 inches from the gable wall at the ridge. I mark 12 inches from the end rafter on the roof deck at the lower end. I pop a chalk line between the two marks. I set the saw blade to cut at a depth of 5/8 inches and trim the plyscore. I now have a foot of overhang at this gable end.

I trim the rest of the roof deck in the same man-ner. The house now has a foot of roof decking hanging over all four sides.

Installing Hanging Rafter

This member is held by nails driven into it through the roof deck. For better holding ability, the nails should be at a fairly acute angle, about 60 degrees.

The four rafters are leaned against the building and a person on the roof pulls them up while sliding them against the plyscore.

I tack several 10d nails 3/4 inch back from the edge of the trimmed roof deck, where the hanging rafter will be installed. I place my hammer at my right side on the deck. I lie on my stomach at the ridge while a helper does the same at the lower end. We lift the hanging rafter with both hands and swing it into position under the roof deck. While pressing the rafter up against the underside of the roof deck with my left hand, I drive the nail I have tacked. I slide down about midway along the rafter and drive another nail. The person at the other end drives a nail there. These three nails will hold the rafter. I drive intermediate nails spaced every 10 inches or so.

The top end of the rafter has been positioned exactly in the center of the ridge. Since the ridgeboard doesn't extend beyond the gable wall, I use the joint between the two pieces of ripped plyscore as a center reference. The remaining three hanging rafters are installed in the same manner.

Hanging rafter

Rake and fascia

Fascia Board

Before the roofing material can be applied, several other members will first have to be installed. One of these is called the fascia; it is attached to the ends of the rafters and on the surface of the hanging rafters.

I trim a 2 x 6 so that, when one end is flush with the outside of the hanging rafter, the other end falls midway on the end of an intermediate rafter. I butt other 2 x 6s to form a continuous surface between the hanging rafters on both the north and south sides of the house. The bottom of the fascia is flush with the bottom of the rafters. Since the rafters have been cut at an angle, the ends are more than 5-1/2 inches and a difference in height is created between the fascia boards and roof deck, but this is inconsequential.

The 2 x 6s used for the hanging rafters are construction lumber and are likely to have imperfections such as splits, loose knots, gouges, etc. I cover these members with a more finished material, in this case 1 x 8 clear cedar or redwood.

The fascia along the north and south sides is positioned so that its top edge is flush with the roof deck. I attach it with aluminum shingle nails. While doing so, I sight down the fascia and bring it into a straight line by shimming cedar shingles between it and the 2 x 6 wherever needed.

The bottom edge of the 1 x 8 fascia will be 1-1/2 inches or so below the 2 x 6.

On the gable ends, the 1 x 8 fascia is a duplicate of the hanging rafter to which it is attached.

The tips of the hanging rafter will be lower than the bottom of the fascia boards. I extend the line of the bottom of each fascia board and trim the hanging rafter with an 8-point handsaw along that horizontal line.

Working from the roof deck, I nail 1 x 3 cedar or redwood flush with the top edge of the fascia boards and hanging rafters. (I make the necessary cuts in this material with a plywood blade.) This member is called a rake. Its purpose is to extend the roof line beyond the fascia and keep water running off the roof from falling on the fascia and walls of the house.

I have used a double fascia, but this isn't at all necessary. A practical alternative is to select the fascia from the construction lumber and set them aside for this use. Among the 2 x 8s used for framing there will often be perfectly suitable clear and unblemished boards.

Although cedar and redwood have excellent rot-resisting qualities, they will discolor; the rake is therefore covered by metal edging to protect it from water. An inexpensive and adequate material is thin-gauge aluminum bent at a right angle. It is usually sold in 10-foot lengths and has a rippled surface to break up the flow of water. One side of the right angle lies over the rake and the other side is nailed to the 2 x 6 fascia with aluminum shingle nails. The edging is attached *only* to the north and south sides of the house before the roofing is begun, and will lie under it. *After* the roofing has been installed, the edging is attached over it along the gable ends. I attach metal edging to the north and south sides of the roof along the entire lengths. I lay lengths of edging with overlaps of an inch or so.

Roofing

For roofs with a slope of 4 inches per foot or steeper, the most common material used is the asphalt shingle. Essentially this is heavy tar paper, the exposed portion impregnated with gravel-like mineralized substances.

Asphalt Shingle

The three-tab shingle is very common. The one in the drawing is the self-locking type. On the back of the shingle, just above the elongated **U**-shaped cutouts, is a band of tar. The heat of the sun plasticizes the tar and gives it an adhesive quality which causes it to stick to the shingle below it. This strengthens each individual shingle by attaching it to another and reduces the chances of wind blowing the shingle back and ripping it off.

Many patterns, types, colors and grades are available. The cost of the shingles for this roof will be about $300. It will probably last for twenty-five years or more.

Installing Asphalt Shingles

Using a notched trowel, I spread a band of plastic cement or cold tar about 1 foot wide down the length of the lower north roof deck. The forward edge of the tar is slightly behind the metal edging. The cold tar itself serves as a cheap adhesive. It sells at $4.50 for a five-gallon bucket.

Tar paper, or 15-pound felt, is sold in rolls 36 inches wide and 100 feet long. Starting at a gable end, I roll out a band 36 inches wide on top of the tar and roof deck, adjusting the downward edge of the tar paper so that it parallels the outer side of the edging and about 1/4 inch back from it. I allow the tar paper to hang over both gable ends, cutting it with a matte knife that has a retractable blade (a razor blade with a handle). I then trim the ends of the tar paper so that it is flush with the gable ends.

If there are any air bubbles under the tar paper, I slit the area and staple the slit ends to the roof deck with 3/8-inch staples in the Bostitch stapler. This will remove the bubbles.

With the purchase of the shingles, I will have also bought what is known as a starter strip. This is roofing with an unbroken mineralized surface. The width is usually 12 inches. It is sold in various lengths, 50 feet not uncommon. I unroll the starter strip, positioning it so that the downward edge lies 1/8 to 1/4 inch beyond the metal edging. This is to keep water running off the roof even farther from the walls and fascia. I use wide-head galvanized roofing nails to fasten the starter strip. I nail the downward side through the edging into the fascia, spacing the nails every 8 inches or so. I nail the top side through the tar paper into the roof deck every 12 inches or so. I allow the starter strip to hang over the gable ends, cutting it from the back side with the matte knife. I then trim the starter strip, also cutting from the back, so that it is flush with or slightly short of the gable ends.

If the starter strip isn't long enough to cover the roof deck in one length, I lap it 1 foot, joining the lapped ends with cold tar. I nail the bottom piece and spread tar over it to fasten the top piece.

I place a shingle on top of the starter strip, one side flush with the gable end. The tabs are downward and flush with the starter strip, 1/8 to 1/4 inch beyond the line of the metal edging.

The shingles are delivered in bundles wrapped in paper. On this paper are installation instructions, which vary with different manufacturers. I use four roofing nails to fasten the shingle.

I place these nails (wide-head, 1-1/2 inches long) 1 inch or so above the tabs and spaced evenly along its length. The end nails are 1 inch or so back from the ends of the shingles.

At the end of the first shingle is half of an elongated **U**. I butt the second shingle to the first. Where they butt, each shingle having half a **U**, a full **U** is formed.

I cut a shingle in half, cutting from the back side. (The top side is mineralized and much harder to cut. It also dulls the razor blade quickly.)

I place the half shingle so that its downward side lies just above the **U**. An end of the shingle is flush with the gable end. The opposite side has half a **U**. About 5 inches of the bottom shingle remains exposed. I nail the half shingle with three nails 2 inches or so above the **U**.

I continue the first course of shingles for about 10 feet.

I continue the second course with full shingles in the same manner.

I start the third course with a full shingle exactly as I laid the first.

Before starting the fourth course, I lay another band of tar paper, lapping it over the first by a foot or so.

I position bundles of shingles all along the 40-foot length in amounts I estimate using in that area.

I am stretched out on the deck while shingling, propped on an elbow with my nail apron on my left side, where nails are easier to remove.

I do not cover the entire roof deck with tar paper unless the day is calm. If a wind comes up, the staples will not hold the tar paper. I therefore do this in sections.

I do not continue all the way across with each course since that would involve a significant amount of needless moving about. I will remain in the same area as long as practical, nailing shingles and beginning new courses. The limiting factor is that no shingle should be installed that extends farther in its row than the shingle below it.

I will start each course at the west gable and alternate rows with full and half shingles. I use the other half shingles at the opposite end of the row.

I continue installing shingles until the top half crosses the ridge. I fold this over and nail.

The south side of the roof is done in the same way, and the last course has part of the shingle

Matte knife and notched trowel

Rolled roofing on ½-inch Insulite over roof deck

folded over the ridge and nailed.

I lay a starter strip along the entire length of the ridge so that half lies on each side and nail both sides, spacing each nail 12 inches or so. This is called a cap. The nails are an inch or so back from the edges.

I cover the gable ends with metal edging, using aluminum shingle nails which go through the edging, roofing, and into the 2 x 6 hanging rafter.

I lap sections of edging 1 inch or so. At the ridge, I make an 18-1/2-inch cut on the side of the metal edging that will lie against the hanging rafter and fold the edging over the ridge. I nail this down after installing metal edging from the other side since the lap should always be with the higher edging over the lower so that water can run off freely and not be trapped under the edging.

In addition to protecting the rake and fascia from rain running off the roof, the metal edging over the shingles along the gable ends serves the purpose of protecting these shingles from wind, which might otherwise lift them off, rip them off, or drive rain between them and the roof deck and cause leaks.

The aluminum metal edging is thin; during installation it will frequently "ripple" and not lie flat against the rake. Nailing it to the rake will only cause other ripples and make these more apparent. Most of this can be avoided if the edging is

bent by hand to a sharper-than-90-degree angle. This should be done carefully, since the edging will crimp if more than light pressure is applied to bend the angle farther.

ADDITIONAL INFORMATION

In selecting colors for roofs, keep in mind that white will reflect heat and darker colors will absorb it. A black roof will make for a hotter house than a white roof, all other factors being the same. The effect of a black roof can be reduced by placing sheets of Insulite over the plyscore. These sheets needn't be 2 inches thick; 3/4-inch Insulite costs 7 cents sq. ft. and is a reasonable choice.

With these thinner sheets of Insulite, aluminum foil is often used. This reflects heat and contributes to a better-insulated roof.

The thin Insulite is attached to the plyscore with roofing nails, the foil with staples.

There is of course a great variety of roofing materials. In general, if the slope is 4 inches to a foot or steeper, some form of shingle is used. If the slope is less but not under 5/8 inches to a foot, split sheet is used.

Split sheet is the same material as asphalt shingles but is manufactured in continuous lengths 36 inches wide. It is delivered in rolls 36 feet long.

Half the sheet is heavy tar paper, the other half tar paper impregnated with a mineralized surface. The mineralized half will remain exposed; the other half lies under the sheet above it.

I unroll the split sheet and lay the edge of the mineralized half 1/8 inch beyond the metal edging. I nail the tar-paper half with roofing nails spaced every foot.

To make a joint on the same course, I allow a lap of a foot or so.

I continue in this way, aligning the second course with a chalk line an inch or so from the top of the mineralized half.

I continue courses toward the ridge until the tar paper is less than 9 inches from it. All courses are nailed to the roof deck through the tar-paper half.

I roll back all the mineralized halves.

With a notched trowel, I spread a band of tar over the roof deck under the first course and then on successive tar-paper halves.

I remove the tar from the buckets by dumping globs of it at intervals before beginning to trowel it.

As I finish tarring each course, I flip the mineralized half back on the tar and cause it to lie flat by walking over it.

I nail through the mineralized surface every 8 inches or so along the bottom of the 40-foot side. I nail the gable ends as well.

I do halves of the roof in this way.

I cut the split sheet from the back to get a roll of continuous mineralized surface 18 inches wide.

I tar both sides of the roofing along the ridge and fold the mineralized half over the ridge to form a cap.

I install the aluminum edging along the gable ends in the same way as with shingles.

For roofs with a slope of 5/8 inches per foot or less, a "hot" roof is required.

This roofing is composed of layers of tar paper and hot molten tar. The more layers, the more expensive the roof and the less likelihood of leaks. The final layer is often covered with gravel on hot tar, which makes it adhere.

The best roof by far, and incidentally the least expensive, is the one made of split sheet. I've never known these to have a problem with leaks and a minimum life span of twenty-five years can be expected. Unfortunately, split sheet should not be used in steeper slopes since the weight of the roofing tends to cause the sheets to work loose from the nails.

Shingles have the disadvantage of leaking in high winds and rain since the wind will often blow them back and drive water under them. Very often some blow away. If asphalt shingles are used in regions where high winds can be expected, it's a good practice to drop an additional blob of tar under each shingle as it is installed.

Personally, I do not like the appearance of asphalt shingles. However, a recent innovation is a product called random width shingles. The tabs of these shingles aren't uniform. If the color is tan, they look very much like a roof of cedar shingles, which I find pleasing.

An alternative cap for the asphalt-shingle roof is to cut the shingle in half and lay the half shingle over the ridge, nailing it in the same fashion. The cap may go from one end of the ridge to the other or start from each end and meet at the center. In this case a second shingle is cut, the upper half discarded, and the piece of shingle nailed over the joint between the two rows.

I would avoid using cedar shingles as roofing. The price per shingle is relatively high and, since only 4 inches of this kind of shingle should be exposed on a roof, this expense becomes even greater. Cedar shingles will deteriorate on the roof much more quickly than asphalt and will take much longer to install. They are also a dangerous fire hazard. They burn rapidly, and I have seen them flung a hundred feet from a burning roof and set fire to neighboring houses.

The more expensive roofs of slate or clay tile last longer than a lifetime. These are usually pre-drilled with holes in the unexposed portions and installed like shingles.

"CLOSING IN" THE HOUSE

10

Closing in the house means finishing the exterior completely. One is at the mercy of the weather before this is done and, although it is now possible to begin interior work, finishing the exterior should have priority.

The first step toward closing in the house is the installation of the windows. Windows today are made of wood, aluminum, or steel. They are composed of the sash or movable member, the frame in which the sash is contained, the casing which trims the exterior of the frame, and hardware by which the movement of the sash is effected.

The windows of this house will be made of wood. The sash movement will be "awning," which means that the bottom of the sash moves outward.

The movement of the sash is controlled by a handle which, when rotated to the right, opens the window.

In addition to the awning window, four other types are in common use.

Double-hung windows are two sashes operating in a vertical plane. The top sash is toward the

Awning window installed

outside of the house and slides between vertical guides called stops. It was formerly controlled by iron weights housed behind the frame and was attached to the sash by a rope or chain over a pulley wheel mortised into the jambs. The weights have been replaced by spring or friction hardware.

Double-hung windows now also have aluminum over the wood in the channel where the sash slides and also a factory-installed weatherstripping arrangement. This is usually a **V**-shaped strip of metal that fits into a corresponding groove in the sash.

The strips which divide glass in the sash are called muntins. If the top sash of a double-hung window is divided into six panes and the bottom sash is one piece, the window is described as six over one.

Muntins were formerly wood but plastic muntins are now common. Some of these are removable and called snap-in muntins. This simplifies cleaning or painting the window.

Anyone who has ever tried to open a double-hung window in an older house has probably experienced difficulty. Sticking is very common, even in the better-made ones. If sticking is not a problem, the windows are too loose and rattle. They also take a great deal of wear, with the result that the frame around the sash often loosens. In older windows, putty on the outside of the glass cracks and falls out.

My own opinion is that the basic design of the double-hung window is faulty in that a wooden sash must slide between wooden guides, both of which swell and contract. In addition, the stress in operation is on the sash rather than a more durable member. I would avoid using them.

The casement window may be one- or two-sash. It pivots from the outer side and the inner side moves outward.

This type of window is frequently used with masonry walls. Only the more expensive kinds have a frame. The cheapest type is steel. An arguable advantage of this type of window is that the entire area of the window can be opened fully. I say arguable because I think that the amount of air which enters a house will depend much more on factors other than how much of the window can be opened. When there is no wind, other things being equal, little or no wind will come through any window. When there is a wind, air in sufficient quantities will enter through all open windows.

The metal casement windows invariably warp, so gaps at the center are a usual occurrence. This makes for leaks and drafts.

The only casement window I know that has stood up well is a wooden one manufactured by the Andersen Co. of Bayport, Minnesota.

In construction, as well as other industries, excellent products are rare and these products become known to people working in those industries. More than fifteen years ago, I was turned on to Andersen windows and have never used any other kind, even in the cheapest houses I have built. My experience has been that their windows are far superior to any others I have used, and an excellent product deserves that response. I don't know anyone connected with the Andersen Co., own no stock in it, and recommend its products solely because of their quality. My opinion was reinforced a short while ago when I happened to be in a house I built many years ago. It had Andersen windows and they were as good as the day I installed them.

The horizontally sliding window is another type; as its name implies, the sash slides in a groove in a horizontal movement. The sash is usually removable by sliding it to the side and then lifting up and inward. This is for ease in cleaning and painting.

This window has a disadvantage similar to that of the casement window, however, in that, when there are two sashes the middle of the window where they meet does not make a tight joint, so there are subsequent drafts and leaks. This has been partially overcome with a locking device at the center that draws the sashes together. Some sort of weatherstripping is provided to make a seal between the two when locked but doesn't work too well after some use.

The hopper window is the reverse of the awning and pivots from the bottom. The sash tilts outward at the top when open. Its most frequent use is in basements.

The most practical window for me is the awning type. I have never known an Andersen window of this type to stick, leak, or have drafts. Its design also allows the window to remain open during most rains without water entering the house.

All windows have certain basic sizes. These basic windows can be joined together to form units of almost any size desired. The member which joins two units together is called a mullion. (For ease in handling, window units larger than 12 feet should be assembled on the site.)

Awning, hopper, and casement windows are

operated by crank hardware or a type called push-out.

The crank, which costs $5 more per unit, has already been described. It locks automatically when the window is cranked shut.

The cheaper pushout has the inconvenience of requiring that the screen on the inside be swung up before the sash can be pushed out or pulled shut by a handle which when fully depressed also locks the window.

The screens of double-hung windows are on the outside, which means additional labor installing them. It also exposes the screening to the weather, which hastens deterioration.

Most windows today are manufactured with an insulation feature in mind. The simplest and cheapest of these is the "piggy-back" type, in which a removable sash is placed over the first sash and attached to it by swing pins or other types of simple hardware which secure it adequately. The window can then be opened or shut as before, but the double pane of glass is probably the single most important antidote to loss of heat.

A more expensive alternative is to have the sash glazed with double glass at the factory.

An even more expensive alternative is a type of glass known as Thermopane. It is an excellent product that is strong, acts well as an insulator, and doesn't require any additional treatment. However, a 4 x 4 pane is likely to cost a couple of hundred dollars.

A recent innovation to the Andersen window is the application of a white plastic primer to the sash and sill. This is fine if painting is projected but creates difficulties when painting is avoided.

An Andersen window roughly 3 x 2 feet, with crank hardware and screen, will cost approximately $41.

The casing or trim of a window is optional as to width and style. It is usually 1-1/4-inch stock, either square-edged or ogee.

The width of the window and door frames can be specified when ordering them. My practice is to use 4 inches for all, the width of the 2 x 4 and sheathing combined. The inner edge of all the frames will therefore be in the same plane as the inner edge of the 2 x 4. Later, after various interior wall coverings are applied, I will rip pieces

to a thickness that is slightly greater than the thickness of the particular wall covering and add this ripping to the window, an act called furring. I do this to enable me to install trim around the frame on the inside of the house. The ripping is made slightly thicker to allow for variations in wall thicknesses.

I find this quicker and easier than going through each room, determining the width of the frames in that particular room, ordering different widths, and keeping track of them. It also permits flexibility in that the wall covering may be changed from the intended one with no additional work.

Installing Windows

I staple tar-paper strips on each side of the r.o. They are about 8 inches wide and extend a few inches above and below the opening. Their function is to make a seal between the back of the casing and the sheathing.

No strip is necessary at the top since a drip cap will be installed later to prevent leaks. No strip is necessary at the bottom since it is highly unlikely that rain will drive under the sill. The joint here will later be caulked to prevent drafts.

I insert the window into the r.o. from the outside of the house. The bottom of the frame or the sill is down. I press the window forward so that the back of the casing lies flat against the tar paper.

I place a level on top of the top member or head. If the window is not level in the opening, I tack a 16d nail at a slight outward angle through the highest side casing. I then start another 16 through the opposite side or jamb, raise the window to a level position, and complete nailing it.

For windows with a height of 4 feet or less, I use three nails on each side. If the window is longer, I use additional nails proportionate to the additional height.

With the purchase of a window, a member called a drip cap is delivered and included in the price. Drip caps were formerly made of aluminum but are now made of a malleable rubberlike plastic. The drip cap sits on top of the head piece of casing. It has two bends. The forward bend forms a right angle with the outward edge of the head casing. The back bend makes a right angle between the inner edge of the head casing and the wall. I install it by nailing through the portion that lies against the sheathing.

Every window is installed in the same manner.

Exterior Doors

The second step in closing in the house is the installation of the exterior doors.

Two types are indicated on the floor plan. On the south wall is a sliding door. The number is 6068x. The 6 feet 0 inches refers to the width, the 6 feet 8 inches to the height, and the x is the position of the stationary half of the sliding door when viewed from the outside of the house. It is also an Andersen product.

The unit is delivered with the wood frame assembled. Once the frame has been installed in the r.o., the doors are placed in position and adjusted. This is a simple process, and full directions accompany the unit. All holes are predrilled. A plug on the movable door is located on the left bottom side. The plug can be lifted out. Behind it is a screw. Turning this screw will alter the setting of the door and is the means by which fine adjustments are made so that the door will glide smoothly.

This particular unit was glazed with 5/8-inch-thick glass and cost $369 at the lumber yard. The screen was included. (Sliding doors are available at half this cost. The frames are aluminum and the glass thinner.)

On the west side of the house a hinged door is indicated.

Two types of exterior doors are almost always used, panel or flush (see page 133 for description of both types). Both are 1-3/4 inches thick.

The panel door is the more expensive and will range in cost from about $40 to $80, depending on the amount and kind of detail used in its center area.

The flush door is available either as "solid core" or "hollow core." Solid-core doors are slightly cheaper than the cheapest panel doors; exterior hollow-core doors will usually cost about $25.

Both panel and flush exterior doors require a frame. It is usually made of clear pine that is 1-1/8 inch thick and referred to as 5/4 stock. The sill, or

bottom member, is frequently either clear fir or more expensive oak. The jambs of the frame are dadoed to receive the sill. Dadoing involves making a U-shaped groove whose depth is 3/8 to 1/2 inch and whose width is the thickness of the sill, 1-5/8 to 2 inches. The dado is at about an 8-degree angle, sloping down toward the outside of the house to create drainage action away from the door during rains.

Because of the angle of the sill, its thickness, and the fact that the dado is not cut at the very bottom of the jamb but an inch or so above it, the top of the sill at the back will be about 2-1/2 inches above the subfloor.

The finished flooring is 25/32 inch (or, for practical purposes, 3/4 inch) thick. The top of the sill at the rear should be positioned so that it will lie 3/4 inch above the subfloor. This would make its height even with the finished floor. It is therefore necessary to remove 1-3/4 inches under the sill to allow the frame to drop down and leave 3/4 inch of the sill above the subfloor.

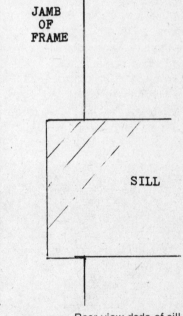

JAMB OF FRAME

SILL

Rear view dado of sill in door jamb

Installing Sliding Door

With an 8-point handsaw, I cut out the shoe which lies within the r.o.

I staple tar paper on each side of the opening.

I insert the frame into the opening, then level it as I did the window. I tack it in this position and check the sides for plumb before completing the nailing. This additional step should be done since the frame is rather large and may be out of square.

The bottom of the frame, or sill, is wood and lies flat on the subfloor. On top of the sill is an aluminum member called a saddle which rises from the outside at an angle of about 9 degrees. This sill is 3/4 inch higher than the subfloor.

With the sliding doors comes a second sill made of oak; it is predrilled for wood screws. After the finished floor is completed, this member will butt the first sill.

An exterior door frame costs about $20. It is simple to make on the site. However, the materials will cost more than half that amount and it doesn't pay for me to make it unless I am making more than five.

I remove the shoe from the opening.

I stand the frame in the opening and mark the outline of the sill on the subfloor.

I remove all nails within this area.

I set the depth of the saw to 1-3/4 inches and cut what I have marked. The power saw will not be able to cut beside the jacks, and I complete this with a sabre saw and wood chisel.

I remove the piece of plyscore.

The boxing board is now exposed. I reset the depth of the saw to cut at 1-1/4 inches since I have removed half an inch of plyscore. I make a number of cuts across the boxing board. I then remove

Sill of sliding-door frame

wood from the boxing board with a wood chisel to a depth of 1-1/4 inches.

I go under the house and nail a 2 x 8 across the sills to support the edge of the plyscore.

I staple tar paper to the sides of the r.o. and install the frame as for a window.

The door frame does not come with a drip cap. I nail aluminum edging the o.o. width of the head piece of casing. One side lies against the sheathing and I nail through it into the header behind the sheathing. The other side lies flat on the casing and extends 1/2 inch beyond it. After the exterior wall finish is applied, I will bend this extension down over the front of the head casing.

Boxing in the Eaves

The third step in closing in the house involves finishing the underside of the roof that extends beyond the walls of the house. The most common manner of doing this is called "boxing the eaves."

At the northwest corner, I lay a level on the underside of the 2 x 6 behind the fascia, bring the bubble to center, and make a mark on the sheathing that corresponds to the bottom of the 2 x 6.

I repeat this about midway along the 40-foot side and then at the northwest corner. I pop a chalk line between the marks so that I have a continuous chalk line on the sheathing that corresponds to the bottom of the 2 x 6 fascia.

I nail 2 x 4s on top of the chalk line, extending their ends to each of the 2 x 6 hanging rafters. I add a cross piece of 2 x 4 8 feet o.c. to provide a nailing surface for the ends of the plywood I am about to cut.

The member which is now to be nailed to the undersides of the 2 x 4s and which lies between the fascia and walls of the building is called the soffit or plancier.

For ease while installing the soffit and because both of its sides will later be hidden by trim, I rip its width 1/4 inch less than the actual i.d. width between the back side of the fascia and the wall sheathing.

I rip the soffit out of 4 x 8 sheets of half-inch exterior plywood, gis (this stands for "good on one side" and is cheaper than plywood which has been filled and sanded on both sides).

I nail the soffit to the 2 x 4s, butting each length. It extends to the outsides of the hanging rafters.

I establish chalk lines on the gable walls that correspond to the bottoms of the hanging rafters and nail 2 x 4s through the sheathing and into studs on top of the chalk line.

At the ridge, I nail a 2 x 4 between the bottom of the hanging rafter and the cleat for nailing that parallels it which I have installed along the gable wall. The boxing boards that rise from the north and south walls will meet at its center and the piece will provide a nailing surface for both.

I rip half-inch exterior plywood at least 1/4 inch narrower than the width between the gable wall and the fascia and use aluminum shingle nails to install it.

I butt a second piece of plywood which I have cut so that its higher end is exactly at the center of the ridge. I reverse this, starting from the southwest corner, to complete boxing in the gable end.

I continue around the house and install soffits.

The gable end detail shows the area to be closed to complete boxing in the eaves. A vertical piece of pine is beveled to conform to the slope of the soffit between the gable wall and the outer side of the 2 x 6 hanging rafter and is nailed to the 2 x 4 cleat.

I cut a triangular piece so that its hypotenuse butts the underside of the fascia and hanging rafter and the area is closed in. I repeat this at the remaining three ends on the gable sides of the house.

While installing the boxing boards, I have butted their sides against the backs of the fascia boards. I use a 3/4 x 3/4-inch redwood strip to cover this joint.

When I have installed the exterior wall covering I will place a similar strip between the wall covering and the boxing boards.

A common practice of architects is to indicate ventilation of the eaves. This is done by cutting strips from the soffit and nailing screening over them. This side will be up and not exposed when the soffit is installed.

The purpose of ventilating the eaves is to provide movement of air which would reduce the build-up of humidity and thereby lessen the chances of paint flaking or peeling from the exposed surface of the soffit. It will also help to prevent excessive build-up of heat in the attic.

I find that this has very minor value for preventing heat build-up and none for peeling paint. I omit these vents unless specified.

If painting is projected, I would not use expensive wood for the fascia, soffit, or trim.

Exterior illumination is often installed in the soffit. No preparation for this is necessary at this time.

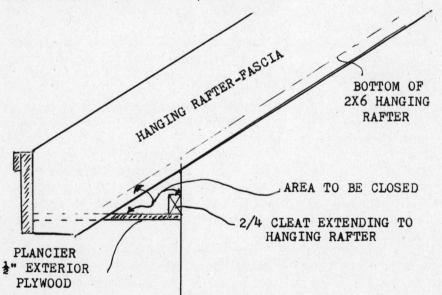

Gable end detail

ADDITIONAL INFORMATION

To replace a broken window pane, knock out as much of the glass as possible with a hammer. Old putty is removed by chipping it out with an old wood chisel or screwdriver. As the putty is removed, small metal pieces (glazing points) that are either diamond-shaped or triangular will be seen. An end of this point is embedded in the wood surrounding the glass and the other end extends above the glass to hold it in position. These are removed by lifting them up with the end of a screwdriver. After the old putty has been completely removed, the opening for the glass is measured. By convention, the width is always given first. In most places that sell glass, it will be cut to size without additional cost. If more than half a dozen panes are to be replaced, it will pay to buy a glass cutter and the glass and cut it yourself.

For each pane, I buy the glass in the nearest dimension greater than the opening. I lay the glass on the opening and with a glass cutter score it 1/8 inch smaller than the side of the frame, which acts as a reference line. After scoring the glass, I grasp the nearest end between my thumb and forefinger and snap it off. If it will not snap with light pressure, I tap the underside of the glass along the score mark until a crack develops. The piece will then either fall off or it will snap off easily.

It is not necessary to press down hard on the glass cutter to score the glass; the glass is likely to crack and may cut the person attempting it. A light pressure is sufficient. The cutter is held at about a 60-degree angle and drawn to the operator. If it is scoring the glass, a scratchy sound will be heard. If it isn't, change the angle to a steeper one. Dipping the cutter in kerosene will often help. This method is for cutting single-strength glass only.

Thicker glass is scored first in the same way but it will not snap off easily; it is best to tap the underside along the scoring line gently with the ball end of the cutter. The tapping should be continued until a crack develops.

The cut pane is laid into the opening. The metal points are inserted with a screwdriver or putty knife so that one end is in the wood and the other end above and snug to the glass. The points should be spaced every 8 inches or so.

Dap Co. makes a fairly good glazing putty. This is laid on the outside between the wood and glass and depressed with a 1-1/2-inch putty knife. The knife is then turned sideways and with firm pressure moved along the putty to form a smooth tapered line.

The key to shaping the putty is to first work it into a ball in your hand in order to mix the oil thoroughly; then, when smoothing it, draw the putty knife toward you with smooth, even pressure. Shape the corners last. The slope of the putty is down from the glass.

To repair a broken sash cord of a double-hung window, remove the stop at the inside of the frame. These are usually fastened with finishing nails. A putty knife slipped between the stop and frame will often loosen the stop enough so that a flat bar can be inserted without marking the stop or frame.

When the stops on both sides have been removed, the sash is free to swing out from the frame.

On each side of the frame, in the channel where the sash slides, will be a screw and plug. This plug is a piece of wood cut from the frame. Remove the screw and the plug will come out.

Remove the broken sash cord. The sash will have to be raised to do this, since the weight behind the frame can be reached only when the lower sash is up.

The weight is removed through the opening left by the plug.

The chain (much longer-lasting than rope) is threaded through the pulley at the top of the frame until it appears at the plug. This end is tied to the weight or hooked to a coil which acts as a knot and keeps the chain attached to the weight.

The chain is cut about 4 inches longer than twice the height of the sash.

The weight is returned behind the frame.

The other end of the chain is attached to the sash by knotting or using the coil. It lies in a groove in the sash milled for this purpose.

The sash is returned to the frame and the stops renailed.

The upper sash is repaired in a similar fashion. However, to remove it, the lower sash must first be removed and then the guide behind it as well. This guide is a narrow piece of wood press-fitted into a vertical slot along its entire length. It is pried loose by inserting a screwdriver between the guide and frame and prying it out of the groove.

I've made all the windows for a house on the site. It took me two full weeks, and I once ran a window factory and am pretty well up on their manufacture. The materials I used cost $400 less than the cost of the equivalent windows, but it was definitely not worth it for me to have made them since my time applied elsewhere is worth more than $200 per week. The point of this is, of course, that one cannot compete with mass production and almost always it will be economical to buy already-fabricated products rather than making them on the site. (There are exceptions, such as kitchen cabinets, and I will discuss these as they arise.)

FINISHING EXTERIOR WALLS

11

The material which will be used to cover the ply-score will be permanently seen and exposed to the weather. These factors should be considered along with economy in selecting the exterior finish.

Among woods, cedar and redwood stand up best because of the natural oils they contain. I have seen redwood siding more than a hundred years old in excellent condition. Board cedar resists deterioration about as well. Cedar in the form of shingles is good, but with an average life of thirty or forty years. Some woods, such as red tidewater cypress, have excellent rot-resisting qualities but their availability is very limited and they are usually much more expensive than the others. Pine has been used frequently, but it requires constant maintenance and even then will cup, warp, split, and rot over a much shorter period of time. The same problems occur with many other woods that have been used. All this reduces itself to the fact that if wood is selected as the exterior covering, it will most likely be either redwood or cedar. I consider them equal in value and even find it

hard at times to distinguish between them because of their similarity in appearance.

In board form, they cost about the same, approximately 45 cents a board foot.

Cedar shingles will probably cost about one third more than cedar in board form.

Brick or an equivalent masonry veneer would cost about $1.50 per square foot *installed,* including 2-1/2-inch-wider footing to allow for it.

A stucco finish would be closer to a dollar a square foot.

Among the metal products, aluminum siding with a baked enamel finish has come into widespread use. Its price varies a great deal between different localities, and even in the same area one contractor may ask twice as much as another. The probabilities are that the cost will be somewhere in the neighborhood of $1.40 per square foot.

Another widely used type of exterior finish is asbestos in the form of a shingle or sheet. This is the cheapest material and runs about 40 cents per square foot installed. It has an added advantage of requiring no maintenance. The colors tend to fade slightly over the years.

Installing Cedar Vertical Siding (Exactly the Same for Redwood)

This cedar siding is 1 x 8. Each board is installed with the groove inserted into the tongue of the board already nailed. The purpose of the **V** is decorative and also serves to mask imperfections that may exist when boards are in position. The cedar is sold in multiples of 2 feet starting from 8 feet. The longest standard lengths are 16 feet. Longer lengths are difficult to procure and a surcharge is often placed on them. Standard widths are 4 inches, 6 inches, and 8 inches. Wider boards are available to 12 inches but, again, a surcharge is common.

I staple 15-pound felt around the northwest corner, half on each wall. On the north wall, I staple another length overlapping the first by 6 inches. The top of the tar paper is at the soffit, the bottom an inch or so below the sheathing. During rains the back of the siding will often become moist; the purpose of the tar paper, which will cover all of the sheathing, is to keep this moisture from reaching the sheathing or members behind it and creating condition favorable to rot. It also helps prevent dampness inside the house.

I use a table saw to rip a 10-foot board and remove the **V**.

I start a nail into the top of the ripped board, align the ripped edge with the sheathing of the west wall, and tack it. The top of the board butts the soffit. The bottom extends below the mud sill.

I start an aluminum shingle nail at the center of the mud sill, plumb the board with a 4-foot level, and finish nailing it. I space two more nails across the board midway along the height and another nail at the top and bottom. I will use aluminum shingle nails for all the siding since they hold well and will not bleed.

I insert a second board into the tongue of the first and nail. If needed, I drive additional toenails along the tongue to make a tight fit.

I continue to install boards along the south wall in this manner until the frame of the first window falls within the width of the next board.

I mark the piece to be cut from the board by first butting it to the frame, the top at the soffit. I place marks on the board that correspond to the top and bottom of the frame. The tongue of the board is against the side of the frame.

I measure the distance between the side of the frame and the end of the tongue of the board already nailed. I draw a line between the two marks equal to this measurement.

To remove this piece, which is that portion of the frame that lies within the boards, I place the board on horses and rip down the vertical line with a plywood blade in the Skil saw that is set to cut at about a 45-degree angle. The result of this is that the underside of the cut, which will lie against the wall, tapers away from the line. The purpose of angling the cut rather than making it straight is for ease of installation. If the cut were straight, the frame would prevent it from being positioned.

I complete the cuts with a Skil jig saw, Model 514.

With the beveled cut, the board will slip into position. I have sawed directly on the vertical line.

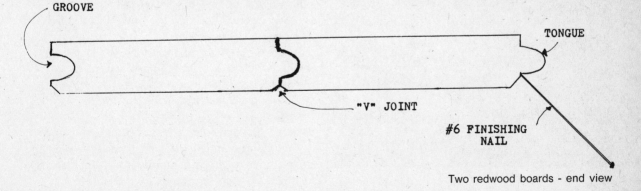

GROOVE

TONGUE

"V" JOINT

#6 FINISHING NAIL

Two redwood boards - end view

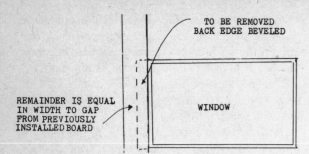

Notching around window, 1/8-inch–3/16-inch tolerance

This will leave a slight gap between the frame and board which I will later fill with butyl caulking.

Because of wind I keep stapling lengths of tar paper as needed rather than covering the wall completely at one time.

I continue with short lengths above and below the window. The bottom of the top boards should sit on top of the window frame and a gap of a quarter-inch or so should exist between it and the soffit. There is no need to make a tight fit at the top since this will be covered with molding.

The bottom board should be snug against the bottom of the window sill. It should extend at least an inch below the mud sill and will be trimmed later.

The shorter boards are continued until part of the next one lies beyond the frame. It is marked in the same way as the first and the portion of it that falls within the frame area sawed away. It is not necessary to bevel the vertical cut on this side

Jig (sabre) saw

since the board is free to slide into the top and bottom tongues without the frame obstructing it.

The rest of the vertical siding is installed in the same manner down the length of the north wall.

At the corner the last board is ripped to a width that will make it flush with the sheathing on the east wall.

I use the other ripped piece for the first board along the east wall. The top is cut at an 18-1/2-degree angle and butts the soffit.

In cutting boards for the gable walls, the high end of one is the low end of the succeeding board. The angle I have set on the protractor remains constant, but the overall length of the board increases and I mark each before installing the one that precedes it.

As I pass the ridge, the situation is reversed in that each successive board now becomes shorter, and I reverse the marking to allow for it. The angle is the same.

Above and below the sliding door, where the width of the frame is more than 6 feet, I will either cut the bottom and top pieces from the same board or measure the distance from them to the end of the frame to make sure that the pieces above and below are in the same plane. Over longer widths, because different boards may not be exactly the same width or one joint may be tighter-fitting than another, these pieces may develop misalignment and the full board that will complete going around the frame will not fit properly. If the boards above and below the window are not aligned, I can correct the situation by making slightly looser or tighter joints above or below as needed to bring the two back into alignment.

The vertical siding is installed in the same manner around the rest of the house.

I pop chalk lines along the bottom of the siding that is a quarter-inch or so below the mud sill. I set the depth of the Skil saw to 7/8 inch and trim along the chalk line all around the house.

I lay a bead of butyl rubber caulking over the siding and against the sides and bottoms of all frames.

I close the gap between the top of the siding and the soffit with molding. Each length of molding butts and is continuous around the entire house. I use shingle nails spaced every foot or so.

When installing vertical siding, most of the boards will be quite straight and fit together easily. Occasionally there will be a warped board. When this occurs, the board is first nailed where it fits properly. A scrap is then cut in a diagonal. Half is tacked beside the board where it is to be shifted into the correct position. The second half is slid between the tacked piece and the board, the narrow end up. The second piece is then tapped forward and acts as a wedge, forcing the warped board to the one already nailed.

I use this when the board is really quite warped. Most often I tack a cleat, lay a ripped piece against the warped board with its groove in the tongue, and pry the board into position with a flat bar.

When the board is only slightly warped, a finishing toenail will usually drive it tight to the nailed board.

When marking a board to be cut around the window frame, the cross cut is marked with a T square. I make the line for the ripping cut by extending the pencil to the width and draw the line freehand by using my third finger as a guide while I slide it along the edge of the board. This takes a little practice but also saves a good deal of time marking lines. Ripping is required a multitude of times, and developing this technique is worth the effort.

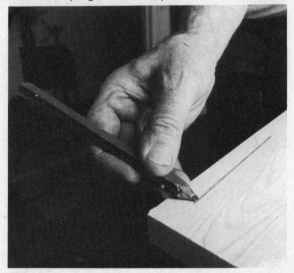

Marking for ripping

Beveled Siding

This type of exterior covering is the same wood as the vertical siding. It is milled as shown in the illustration and is installed horizontally. Its cost is about the same as the vertical siding, the choice between the two is purely for reasons of appearance.

End view - bevel siding

Installing Redwood Beveled Siding

I cut an end of a 10-foot length of square-edged 1 x 3 redwood at an angle of 18-1/2 degrees. I place this on another 10-foot length and nail the two together to form a right angle. The lower end of the angle cut is flush with the top of the straight cut.

I tack the "corner boards" over the corner and plumb. I then nail the corner boards through the sheathing into the corner post. I trim the bottoms so that they are 1/4 inch below the mud sill. I do the same at the remaining three corners.

I butt a length of siding against the corner board and tack it so that its bottom is flush with the bottom of the corner board. I lay the 4-foot level on the length of siding and bring it to level, then nail. I use one shingle nail on the beveled portion of the board and another on the flat and exposed surface. I nail every 16 inches into a 2 x 4 member of the wall, using aluminum shingle nails throughout.

I lay a bead of butyl caulking against the edge of the nailed board and butt a second to it. I squeeze this board against the first, nail, and remove the excess caulking. (Turpentine is a solvent for the caulking and will help remove excess if necessary.)

I continue to the northeast corner board so that the beveled siding lies between both corner boards and is also level and 1/4 inch below the mud sill.

I start the second horizontal course with a board of a different length so that the joints between boards will vary. I tack a couple of number 4 finishing nails where the bevel ends, rest the board on them, and nail.

On the gable ends, I install the molding between the sheathing and soffit first, then butt the siding to it.

The balance of the installation of horizontal beveled siding is the same.

Asbestos Sheets and Shingles

Asbestos shingles are probably the most widely used exterior wall covering in the country. I can think of no other reason than their relative cheapness to account for this. Aside from aesthetic considerations, they last indefinitely and require no maintenance. However, because of their porosity, the unexposed side of the shingle will be as wet as the exposed part during a rain. In spite of the tar paper that is installed behind them, this makes for a humid house. Asbestos shingles also make a "cold" house, in that heat from inside escapes

through them easily. They are very brittle and will crack even under a light impact.

They are sold by the square foot and presently cost 20 to 25 cents. Standard thickness is 3/16 inch, 12 inches high, and length varies from 16 to 24 inches. They are also available in 2 x 8-inch sheets and other larger dimensions.

Installation of Asbestos Shingles

In handling asbestos shingles, keep in mind that they are brittle and will break almost as easily as glass. All the cutting necessary is done with the asbestos shingle cutter shown above. It costs about $35, but frequently the lumber yard where the shingles are bought will send along a cutter free of charge.

A typical asbestos shingle is 12 inches high and 18 inches long.

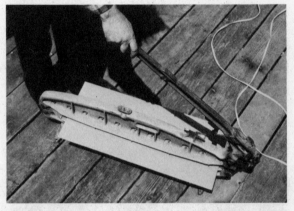

Asbestos shingle in shingle cutter

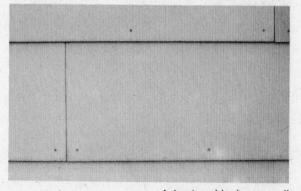

Asbestos shingles on wall

Three holes are predrilled 1 inch above the bottom. Shingle nails the same color as the shingle are sold with them and included in the price.

With the shingles and included in the price are "tabs," rectangular pieces of tar paper 3 x 12 inches. I place these in my left back pocket. I staple a horizontal length of tar paper on any wall. The bottom lies at least 1/4 inch below the mud sill.

I fasten corner edging to each corner with shingle nails.

Bull-nosed metal corner for asbestos shingles

The bottom of the metal is 1/4 inch below the mud sill.

I pop a chalk line on the tar paper 12 inches above the bottoms of the metal corners.

I insert a full shingle into the groove in the metal. Its top is on the chalk line. I nail through the three

predrilled holes. Before driving the third nail, I slip a tar-paper tab behind the shingle so that half remains exposed.

I butt a second shingle to the first and nail. The joint between the two shingles has a tab under it. I continue the first course of shingles in this manner, placing tabs at each joint until the bull-nosed corner falls within the length of a shingle.

I butt a shingle to the one last nailed and mark it

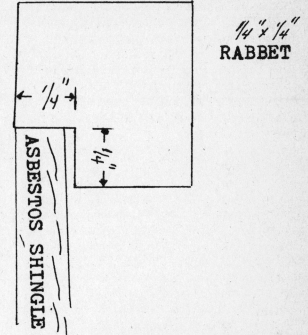

1/4" x 1/4" RABBET

ASBESTOS SHINGLE

Upper closing strip for asbestos shingles

to correspond to the position of the bull nose. This is the width to which the shingle must be cut; for ease in cutting, I mark both the top and bottom.

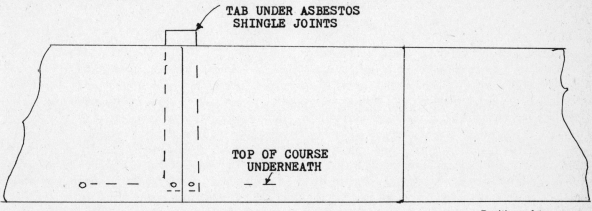

TAB UNDER ASBESTOS SHINGLE JOINTS

TOP OF COURSE UNDERNEATH

Position of tar paper

I raise the arm of the shingle cutter, which opens the jaws. I insert the shingle between the jaws. I shift it so the marks are over the tapered knife, then press down on the handle; the top jaw pressing down on the lower knife edge will cut through the shingle. If the shingle doesn't break in a clean line, it can be trimmed in the same way. I nail this last piece to fit between the bull nose and full shingle and complete the first course.

I start the second course with half a shingle at the northeast corner. I insert a nail into the first hole and slide the shingle and nail down till the nail catches on top of the shingle below. I nail it there. I do the same at the other hole, but before I complete driving the nail I slip a tab under the shingle. The bottom end lies 3/4 inch over the shingle below, while the width of the tab is roughly centered on the joint.

The second course of shingles will lap over the first course by 1 inch.

I now have the option of popping another chalk line to use as a reference for the tops of the second course shingles or using the predrilled holes. Over a 40-foot length, unless one has installed asbestos shingles many times, the chalk line is more reliable as a means of alignment.

Courses of shingles are now laid until a frame falls within the area of a shingle.

The portion of the shingle to be cut away is marked in a similar manner as siding.

To make any cut other than a straight line across the length or width of the shingle, the device at the front of the shingle cutter is used. If a 3-inch square is to be removed from the corner of the shingle, the shingle is first laid under the hooked metal piece. The side of the line where the cut is to be made is laid on the outside of the hook. The shingle is positioned also so that it lies 1/4 inch or so behind the end of the hook end and therefore only 1/4 inch or so of the cut will be made. The handle is lowered. This causes the hook to come down and remove a bit of the shingle equal to its width and only 1/4 inch into the shingle. The purpose of making a series of very small cuts rather than fewer larger ones is to avoid cracking the shingle, which is extremely easy to do. If the shingle happens to be wet, I don't even attempt to cut it since the little strength it does have is even further weakened.

I slide the shingle forward another 1/4 inch, cut again, and continue this until I have the length of cut I desire.

I then turn the shingle at a right angle and cut the second line in the same manner.

The north and south walls are closed at the top with molding. The molding should be pressed against the shingle but nailed to the 2 x 4 nailer above the soffit and not through the shingle, since it will most likely crack if this is attempted.

At the soffit of the gable walls, I first install molding that looks like this when viewed from the end:

Cedar shingles

I mill this piece myself, but the same result can be achieved by nailing two strips of molding together. Its shape allows the tops of the shingles to fit behind the molding and keeps them in position. Simultaneously, it closes the gap between the wall and soffit.

Installing Cedar Shingles

Cedar shingles are packaged in bundles which should cover 1/3 of a square, a square being an area 10 x 10 feet. A metal band ties them and Wiss shears will cut the metal.

Most of the cedar shingles used are 18 inches long and will usually vary in width from 2 to 12 inches. They may also be 24 inches long. There are two main grades. Number 1 is adequate. When number 1 shingles are trimmed to be rectangular they are referred to as resquared and rebutted.

The better stock is used for these and the shingles sell at a premium. Number 2 shingles, which are mainly used under shakes to provide a "shadow line," are much too poor to use as an exposed surface.

Eighteen-inch shingles are often installed on walls with 7 inches exposed. I will use these for the walls of the house. Since none of the nails will be exposed, I use number 3 common galvanized, which are more often called shingle nails.

I staple a horizontal band of tar paper, going around the northwest corner and along the entire north wall.

I install corner boards the same as I did for the beveled siding.

I run a string between the bottoms of the corner boards on the north wall.

I butt the first shingle to the corner board; its bottom lies along the string. A second course will go directly over this first one. The shingle needn't be aligned all along the string, though at no point should it extend below it. I butt the second shingle to the first. The important thing here is that there not be a large gap between the shingles.

I nail the shingles with two nails about 6 inches up from the bottom. If I get a wide shingle, say 6 inches or more, I'll use three nails, with even wider shingles, possibly four.

To trim the side of the shingle, I simply score it deeply with a matte knife and split. Any straight scrap of wood can serve as a straightedge, I will trim the sides of shingles only when they would be very much out of plumb were I not to do this.

I install the first course.

I begin the second course with another shingle directly over the first. I want the side of this shingle *not* to lie over a joint below it and prefer it to be at least an inch away. I continue to install shingles directly over the ones below. Now, however, I want to assure three things:

1. The joints between shingles should be tight.

2. When the joints are tight, the bottoms of the shingles should parallel the string and lie adjacent to it.

3. The joints of the second course should not lie over joints of the course underneath and preferably should be about an inch from them.

No measuring is necessary for any of these;

they should be gauged by eye.

If the bottom of the shingle looks fairly square, the butting side must be trimmed, which can be done with the matte knife if more than 1/4 inch is to be removed. If less, a block plane or sharp hatchet is quicker. (The block plane is a small plane used in one hand. Mine is a Craftsman, the least expensive I could find.)

If the bottom is to be trimmed, a situation that occurs much less frequently, the jig saw (more often called a sabre saw) is best.

I select those shingles whose width permits joints to be staggered.

I complete the second course. In doing this I make the fit along the 7 inches that will be exposed and spend little time on the 11 inches that will be hidden.

I tack a straight 1 x 3 6 or 8 feet long onto the shingles with finishing nails. The top of the 1 x 3 is 7 inches above the bottoms of the shingles.

I butt the first shingle of the third course against the corner board. If necessary, I trim the shingle so that its side butts the corner board along the entire length and its bottom sits on the 1 x 3 along its width. The 1 x 3 acts as a straightedge, although it is a waste of time to try to align each shingle perfectly. What is important is that joints do not lie over each other and create leaks.

As I come to the end of the 1 x 3 with shingles, I shift the straightedge farther down the course until it reaches the corner board.

An alternative to using the straightedge is to pop lines at the beginning of each course that are seven inches above the bottoms of the course below. This method usually results in less-well-aligned courses.

The shingles around the window frames are cut with the sabre saw.

Occasionally, when the top of the window frame is reached, only a tiny portion of the shingle will be exposed if the 7-inch exposure has been kept to. If less than 1/2 inch is involved, I would expose more than 7 inches.

Along the north and south walls, the shingles are continued to the soffit until less than 7 inches would be exposed if another course were added and the gap between the shingles and soffit closed with molding.

The shingles are continued to the soffit along the gable walls and the gap between them and the soffit closed with the same molding.

Instead of molding, shingles are frequently installed horizontally and serve the same purpose.

I caulk the joints at the corner board with butyl rubber and all other joints around windows (except the top) and door frames.

ADDITIONAL INFORMATION

The cedar siding will not deteriorate if left as is, but it will usually blacken on the north side of the house and turn silver-gray on the south. This is of course a generalization, but one that holds true over a wide variety of climates. The blackening occurs when wetting is frequent and drying out occurs less often. When the cedar is both wetted and dried frequently, the result is a silver or driftwood effect. Since more sun will usually be on the south not the north side, the generalization has validity.

A product called Woodlife, which is primarily used to help wood resist rot and does this well, also helps avoid blackening. If used, it should be applied every two years. It costs about $4 per gallon and will cover about 700 square feet to the gallon. I apply it with a mop. I would not recommend any other product for cedar or redwood.

Another method of handling discoloration is to use an oil-based stain. The color of the wood is lost but uniformity is achieved. This also has to be repeated every two or three years.

I would use paint only if I desired color. Paint doesn't protect wood and in fact helps it to rot. An example of this is often seen at the base of posts such as those at the front entrance to a house. Moisture forms under the paint and is retained. This condition leads quickly to rot and newly painted posts that look in excellent condition have actually rotted at their base. Paint is a cosmetic and nothing more. Once it has been applied, it must be reapplied every two or three years, not to preserve the wood but because the paint itself has peeled or blistered and powdered. It is the deteriorated paint that has to be replaced. If colors are desired, a better alternative to paint

almost always is some form of stain, which is usually longer-lasting. It is also cheaper, since it will cover much larger areas per gallon. Personally, if I used cedar or redwood for the exterior, I would leave it to age naturally.

Cedar and redwood are very soft woods and will splinter, scratch, and damage easily. They must be handled with care.

When installing asbestos shingles, it is sometimes necessary to make a hole for the nail in a partial shingle. Near the end of the handle of the cutter is a pin. The shingle is placed under the pin and the handle dropped. This pierces a hole in the shingle to accommodate a nail.

Almost as soon as the asbestos shingle gets wet in front it will become wet in back. Because of this, the tar paper should be applied very carefully to ensure that the sheathing is completely covered.

If a very small amount is to be removed from a shingle, the shingle cutter doesn't work too well. A better alternative is to place a composition blade (the same one used for cutting concrete block) on the Skil saw. It will then cut as well as a steel blade through wood.

The composition wheel should be used on asbestos shingles outdoors, since it is dangerous to breathe in asbestos dust.

If asbestos sheets are used instead of shingles, the composition blade is also the best way of cutting the sheets. Marking is the same as for marking sheathing and the cutting is similar.

Cuts may also be made with a metal-cutting blade in the sabre saw, but this takes much longer and uses up a lot of blades since they become dull quickly.

To replace broken asbestos shingles already installed, break the shingle with a hammer and remove nails and pieces. Slip a new shingle under the one above until it hits the nails of that shingle, then nail the replacement shingle.

To replace rotted cedar shingles, drive a flat bar under the rotted shingle so that the **V** of the flat bar hits the nails holding it. Continue to hammer the flat bar against each nail till it is sheared.

Slip out the rotted shingle and replace it with a new one. Face-nail the new shingle. In face-nailing, the nail will remain exposed and be located just under the course above. The nail should be aluminum to prevent bleeding.

Of the four exterior finishes discussed, redwood beveled siding or vertical cedar siding would be my choices; these two types of siding give the best value.

At any point after the exterior of the house has been completed, the surveyor should be notified and a survey made.

WASTE DISPOSAL

12

The exterior of the house has been completed but some outside work remains; when weather permits, this has priority.

A means for the disposal of wastes which pass through the plumbing system must be provided. In cities and many suburban areas a municipal sewage system accomplishes this by channeling

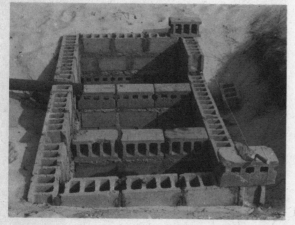

Septic tank without lid

the wastes into a 4-inch cast-iron pipe which is then hooked up to the sewer line. However, millions of homes have no sewer lines available and the probabilities are that millions of other homes will be built with the same situation. In these cases waste disposal is accomplished through the use of a septic tank and cesspool or dry well.

This septic tank is 5 x 10 by 4 feet deep, the equivalent of six courses of block. The dimensions are the minimum size required by many Health Departments. Formerly, three compartments were necessary, but this requirement has been changed to two.

Two types of concrete blocks are used; the ordinary stretcher block and the septic-tank block. The latter has a small hole placed toward the inside of the tank. The opening then slants down into a larger hole identical to the hole in the stretcher block. The presumable purpose of this is to permit the effluent in the tank to drain down and away from the tank. This is an insignificant refinement and the only practical result of using septic-tank blocks rather than stretcher blocks is to pay about twice the amount for the septic-tank blocks.

The tank in the photograph has a lid made of five 2 x 5 foot slabs of 2-inch reinforced concrete with a rabbeted joint along the longer sides. Embedded in the slabs is a steel ring for removal of the slab should this be necessary at a later date. The slabs were very heavy; three men had a hard time moving them into position. The total cost of the lid was over $100 delivered. An equivalent lid fabricated on the site would have cost less than $25, but the bureaucratic idiocy of this particular Health Department made the use of these specific lids mandatory.

The septic tank operates on the principle that anerobic bacteria feed on the solids in the wastes and render the whole harmless. These bacteria function in an airless environment. Grease and detergents interfere with their proper functioning and therefore those wastes originating at the kitchen sink and washing machine will be channeled to the dry well and the remaining wastes to the tank.

An important aspect of pollution is a factor called the biochemical oxygen demand—the amount of oxygen the solids in the waste will remove from the effluent. The liquid is said to be polluted when the oxygen falls below a certain level and is incapable of supporting most types of marine life. In attacking and decomposing the solids the bacteria remove the oxygen-consuming organisms and thereby render the waste harmless. The liquid then seeps from the tank into the surrounding soil.

Installing the Septic Tank

When marking out the area of the site to be excavated, I also stake out a 9 x 14-foot area for the septic tank and have the hole dug while the site is being prepared.

Some Health Departments require that the location of the tank be at least 100 feet from the nearest well and 10 feet from the property line. I also try to place it nearest a bathroom and at the rear of the house, where it is least conspicuous.

If the hole is to be dug manually, two men can usually do it in four or five hours in average soil. A pointed shovel should be used; shovelfuls of loose soil should be slid along the ground and

lifted only when necessary.

I bring the blocks to the tank in a wheelbarrow and place them around the hole.

I set up the builder's level near the hole.

I lay a septic-tank block in a corner of the hole and level it with a spirit level. No footing is needed and the block is laid directly on the soil. Soil is added or removed to level it.

I place the rod on the block and take a reading. I want the block to be about 42 inches below grade. Since five additional courses will be laid and the lid is 2 inches thick, this will place the top of the tank at grade.

I lay a second block 10 feet o.o. from the first. I take a height reading with the builder's level and adjust the second block so that it is level with the first.

I lay blocks in the third and fourth corners to attain 5 x 10 feet, then shift the blocks till the diagonals are equal and I have a rectangle with the same dimensions.

I stretch string between corners and lay the first course of blocks directly on the soil. The blocks are butted and no mortar is used. The holes face out and are parallel to the ground.

I lay a course of stretcher blocks midway along the 10-foot sides to start the two compartments; the blocks here are also butted without mortar and the holes in the blocks placed vertically.

I lay another septic-tank block in each corner and stretch strings.

I lay a second course of stretcher blocks for the partition. These blocks extend between the strings on the 10-foot sides and are flush with the outside of the septic-tank blocks. This ties the partition wall into the 10-foot walls and also staggers the joints between courses.

I build up four courses in the same manner.

On the fifth course, I lay the septic-tank blocks with mortar, their holes up and down, the sides solid. The sixth course is also mortared and the blocks are also solid at the sides.

For the fifth and sixth courses of the partition wall, I lay the stretcher blocks with their holes on the sides so that effluent can flow between compartments when the liquid level reaches that height.

The last two courses of the walls are solid, to keep the liquid from seeping out of the tank no less than 16 inches below grade.

I position the five sections of the lid on the walls of the tank.

I will later cut a hole in the side of the tank for the entry of a 4-inch cast-iron waste line. It makes no difference which compartments the pipe enters. I will pack mortar between the pipe and hole to seal the opening. I will back-fill when this is done.

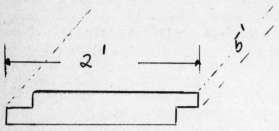

Precast concrete lid for septic tank, 2 feet by 5

Installation of Dry Well

This is simply a hole in the ground with loose block walls to permit liquid to seep out of it into the surrounding soil. I will locate it as near the kitchen sink and washing machine as practical. I use only stretcher blocks for the walls.

I dig the hole. A 5 x 5-foot hole 4 feet deep should be more than sufficient. The hole should be at least 5 feet deep, which would place the top of the dry well at least a foot below grade, less 3 inches for the lid.

I lay the four corner blocks directly on the soil. The holes are on the sides, to permit the liquid to seep out. I lay the first course in this manner and do the same for the three following courses. No mortar at all is used. I lay the fifth and sixth courses with mortar and the holes in the blocks up and down so that no liquid will seep out at this height.

I back-fill.

I drive two stakes 1-1/2 inches from the outside of each wall. I cut two 2 x 4s to a length of 5 feet and nail them to the stakes. I nail two studs to the ends of the 5-foot lengths, then nail the studs to the stakes. The tops of the 2 x 4s are 3 inches above the walls. This makes a 5-foot-square form around the walls of the dry well.

I chisel 3/4 inch from two opposite walls at roughly midpoint and lay a scrap piece of 3/4-inch pipe, which rests in the chiseled portion of the

block. I then place two scraps of plyscore about 58 inches long across the pipe, their ends resting on the walls. I lay as many scraps as needed to cover the hole, each supported by pipe underneath. I cover the plyscore with tar paper to keep concrete from falling between joints in the plyscore and holes in the block.

I place a few stones around on top of the tar paper and lay scraps of metal lath or scraps of 1/2-inch-diameter reinforcing bars on them. The bars or lath should be 1 inch above the tar paper.

I mix concrete (one part Portland cement, three parts sand, five parts gravel and seven gallons of water per bag of cement), pour into the form, and screed.

I will later cut a hole under the lid to permit entry of a 1-1/2-inch copper pipe. When this is done, I will cover the dry well completely.

ADDITIONAL INFORMATION

Prefabricated septic tanks and dry wells are manufactured; the complete cost of installation is likely to run between four and five hundred dollars. The cost of materials for what I have described is about $120, to which must be added three man-days of labor.

Most plumbing codes require that cast-iron waste lines be used within the area of the house. Once outside the house, this is no longer necessary. In the photograph there is a 4 inch cast-iron waste line. I used this because the tank was only 10 feet from the house. If it had been farther away, a better alternative would have been a plastic pipe called Orangeburg. It is much cheaper than cast iron, the sections are simply pressed together, and the laborious work of making leaded joints between lengths of cast-iron pipe is avoided. Orangeburg, however, is fragile compared to cast iron and should be laid in a trench.

Almost always, I find it a good practice to build septic tanks larger than the minimum required. How long a tank will last before cleaning is needed depends on the amount of plastic material flushed down the toilet, the type of soil into which the effluent seeps, the water table, the number of people living in the house, etc. I've seen some tanks last twenty years and others four years before cleaning became necessary. The first signs of this need are the odor around the tank and wetness of the soil. The toilet bowl will flush slowly and gurgling will occur in the waste line. In some areas septic tanks are cleaned by flushing them out with water and pumps. If it's available, I recommend this service.

As soon as the septic tank has been installed, the local Board of Health should be notified. One section of the lid should be left off so the interior is visible to the inspector.

ROUGH PLUMBING AND WIRING

13

Any time after the exterior of the house has been completed to a point where the weather isn't a factor, the initial wiring and plumbing may begin. This is known as the "roughing" and includes all that should be done before the interior walls and floors are completed.

It is beyond the scope of this book to demonstrate the wiring and plumbing since this would require a book in itself. However, a number of facts will be helpful.

Plumbing Information

The responsibility of the plumber in the roughing stage will be to bring hot- and cold-water lines to the sink, basin, and tub. These will most probably be 1/2-inch copper. At the tub, he will also provide a line to the shower. If there is a dishwasher, he will provide a hot-water line to it. If there is a washing machine, he will bring the water lines to that and also a cold-water line to the toilet. All the water lines should be pitched or sloped to permit drain-

age and be equipped with valves. The plumber will install waste lines from all fixtures. These will probably be 1-1/2-inch copper, except for the toilet, which is 4-inch.

In the walls he will install vents for the fixtures; these will usually be 1-1/2-inch, 2-inch and either 3-inch or 4-inch copper, depending on the code in that area. He should run a pressure test to determine if there are leaks in the roughing system.

It is the plumber's responsibility to run a sewer line from the bathroom and make the connection to either the septic tank or municipal sewer.

He will also run a main to the water source and make the connection, either 3/4-inch or 1-inch copper.

After the walls and floors are completed, he will install the fixtures and appliances and be responsible for the plumbing inspections.

If a one-piece molded shower stall is projected rather than a tub, it will have to be placed in position before the interior walls of the bathroom are framed. The plumber should have this delivered to the site early in the framing.

"Knockers" should be obligatory. These are 1-foot extensions on the water lines which are capped and prevent knocking sounds when the water is turned on.

If gas is projected, he is responsible for the installation. Copper tubing may be used in most suburbs and rural areas; 3/4-inch black iron pipe is often mandatory in cities.

The tub can be positioned any time after the subfloor is completed and should be in place before the bathroom walls are started.

Cleats for a shower-curtain bar around the top of the tub are the carpenter's responsibility, as is the backing for a wall-mounted sink.

The total cost of the labor and materials for the plumbing should be in the neighborhood of $2000.

Electrical Information

The rough wiring may be started any time after the interior walls are completed.

In most areas today, a 100-ampere service is the minimum required, and this is what a three-bedroom house will normally require. If the appliances and heating are all electric, this house would need a 200-amp. service. The difference in cost between the two is about $150, which is small compared to the advantages of a larger capacity. The larger capacity will permit the addition of other electrical appliances and minimize the chances of overloading any particular circuit, since in a normal 200-amp. main there is room for forty circuits and only eighteen or so would be used on the initial installation.

It is the responsibility of the electrician to install the main and a mast at least 14 feet above grade. The main wire will be in the conduit; he will expose three wires for the utility company, which is responsible for hooking these into the power source at the pole.

It is also the electrician's responsibility to provide a meter base at eye level on the outside of the house behind the main and the utility company's responsibility to install the meter.

In the roughing stage the electrician will run appropriate sized wires (#14 for light circuits, 12 for utility, and greater-diameter wire as needed for the hot-water heater, electric stove, etc.), through the walls for the most part, and leave their ends 8 inches or so beyond metal or plastic boxes whose outer edges will be in plane with the finished interior wall or slightly behind.

A normal circuit which would feed power to a number of lights would have a 15-amp. circuit breaker (a type of fuse) in the main. The circuit which might feed the refrigerator, toaster, etc., would probably have a 20-amp. breaker. The electric stove, a 220-volt installation, would have a 50-amp. breaker. It is the electrician's responsibility to determine the load on each circuit and provide the appropriate wire and breaker.

After the interior walls and ceiling have been completed, the electrician will install all outlets, switches, fixtures, and appliances. He will also connect all circuits at the main and provide all switch and outlet covers.

He is responsible for the electrical inspections.

In suburban or rural areas, he will most probably use a plastic-sheathed wire called Romex. In cities, the wire will most probably be enclosed in a thin metal pipe called conduit or in a flexible metal sheath called BX. The size of the wire would be the same no matter what its outer cover.

The total cost of materials and labor for electrical work in this house (including electric heat in each room and thermostats but not lighting fixtures) would be around $1600.

If the plumbing and wiring is subcontracted, a common arrangement is to pay one-third the amount in advance, one-third on completion of the roughing, and a third on presentation of the documents attesting to the satisfactory completion of the work.

ADDITIONAL INFORMATION

A plumber and helper should complete all the plumbing for this house in three or four days. An electrician should complete the wiring in less than three days, with a few hours assistance by a helper.

The physical execution of both wiring and plumbing is simple, so much so that when an inexperienced person is directed to do a specific item, he has no difficulty executing it. However, the key to both trades is information, and this information is rather extensive, particularly for wiring. It is available in a great many books but in a form that I believe is useless for anyone buidling a house. There is no book that I can recommend, since none that I have read gives a step-by-step demonstration of how plumbing and wiring are actually done.

The plumber and electrician are responsible for arranging their respective inspections and securing documents of approval. When all inspections and documents have been secured, they are presented to the Building Department and a Certificate of Occupancy will be issued.

INSULATION AND CEILINGS

14

The purpose of insulation is to maintain interior temperatures and the material most widely used for this is fiberglass. It is enclosed in tar-backed paper or aluminum foil the i.d. width of a standard bay (area between joists or studs) 14-1/2 inches, and manufactured in rolls or 4-foot bats. These are installed by inserting the roll or bat in the bay and stapling extension tabs on each side to the underside of the joist. The paper or foil always faces the inside of the house.

Standard thicknesses are 2, 4, and 6 inches. I will use 6-inch insulation for the ceiling and work from a 5-foot step ladder.

I slice through the paper at the back of the insulation with a matte knife to cut pieces.

I insulate the walls in the same manner with 3-1/2-inch bats.

In both instances, I remove insulation that covers electrical boxes.

The cost of insulating the house is under $200. Savings in fuel plus the added comfort of more stable temperatures makes this a highly desirable feature. One person can install all of it in less than a day.

Insulation is not a good soundproofing material, despite widespread belief to the contrary. However, it does change the quality of the sound from echoy to nonreverberating and muffles it slightly. No useful purpose is served by insulating interior walls; if soundproofing is desired, soundproofing

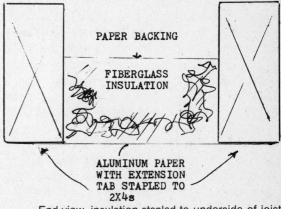

PAPER BACKING

FIBERGLASS INSULATION

ALUMINUM PAPER WITH EXTENSION TAB STAPLED TO 2X4s

End view, insulation stapled to underside of joist

material such as acoustical tile should be used.

A good practice is to remove clumps of fiberglass from a bat and stuff it around windows and exterior door frames to cut down air seepage.

As a complement to insulation, heating "experts" recommend that thin plastic sheets be stapled over wall insulation to act as a vapor barrier. Since this will cause condensation to occur in the walls and rapid rotting, it is an unsound practice.

Some people react to fiberglass with a fair amount of itching. The use of a long-sleeved shirt and gloves while installing it will avoid this.

Ceilings

Formerly most ceilings were plaster, but this has been supplanted by a material that contains gypsum between paper sheets. It is called sheetrock and manufactured in sheets 4 x 8 feet, 10 feet, and 12 feet (standard sizes). Thicknesses range between 1/4 and 5/8 inches in 1/8-inch multiples (also standard dimensions). A 4 x 8-foot sheet, 1/4 inch thick, costs about $1.25. Longer and thicker sheets are proportionately higher.

Sheetrock which is treated to be fire-retardant is called Type X. Type X will usually be 5/8 inch thick. It has been tested and rated "one hour," which means the sheet will delay the spread of fire for an hour. (These sheets are heavy and should be handled one at a time.)

Most building departments require that the wall which separates the garage from the house be one-hour on the garage side. This would also include one-hour studs, door, lock, etc., but this is not often insisted upon in residential construction. Treated one-hour studs cost about 50 percent more than untreated ones, one-hour doors cost four times ordinary ones, and a one-hour lock (which has a longer-than-ordinary tongue) is three times the cost of the normal equivalent.

Despite propaganda from plasterer's unions, sheetrock is as durable as plaster, is far easier to install, requires much less labor, and is probably the least expensive building material in use today.

It is also manufactured in smaller sheets with holes for use with plaster and called plasterboard.

Sheetrock can be shaped into curves by applying water with a sponge. An end is fastened to a member with nails and the wet sheet bent slowly and nailed to successive members forming the skeleton of the desired curve. While wet, sheetrock is very fragile and only very light pressure should be applied to shape it. The sheet should be allowed to dry thoroughly before further work is done on it.

I follow the premise that having as few joints between sheets in the ceiling as possible is an optimum consideration in selecting lengths. These joints must later be hidden, and the labor involved in doing this is much greater than the disadvantage of handling longer sheets. I therefore select 4 x 12-foot sheets for the bedrooms.

The longer the sheet, the more difficult it is to handle. This is particularly true for ceilings; when no additional joints are involved, I will use shorter sheets. Therefore, rather than using two 12-foot sheets and a 6-foot piece to cover the ceiling, which is 30 feet at the easterly end of the house, I will use three 10-foot sheets.

The function of the ceiling is purely cosmetic and I would prefer to use 1/4-inch thickness. However, the thinner the sheet, the more apparent will be the variations in plane of the ceiling joists. If the joists are very straight, an unlikely prospect, I would use 1/4-inch. With ordinary lumber, 3/8-inch should be sufficient. If the joists are more curved than ordinary, I would use 1/2-inch. If they are very much out of plane, I stretch a string from wall to wall directly under the joists and furr down the worst ones, then use 3/8-inch. On the whole, 3/8-inch sheets will usually produce a ceiling without marked waves.

Other Ceiling Materials

Wooden ceilings were formerly widespread and have begun to reappear recently. They are installed in a similar way to wooden walls. Of this type, my favorite is 1 x 4 fir, tongue and grooved. One side has a **V** joint, the other a **V** joint and a cosmetic mark along the center called a bead. The board is known as bead and center bead. In the late nineteenth century it was widely used for ceilings and walls and was finished with orange shellac and varnish. One room in my own house has this. It was done fifty years ago and is still in very good condition.

A wide variety of composition materials is manufactured for ceilings. Among these are perforated tile in 9-inch or 12-inch squares used primarily for soundproofing, various Cellotex squares or rectangles and a product called Marlite, which is Masonite with a baked enamel finish. These materials usually have a tongue and groove along their sides and are either nailed or stapled on tongues that will be hidden.

Since these materials are usually less than 16 inches and have little or no structural strength, the spans are decreased to the size used by means of furring strips that are nailed at right angles to the joists and spaced accordingly. The larger rectangles are often sold with metal strips that are hung from the joists. The strips are bent to a right angle and the rectangles are simply laid on them.

When smaller tiles are used, I nail 1 x 2 furring strips around the perimeter of the ceiling. I nail a strip down the center of the ceiling, then measure outward 9 or 12 inches from both sides and nail the other strips until I am less than 9 or 12 inches from the perimeter. I mark 9- or 12-inch multiples measuring from the center along the furring strip at the center. This marks out a uniform ceiling and the tiles around the perimeter will correspond in size.

Most of the tiles can be cut with a matte knife or sabre saw. I use a plywood blade in the table saw for cutting Marlite, and begin the ceiling with the cut pieces at an end.

Installing 3/8″ Sheetrock Ceiling

I will nail the first sheet at the northwest corner. I place horses under the area with several scaffold boards on them. Ideally, when standing on the boards, my head should just graze the joists.

The floor of the room in which the ceiling is to be installed should be swept clean first to avoid tripping over scraps. The sheets are bulky and the room should be cleared so that needless items don't interfere with their handling.

When sheetrock is delivered, I stack it flat on the floor in the center of the room whose ceiling I plan to do last. It is packaged in pairs, the yellowish-white finished surfaces against one another and the gray backs exposed. To separate the sheets, I tear a band of paper from each end.

The corners of the sheetrock break very easily. This occurs most often when someone drops rather than places an end on the floor. Every broken corner will mean about twenty minutes of additional work later to repair it, and it should be handled with care.

I turn the sheet with the smooth finished surface up and make all cuts from this side.

The bedroom is 12 feet and so is the sheet. However, either wall of the bedroom is bound to vary somewhat from that 12 feet. In places it may be more, in places less, and with ordinary care I would expect that the variation will never exceed 1/2 inch. I could therefore trim 1/2 inch from the sheet and have it fit easily, but trimming this small amount from the end would mean I would have to recut five or six times since small pieces rarely break off cleanly.

The drive for accuracy is never so misplaced as when sheetrock is cut to fit "exactly." Many times I have held up a heavy sheet with my head while trying to cram a tight sheet into place only to have the edges broken or having to put the sheet down and recut it. A gap should be left between walls and sheets to avoid this.

I mark 1 inch along both long sides and lay my 4-foot level across the sheet as a straightedge. I score the surface of the sheet. I slide the sheet to me so that this end is beyond the stack, stretch my fingers to cover as wide an area as possible along the knife mark, and press down. The scored 1-inch piece breaks along the cut. It is now held to the sheet by the paper at the back. From the underside I cut the paper, following the crease made by the turned piece.

Occasionally the break is not clean and an irregular chunk of gypsum still remains along the cut. I remove this by whittling with the matte knife. It comes away very easily.

I fill my nail apron with lath nails. These are 1-3/8-inches long, blue, with a wide head and annular rings on the shank for increased holding power.

I tack a 2 x 4 cleat to the north and partition walls, 1/2 inch below the joists. The cleats serve the purpose of holding up the ends of the sheet while positioning it.

Three people are needed for installing 12-foot sheets.

If three people are installing the ceiling, I would finish nailing each sheet completely before going on to the next.

If a fourth person is available, I would nail only enough to hold the sheet, (ten nails or so) and have that person finish nailing and make sure that all heads are below the surface and that hammer marks are left.

We lean the trimmed sheet against the scaffold boards. The long side is on the floor and the finished surface faces us as we stand on the boards. One person is at the center of the sheet, the other two 1 foot from the ends. We lift, turn the finished surface down, slide the sheet between the cleats and joists, and raise it against the joists. We shift the sheet so that a side is against the west wall and the ends 1/2 inch or so from the north and partition walls. We hold the sheet against the joists with the tops of our heads. This leaves our hands free to nail.

Nails are spaced along the joists every 8 to 10 inches. They are driven down *into the sheet and a depression around the nail head must be left.* It is called "leaving a hammer mark." Nails will be hidden later by a material called joint compound. If nail heads are above the surface of the sheet, this cannot be done, and the nail will then have to be driven down to leave the hammer mark.

The gaps at both ends between the wall and sheet will later be hidden by the thickness of the wall covering, by a molding, or both. This is true around the entire perimeter of the ceiling, and all sheets should be cut so that they are at least 1/2 inch away from the sides of the plates. No tight fits should be attempted since this is not only meaningless but will also cause difficulty if the sheet is even slightly longer than the area to be covered.

The first joist was positioned 47-1/4 inches from the east wall. This leaves the 12-foot side of the sheet midway on that joist.

The long sides of all sheets are tapered down so that when the next sheet is installed, the joint between the two forms a flattish **V**-shaped depression. This joint will be covered later.

To cut sheetrock lengthwise, I pop a chalk line on it for the desired width. I score the line with a matte knife, raise the sheet so that it stands on its side, hit the back along the scored line with my knee, allowing the botttom to lie flat on the stack. The sheet is now bent into two pieces and held by the paper on the back. It is creased along the line I scored on the finished surface and I cut through the paper along this crease. This completes cutting the sheet into two pieces.

The cut side of a piece should always be adjacent to a wall so that the **V** joints are toward the inside of the room.

About ten nails will hold a sheet and I only use this many at this time. I reposition the scaffold for the next sheet.

One should be able to locate 16 inches o.c. by eye and without measuring. This becomes relevant when the sheet is held against the joists

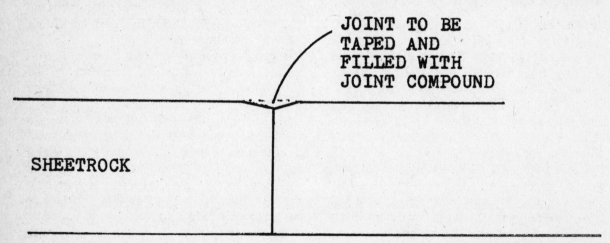

JOINT TO BE TAPED AND FILLED WITH JOINT COMPOUND

SHEETROCK

Tapered sides of sheetrock

for nailing. The positions of the joists along the sides are no problem to find but the intermediate ones are hidden. It's not much fun holding a sheet up with your head and driving a nail, only to find that it has not entered a joist. If there is any doubt about ability to space the joist by eye, light pencil marks should be made on the face of the sheet along 16-3/4 inches and 32-3/4 inches, which mark the center of the hidden joists.

Any electrical box in the ceiling will be 1/4 inch below the joists. I measure its location before installing the sheet and omit nails in the area of the box. After the sheet is nailed, I take my hammer and knock a hole in the sheet that corresponds to the center of the box sheet. The outline of the box will usually appear on the surface while doing this.

The keyhole saw in the photo cost $1. After a few cuts into sheetrock, the teeth become dull. They are still sharp enough for cutting sheetrock but not for much else. When they are too dull for even sheetrock (this will be after using it only for this purpose for several houses), I throw the blade away. Incidentally, all steel tools dull very quickly when sawing or drilling through masonry materials and only cheap throwaway kinds should be used for this.

I make a cut on the outside of the box, pry the tip of the keyhole saw through the cut, and saw out the sheetrock that covers the box. The sheet is now free to be pressed up against the joists and the omitted nails are driven.

Some people prefer to mark the location of electrical boxes on the sheet and cut them out before installation. I've found that this takes much longer to do without any advantages.

From time to time I will find it necessary to cut a piece from a sheet when the cut doesn't extend from one side of the sheet to the other. I mark the piece to be cut on the front of the sheet. I cut completely through with the knife along the shorter side, score the other side, and cut from the back to remove the piece.

Joint Compound and Taping

The sheetrock ceiling right after installation is dotted with numerous nails, hammer-mark depressions, joints between sheets, and most probably a number of broken corners and gouges on the surface. These are to be hidden and a smooth unbroken surface achieved. The material used for this is called joint compound and along the seams it is used with 2-inch-wide paper called tape.

The joint compound or joint cement is sold premixed and may be thinned slightly with water. It is also available in powdered form which is

Keyhole saw

Trowel, spackling knife, and tape

mixed with water and allowed to stand for twenty minutes, after which it is ready to use.

Both types adhere well to the surface of the sheetrock, but I have found the premixed kind difficult to work with because of a rather gummy texture which causes "dragging" and never use it. The powdered form is cheaper and works more easily. In the powdered form there is a gray undercoat for the first and second applications. The tan topping is used for the final coat.

Applying Tape and Compound

I will be using a 4 x 16-inch square trowel, and a 3-inch Hyde spackling knife (the latter is more toward the stiff than the flexible side).

In a clean five-gallon plastic bucket, I mix undercoat and water to a consistency of butter at room temperature I allow it to sit for twenty minutes. During this time it will become slightly looser. I cover the mixture with a cloth when not in use to keep foreign material from falling into it and to retard evaporation. Covered, the mixture will be good for at least two or three days and so I mix five pounds at a time.

I place two stepladders under the ends of the seam I intend to cover and lay a board between them. I want the board to be on those treads which will place me 1 foot below the ceiling when I stand on it.

I transfer two fistfuls of compound to the trowel with the knife. The trowel serves as a mortar board.

I remove portions of the mixture with the knife and press lightly into the seam and **V**. What I want is a bed of compound somewhat wider than the tape which lies evenly on both sides of the joint and in the **V** depression.

If the compound sags, I remove it, add more powder, and remix. The compound should retain its shape after being laid. I shift the compound in the depression so that it is roughly flat and wide enough to make contact with the tape throughout the length of the seam.

The tape is sold in rolls and is sometimes perforated. I unroll it on the floor and tear off a length equal to the width of the room or 1/2 inch less. I roll the piece up.

I lay an end into the bed gently 1/4 inch from the end. I want it centered over the seam and flat. I continue to unroll the piece, moving backward along the board as I lay the tape in the bed until the end of the seam.

I turn my trowel at a shallow angle to the sheet at one end of the seam. It is centered over the seam and the far side of the trowel lies against the sheetrock. I then draw the trowel toward me, moving backward on the board in a continuous motion along the entire length of the joint. This removes excess compound above the **V** depression.

While I am moving backward and troweling, I am watching the bed and tape to note whether the entire tape is in contact with the bed. If there is no compound behind the tape at any point, I spread compound to that point by pressing down on the tape in the adjacent area until it does make contact. I then lay additional compound over the point and trowel away the excess.

I now look down the entire seam and remove any compound beyond the depression. This will have to be removed sooner or later to achieve the smooth surface, and it is much harder to remove when dry.

Heavy pressure on the trowel against the sheet is unnecessary and will often scratch its surface.

I have removed all the excess from the seam. However, in places, particularly over nails, there may be hollows, and I fill these with compound on top of the tape if necessary.

Compound is effective only when used in thin layers and it is important not to apply too thick an amount at any given time. Not only will it take a long time for this area to dry, but the chances are it will also "alligator"—break into small multiple cracks similar to dried mud.

I tape all the seams in this manner.

I thicken the mixture to fill the hammer marks and cover the nail heads. For this I use the knife, with the trowel as mortar board. I press compound firmly into the depression, then wipe the area clean of any compound above the surface. Two strokes should be sufficient.

When the compound dries, it will be slightly concave. I will go over the hammer marks three times and do not try to fill them entirely the first time around.

If neatness is not practiced and excess compound not removed right after it has been applied, much more work will be created since the dried compound will have to be sanded away later.

This phase should take a day, but if time remains I will start a second application over the hammer marks, beginning where I first started. The compound here should be dry within a couple of hours, but even if it is slightly moist, the depression can be refilled if applied lightly.

I allow the compound to dry overnight.

I apply the second coat to the seam by turning the trowel sideways to it, pressing the compound more firmly into the depression, then repeating this along the entire length until the compound fully covers the **V**. I then trowel off the excess by drawing the trowel down the entire length in a continuous motion and at a right angle to the seam.

Occasionally, I apply compound to the seam with the knife, packing it fully before troweling off the excess. Either way should work.

I apply the second coat to all seams in the same manner.

I apply the second or third coat to all the nails.

I allow the compound to dry overnight.

For the third coat, I use the tan topping. This is easier to sand, although there is rarely a need to sand at all once the technique I've described is absorbed.

I mix the topping looser than the undercoat since I want only a very thin coat.

I apply the topping in the same way as the undercoat, but in cleaning off the excess I hold the trowel at about a 45-degree angle and press moderately to pack the topping into gaps in the undercoat and leave a smooth finish.

The finished seam may be 6 inches or wider. The topping may extend beyond the width of the **V,** and I often make sure that it does. In general, the wider the joint, the less noticeable it will be, provided the edges are tapered to meet the surface of the sheet and not leave a line which would be the amount the topping is above the surface of the sheet.

The troweled edge pretty well guarantees that a flat surface will remain when dry but the edges of this surface should blend into the adjoining surface of the sheet; this is accomplished by moderate pressure on the trowel against the sheet.

The 4-foot sides of butted sheets have no depression. These seams are more difficult to conceal and for that reason should be avoided wherever possible. Any compound placed on the sheet will obviously be above the sheet. To tape and finish this joint, I first remove any loose material at the joint (which would be broken bits of gypsum or torn paper).

I lay a flat scrap over the joint and hit it a few times with a hammer. I am not trying to create a depression by doing this but to achieve a flat surface as a start.

I lay compound not more than 1/8 inch thick over the joint and apply the tape. I trowel off the excess.

It is particularly important that the surface be left flat and I will add more compound to achieve this. The edges of the compound should not be more than 1/8 inch above the surface of the sheet.

I allow the compound to dry overnight.

I apply a second coat to the joint with a thickness no more than 1/16 inch. Again, I want a flat surface to remain and fill as necessary to achieve it.

I allow the second coat to dry overnight.

I apply topping with the knife from an edge of the dried coat outward from the seam for about 6 inches. I then place the trowel so that one end is on the raised edge of the dried joint and the other on the sheet and draw it across toward me to clear away the excess and leave a smooth band that tapers from the dried edge to the surface of the sheet. I repeat this on the other side of the joint.

The seam will now be 3/16 inch above the sheet where the ends butt, then taper off from this to nothing. Viewed from below as ceilings are, this difference in height cannot be seen.

ADDITIONAL INFORMATION

If all the walls and ceilings in this house were sheetrock, an experienced person could do all the taping and application of compound in three days. I have even seen a man working on stilts do it in two. Most often no sanding is needed and rarely more than fifteen minutes of it. However, while the operation is extremely simple, experience has shown me that it is very hard and time-consuming to learn.

In San Francisco, my students and I took on a large renovation job, a part of which involved installing and taping a thousand pieces of sheetrock. After some instruction and three weeks of working steadily at compound and taping, not one person had achieved good quality or even a third the speed of a professional. Needless to say, there were miles of sanding to do. (A Rockwell orbital sander, heavy duty, Model 305, with fine emery cloth is best for this.)

The greatest difficulty encountered is finding the correct angle to hold the trowel while drawing it toward one and leaving a smooth coat of compound.

Quite often the compound is allowed to get too thick, so that it parted even when the trowel was drawn at the right angle and pressure. Proper consistency is essential. When too loose, the compound will lump behind the paper and cause it to sag. When too thick, it will cause "dragging" and separation. If the compound is not reacting well, the position of the trowel should first be checked; the second source of error is likely to be consistency, which should be altered by the addition of more compound or water.

A great deal of unnecessary work is caused by not cleaning off the excess compound while it was still wet and required only a pass from the knife.

The 4-foot joints were also a major problem. Often the ends were chewed up in handling, and compound was used to "glue" this loose material in the seam rather than removing all loose material before applying any compound. This doesn't work.

The seam was not hammered down so that in places, before any compound was applied, parts were already 1/4 inch or so below the surface of the sheet. In order to taper these joints, a huge amount of compound was needed.

Several people attemped to apply large amounts at one time and alligatoring resulted, as well as poor adherence. It was several days before the area dried enough to permit further work.

In some instances, the bucket holding compound was not covered and bits of plaster and dirt fell into it. Foreign material of this sort sticks in the compound and leaves streaks when trowled. Since very thin coats are best and necessary, even small bits of foreign matter cannot be buried and will be visible.

If the trowel is used in a series of movements rather than more continuous one, a high line of compound usually remains behind wherever the trowel is stopped. This is due to slight differences in pressure between successive movements. Maintenance of the same pressure is best achieved if the motion is continuous.

When the tape was applied to the bed, not enough attention was given to making sure that *all* of the tape was making contact with the compound and that all of the compound was adhering to the sheet.

Normally, when compound is pressed against the sheet, all of it will adhere. This is not always true in seams, particularly when the nailing is rough and chunks have been gouged out of the edges. In these places, the compound must be pressed firmly to assure complete contact with the broken surface. When this isn't done the compound falls and dries on the paper, making lumps far below the surface of the sheet. When this happens, the area should be cut away with a matte knife and then redone *before* the third coat.

Another common problem was mutilated seams. Before the work began I impressed everyone with the need for making hammer marks and one person almost slammed through the sheet while driving each nail along a seam. If there are large and deep gouges, these should be filled *prior* to installing the tape.

Since that job, many of the people who worked there have told me that the greatest difficulty they had was learning to use the trowel—holding it at shallower angles when applying relatively larger amounts of compound and at steeper angles for less. I've also been told several times that after about a month of applying joint compound and learning how, these students wondered why it had been so difficult to absorb the method.

Where sheetrock walls are used with sheetrock ceilings, I fold the tape in half and imbed it in the right-angle joint that would be made between the walls and ceiling. The tape is made with a centered crease to facilitate this. This joint is finished in a similar manner as the 4-foot joints in that the compound is relatively thin and tapered from about 1/8 to 3/16 inch in the corner to the surface of the sheet 6 inches or so away.

The corners of intersecting walls are taped in the same way.

Exterior corners of sheetrock walls are first covered with a right-angle corner guard which has two paper sides stiffened by metal and comes together in 1/8-inch rounded metal called a corner bead. The corner guard is nailed over the corner and compound applied in the same manner as was done with tape.

I have plastered quite a few ceilings. It's probably the hardest work I've ever done. I've installed a variety of other ceilings and all were more expensive and time-consuming than sheetrock. If a plain, economical ceiling is desired, the housebuilder will find sheetrock is by far the most viable material.

INTERIOR WALLS

15

Interior walls today are most often covered by sheetrock or wood.

Sheetrock walls are installed in a similar manner to ceilings; 3/8-inch thickness is sufficient, though 1/2-inch is by far the more frequent choice. Thicker sheetrock does make a stronger wall, but a blow that would knock a hole in the thinner sheetrock is also likely to do so in the thicker. Other advantages are also insignificant. Wall coverings are essentially cosmetic and selection should be governed by that fact.

Wood for covering interior walls is generally either prefinished 4-by-8 plywood sheets scored to simulate boards of various widths or individual planks from 4 to 12 inches wide in 2-inch multiples, called paneling.

The cheapest plywood sheets are 1/4 inch thick and (by use of a photographic process) simulate woods of exotic grains and colors. Some sell at less than $3 per sheet.

The medium-priced sheets run between $8 and $12 and are also 1/4 inch thick. Some have oak veneers which have been stained, sealed, and waxed; others have veneers of pine, cypress, etc. I've never seen one that appealed to me personally, but they are relatively cheap, easy to install, and require little maintenance.

The more expensive sheets are 3/4 inch thick with veneers of mahogany, teak, rosewood, and other hardwoods. They are likely to cost $25 per sheet and up. If these are sought, the lumber yard should be bypassed since they don't usually stock these items and the supplier will often also sell retail.

When purchasing prefinished plywood, nails and moldings are available in corresponding finishes.

Moldings are essentially a device for avoiding the time and effort needed to make well-fitting joints. I prefer to use them as little as possible, but if appearance is not a factor, quarter round molding can be used lengthwise in corners to hide the joint between sheets of plywood of intersecting walls.

Installing 1/4″ 4′ x 8′ Prefinished Plywood

I lay a straight 1 x 3 on edge against the studs to determine whether they are in the same plane. Since the plywood is thin, it will bend when nailed and stud variations will be noticeable after the sheet is installed.

At smaller variations, I remove the portion of the stud that is "out" with a hatchet or furr out those that are "in" with thin rippings.

I place powdered chalk on the edges of all electrical boxes in the walls of the room in order to mark their location.

I intend to start on the partition wall, since this is where I nailed the first stud at 47-1/4 inches. I stand the sheet in the corner, an 8-foot side butting the exterior wall. I push the sheet against the electrical box, so that its outline is marked in chalk on the back of the sheet.

I lay the sheet on horses, the back side up, and drill a 1/2-inch hole in the center of the outline of the box. (As the bit comes through the plywood it tends to split the veneer. By cutting the hole near the center, the face of the sheet won't be damaged.) I cut out the box with a sabre saw, cutting *on* the chalk lines.

This makes a small gap around the perimeter of the box that will later be hidden by the switch or outlet plate. The gap permits the sheet to be adjusted to a plumb position without binding against the box. (The gap between the outside of the box and plywood should not be more than 1/4 inch, or the plate will not be big enough to cover it. However, there is a larger plate known as a "boob plate" to cover it up if this error is made.)

I lay my flat bar on the floor and set the sheet on the tip of it and against the wall. One side is flush against the exterior wall, the other centered on the 47-1/4-inch stud. I lay a level along any convenient score mark and shift the sheet so that it is plumb by pressing down on the flat-bar handle as needed.

The nails are annular or ring nails for better holding strength and I place them along studs about 8 to 10 inches apart. I place nails in the scored marks whenever a stud lies behind them since they are least conspicuous in that location. The scored lines on the face of the sheet are uniform and act as a reference in locating studs.

I continue to the hallway partition in this manner.

Although there is a doorway near this corner, I use a full sheet and cut out the doorway area so that it lies 1/2 inch back from the r.o. I do *not* want a tight fit since the edges of the plywood will later be covered by the trim around the doorway. I cut 1/2 inch wider and higher than the r.o. with a plywood blade, cutting from the back of the sheet to keep from scratching the finished surface.

I butt the cut sheet to the sheet on the bedroom partition wall and nail.

Unless the return studs in the corner are straight and flat, a highly unlikely occurrence, the joint in the corner between the two sheets will have gaps. I do *not* scribe and plane the sheets to make them fit.

I go into the hallway, slip the flat bar behind the nailed sheet where the gap exists, and pry it forward to close the gap. I then slip an end of a cedar shingle into the gap between the back of the sheet and the stud, tap it gently until it is wedged, and break off the protruding part of the shingle. I close all gaps in the corner in the same way.

The hallway partition wall is 10 feet i.d. I therefore rip the third sheet in half. The ripped piece is installed with the factory edge against the second sheet and the ripped edge against the west wall.

I start the west wall with a full sheet and close any gaps in the corner in the manner described earlier.

In cutting out for the window a tight fit is again unnecessary and I cut the plywood so that its edges lie 1 inch back from the perimeter of the window frame.

The final sheet in the room will have to be fitted between two sheets already installed.

I mark the top, center, and bottom width of the area between the installed sheets on the sheet to be cut. I tilt the blade on the table saw to a 30-degree angle or so and cut the sheet so that the finished surface is wider than the back. This will make a "wedge" fit.

If no table saw is available, I would install the sheets so that the last piece is in the doorway corner, where I can remove gaps if necessary from the hallway and where I would be handling a sheet most of which has already been cut away for the r.o. of the doorway.

I make tight fits *only* lengthwise between successive sheets and in corners, the only place where joints will not be covered. The tops and bottoms of sheets, around windows, and the r.o. for the door will be covered by molding.

Individual Boards

Most lumber is derived from two types of trees. The conifers or evergreens with needle-like leaves provide the "softwoods." Deciduous trees, those that shed their leaves annually, are the source of "hardwoods." These categories are not descriptive, since some softwoods are harder than hardwoods.

In general, lumber is darker, denser, and harder the closer it is to the center of the tree. I have used almost-black redwood that was so hard I had to drill a pilot hole before I could nail it. The closer the wood is to the bark, the lighter in color and weight it will be as well as softer.

Because of their availability and durability when exposed to weather, cedar and redwood siding have been widely used for exteriors and more recently for interior paneling as well. Both have the disadvantage of being soft and susceptible to scratches, nicks, gouges, etc. They are priced today at about 39 cents per foot, but because of

the area lost in milling are actually 47 cents a foot "on the wall."

An average-priced prefinished plywood sheet costs about 40 cents on the wall. It does take less time to install plywood than individual boards but this consideration is minor.

There is an individual board competitively priced with plywood. It is Idaho pine, a species of white pine. Unlike cedar or redwood, it is relatively hard and less prone to scarring. Knots are tight, small, and do not occur so frequently that they dominate the wall. These boards are packaged in cardboard cartons; I have rarely found any damaged on delivery. The boards are kiln-dried, straight, and easily installed. Splits and checks are infrequent. I prefer Idaho pine to all other varieties of pine for paneling.

One side of the board is milled with a **V** joint, as is most paneling. Frequently, the other side has an additional milling called butterfly.

The wall in the photograph is fifteen years old. It was a sharp yellow when I first installed it and has darkened a bit over the years. It is in its natural state, and the only maintenance ever done has been to occasionally wipe it down with a damp cloth.

Either side of the board can be exposed.

This paneling is fir, which also has the advantage of being relatively hard. It was installed sixty years ago. The raw wood was sealed with a coat of

Idaho white pine butterfly design

Fir paneling

orange shellac, the nap that was raised removed with steel wool, and a final coat of varnish applied. It is in excellent condition.

This same fir is also milled in 1 x 4s with a center bead on the back which can be exposed if this surface is desired.

It is also produced in 3/8-inch thickness, which is proportionately cheaper and adequate for interior walls and ceilings.

Both thicknesses are competitive with plywood. Fir was widely used around the turn of the century and has recently been revived. It is produced as clear only without knots.

Installing 1 x 6 Idaho Pine Paneling

"Cats," 2-by-4 pieces nailed to horizontally along a 4-foot line between all members, must first be provided as a nailing surface since an 8-foot board nailed only top and bottom is insufficient.

I lay the groove of a board against the west wall in the northwest corner and plumb it. I nail two 8 finishing nails 1 inch down from the top into the plate and another two 1 inch up from the bottom into the shoe. I put another into the board 1/2 inch from the groove into the corner stud and toenail the sixth into the cat. The toenail is located directly above the tongue.

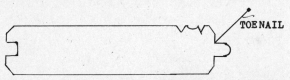

End view - butterfly pine

In nailing all other 8-foot boards I will repeat this with the omission of the face nail 1/2 inch from the groove; this nail is used only in the corner. The thickness of the board that butts will hide it. Wherever a board is 4 feet long or less, I omit the toenail and nail top and bottom.

I split an 8-inch-long scrap down the middle and keep the grooved piece.

I slip the groove of a second board into the tongue of the first. The fit between the tongue and groove is somewhat tight at times and, if necessary, I place the groove of the split scrap into the tongue of the second board and hammer the second board to fit tightly against the first.

If the board is warped and the curve is out at the center, I nail the top first. I start a toenail and face nail opposite the cat. I place the split scrap at the curve, insert the flat bar between the outside of the scrap and the nearest stud, pry the board to the board already installed and nail.

If there is more than 1 inch between the outside of the scrap and stud, I decrease the distance with another scrap against the split piece to effect better leverage action. I nail when the board is in position. More than enough leverage is provided in this way to bring practically any warped board into position, and two nails are usually sufficient to keep it there. My left hand is on the flat bar and my right is free to nail. If the curve is in at the center, I nail it there first, place the scrap at the top, drive the end of the flat bar into the plate directly behind it, and pry from there. I pry and nail the bottom in the same manner.

If a board is so warped that this method is not succesful, which happens very rarely, the board should be cut and used under and above the windows or wherever shorter lengths are required.

I continue to install boards until I am less than 5-1/2 inches from an electrical box.

I stand the next board beside the box and mark its top and bottom on the board. I measure the distance between the inside edge of the tongue of the nailed board and the outside of the box. I mark this width as a vertical line between the top and bottom marks of the box, measuring from the grooved side of the board. I extend the top and bottom marks with a square to intersect the vertical line and cut this out with a sabre saw, cutting *on* the lines. This makes the opening for the box slightly larger than necessary for ease in installing the board, but not so large that the plate doesn't hide the gap (not more than 1/4 inch).

If the box lies entirely within the board, I draw its location on the face of the board, drill a 1/2-inch hole in a corner and cut it out with the sabre saw. (A rough cutting blade, one with widely spaced teeth, does it most quickly.)

It is possible to start a hole in the wood without a pilot hole by using only the sabre saw. The blade is held almost parallel with the surface of the board and eased into the board *very* gently, then raised slowly to a vertical position. (I would be prepared to break a few blades before this technique is mastered. It eliminates drilling a hole and does save a little time.)

A good practice is to cut the pieces above and below the windows from the same board. Boards vary in width and across several feet may cause a misalignment of tongues, so that when the areas above and below the window are covered, the next full board will not fit. The pieces that are the area of the window can be used above the doorway.

I do *not* cut the boards around the window to fit tightly against the frame but leave a gap of 1 inch or so which will later be covered by trim.

It is unnecessary to make the tops and bottoms fit tightly since molding will hide gaps at the top and the flooring and baseboard will cover them at the bottom.

I make all cuts with a combination blade in the Skil saw.

In the corners, I rip the board 3/8 inch less than the width to the intersecting wall. This gap will be hidden by the board butting it on the intersecting wall.

I do *not* scribe and cope the corner board to fit if there are gaps but remove them in the manner described with plywood. Because the stock is 3/4-inch, these gaps seldom occur.

I panel the room and leave the final board to be installed in the corner adjacent to the r.o. for the doorway. Here the board will have to fit in the corner, but only for the distance over the doorway.

I measure the width between the piece of paneling over the doorway and the corner. I set the table saw to cut at a 45-degree angle and rip this width, removing the tongue side of the board. The board is widest on its face along the entire length.

I measure the width between the jack and corner, mark on the board, mark the height of the r.o. also, and cut this piece out from the groove side. The ripped edge will lie beside the jack and be covered later so it is pointless to try to rip in a perfectly straight line, though it does present an occasion for practicing.

I slip the groove of the cut board into the piece over the doorway. Because the board has been beveled, it should slip in without a problem. I push toward the corner stud. At this point the beveled side of the board comes into contact with the board on the intersecting wall. I am interested only in that portion which lies above the doorway, since the tongue-and-groove arrangement is operating only along this length and the remainder of the board can be moved with ease.

If this portion above the doorway becomes tight before it is 2 inches away from the wall, it's too wide. I remove the board and use the electric plane to narrow it, keeping the bevel.

I want this portion to be snug when it is about 1/2 inch away from lying flat on the wall. I place a scrap on it and hammer the portion to lie flat against the wall and drive it forward to make a tight wedge fit.

The remainder of the board can simply be pushed so that it lies flat against the board of the intersecting wall. The joint at the corner can be improved if necessary by toenailing the ripped piece to butt more tightly. The toenails are driven through the ripped edge into the jack of the doorway.

An alternative method for fitting the last board is to remove the underside of the groove by breaking it off with a hammer and simply laying the board flat into the gap. The side in the corner should be beveled, since it is easier to adjust for a tight fit when cut this way.

I use a wooden box about 1 foot high to reach the tops of the boards. I find it more practical than a ladder, since it is easier to move about and leaves the work area more open.

Plaster and Stucco Walls

The masonry wall finished with plaster is still common though in decline. This is one method also applicable to renovation and repair.

I nail wire lath (thin-gauge metal with a small diamond-shaped mesh) to all members of the wall with lath nails, the same used for sheetrock. I cut the lath to expose all openings and boxes. (When cutting wire lath, the exposed ends are sharp and should be bent away from the right hand to avoid cuts.) I apply a mixture of one part masonry cement and three parts fine graded sand seven gallons of water per bag of cement to the lath so that it spreads behind the wire and forms a key. This coat, which is known as the scratch coat, should be 3/8 inch thick. While it is still wet, though firm, I make horizontal scratch marks on the surface with a scrap of the metal lath.

Four or five hours later I spray the wall with water (lightly) and add a second coat made up of neet or any of a variety of cementitious materials with fibers for easy working. A flat surface is achieved by screeding. This is called the brown coat.

I allow the wall to dry before the third and final coat. This coat is composed of equal parts of lime which has been soaked in water at least overnight and plaster. (A retardant may be placed in the mixture which will keep it from hardening more rapidly than an inexperienced person can apply it. Small amounts should be mixed if plastering is new to the person doing it.) I make a circle of lime on a sheet of plywood, sift the plaster inside the circle, add water, and mix.

The third coat is a thin film usually no thicker than 1/8 inch which is spread over the brown coat; it is screeded and troweled with a metal trowel for a smooth finish. The final coat is called the white coat; this is the only place where plaster exists in a plaster wall.

Structolite is a material that has supplanted both the scratch and brown coats as a bed for plaster. It is light, has relatively more bulk for its weight, and is easy to work.

Its application is similar to stucco.

Various materials in some form of gypsum are on the market; they eliminate the need for the scratch and brown coats. Gypsum block is commonly used as the member of partition walls. It is light, inexpensive and meets fire codes.

On the whole, I would avoid plaster walls and use sheetrock when the option is possible.

Stucco

Stucco is essentially concrete. The aggregate is sand alone with granules no larger than 1/8 inch and finely graded. Ten percent of hydrated lime is also added (by weight) to make the mixture more workable. The amount of water used in the mixture is the same as with concrete, though on the lower side since the less water used, the stronger the stucco and the less likelihood of cracks developing.

If the sand isn't graded well, the voids between granules will be too large and require more cement and water, a condition that weakens the stucco.

It is still widely used for exterior walls and is a viable economical covering since the materials cost will be under 15 cents per square foot. Even so, it's not often used for interior walls. I believe this has more to do with the availability of masons than any factors inherent in the material itself.

Unlike plaster, which beginners find difficult to work with mainly because of its quick setting time, stucco is easy to apply. With only a few hours of instruction and practice, most people are able to achieve a speed that would enable them to complete a 10-by-12-foot bedroom in a day with a helper.

The finish of the wall I am talking about, though reasonably flat, will not be smooth. It will have a rough feeling to the touch. This textured effect can be heightened in a variety of ways (see p. 125 for a couple of examples).

If a color other than concrete is desired, this should be produced by mixing mineral oxides into the stucco prior to application.

The final wall will be as tough and durable as concrete. (On one renovation job, stucco resisted blows from a 20-pound sledge for quite a time before breaking.)

Installing Stucco Walls

I nail 3/4 x 3/4-inch wooden strips on the plate at the ceiling and a 1 x 3 to the shoe. I nail the 3/4-inch strips beside all other openings excluding electrical boxes. These strips are called grounds. They are the same thickness as I intend the stucco wall to be and will serve as a guide for screeding. Later they will also serve as nailing surfaces for trim.

I nail sheets of wire lath over all the walls in the northwest bedroom. I use straight Wiss shears for cutting it away from openings and electrical boxes. The ends of the lath should be nailed throughout, the spacing of nails 10 to 12 inches apart. (Chicken wire can be used instead of wire lath.)

I place half a bag of Type 1 Portland cement in the power mixer, 4 to 5 pounds of hydrated lime and eighteen shovelfuls of fine and graded damp sand. I add water and mix for at least five minutes.

I transfer a pile of stucco to a "hawk," a 12-inch aluminum square with a handle at the bottom for carrying. I use a 10-inch trowel. The hawk serves as a portable mortar board.

Hawk

I start at the bottom in the northwest corner, lay the side of the hawk against the lath, push stucco gently against the metal, removing only half a fistful at a time. I do *not* spread the stucco over the lath. My goal is to create a band of stucco on the lath that is about 1/2 inch thick and 3 to 4 feet wide (arm's length). I am pressing gently: if I use too much pressure, the bulk of the stucco will simply fall behind the lath. The first few times this is tried, a layer of tar paper should be stapled behind the lath to help avoid this. (Paper should always be used with exterior stucco for this reason and more importantly to create a barrier between the wood and stucco and prevent moisture from passing to the wood.)

I am also pressing gently to push the stucco through the mesh, where it will harden and form a key—a blob larger than the hole of the mesh—and thereby keep the rest of the stucco from falling off.

Once through the mesh, it is essential that the stucco not be moved until at least several hours have passed. This time allows the key to harden. If the stucco is moved before the key has set, it is unlikely to reset and the stucco will probably fall off the lath.

As I lay the stucco on the lath, I note whether it sags. If it does, the mixture is too thin and I thicken it with a little cement and sand. If it pulls apart, it's too thick and I thin it sparingly with water.

I keep the hawk butted to the mesh to catch the stucco that falls as I build up the band with *small* amounts on each application. Once I have laid that small amount, I *do not* touch it again.

I continue to the ceiling in this fashion and start at the bottom again to make a new band that joins the edge of the first.

I cover the north bedroom wall in an hour or so, working at a slower-than-ordinary pace.

I continue in the same manner until at least three hours or so have elapsed since I began.

I return to the first band. The stucco is still wet but should be firm enough that I can feel the hardness behind the soft surface when I apply more. If any of the original stucco shifts while I do this, I will wait until it hardens further. (I am not referring to the surface stucco but what lies behind it and forms the key.) I have left a very rough irregular surface on the first application, which ensures a good bonding between it and the second.

For the second application, I continue to work from the bottom up, using small amounts, and thicken the coat so that it is at least 3/4-inch throughout.

I select a straight 1 x 3 and cut it an inch less than the distance between floor and ceiling. From time to time I lay this on edge against the stucco to reveal depressions or bulges. I leave the bulges and fill the hollows.

I continue to cover the lath while this second application is setting and work intermittently on walls in this manner until I have covered all of them with stucco at least 3/4 inch thick.

I begin to screed the north wall with short up-and-down strokes when the stucco is firm in back and still wet enough in front so that excesses are removed *without* pulling off stucco behind it. As I screed, I am using only very light pressure against the stucco and removing excess a little at a time.

While screeding, I must *feel* the hardness behind the surface of the stucco through the screeding board.

While screeding, I am also filling any depressions I missed earlier.

If movement of the surface stucco extends beyond a radius of 6 inches while screeding, not enough time has been allowed for the stucco to set.

If the stucco has hardened a good deal and is hard to work, I flick water on it with a brush and make it pliable.

Once the wall has been satisfactorily screeded, which is to say that it is relatively flat, I allow it to set for another half hour.

I now use a float, a rectangular wooden trowel, 4 inches x 2 feet, and go over the entire wall with broad semicircular motions. This removes marks left by screeding and packs the surface. My pressure is still gentle. I fill in stucco wherever needed and work it into the wall with these same semicircular motions and pressure. At no time should the pressure be more than light.

In the corners of the room I use the screeding board to establish a vertical line, then clean by running over the corner with a metal trowel that is shaped at a right angle.

The wooden float leaves a rough texture on the surface. If I wish a smoother one, I can go over the wall with a metal trowel. This will not result in a smooth "plaster" finish but makes the surface less rough.

I can emphasize the textured surface by flicking additional stucco on the still-wet surface.

Swirls are sometimes formed by pressing crumpled newspaper into the slightly wet surface and rotating it.

There are, of course, masonry paints which could be applied to the wall after it has dried (allow at least four or five days), but I would avoid all paints and use the oxide pigments for colors.

The total cost of a stucco wall should not be much more than a sheetrock one when taping and finishing is taken into account. It is far superior in strength and durability and if done properly, cracks will be avoided. For an interior wall, anything that will cause a stucco wall to crack will make a sheetrock wall crack much more easily. With sheetrock cracking will occur along the seams; with stucco, the cracking is more unpredictable but much less probable. Stucco also requires much less maintenance than sheetrock.

Bathroom Walls

Where walls are exposed to sharp and frequent temperature changes as well as a great deal of water and humidity, wall coverings should be suited to meet these conditions. For a long time ceramic tile has been dominant in bathrooms, though its use has spread to other areas of the house.

The cheapest material adequate for bathrooms is a washable wallpaper which is applied on a backing of sheetrock previously finished with joint compound (taping is unnecessary).

A kit for hanging wallpaper sells for about $2. The circular knife and wooden roller may be discarded, but the long-handled brush to apply paste and the narrower one for brushing out air bubbles and smoothing are adequate.

A variety of expensive adhesives is on the market, but cheap wheat paste is perfectly suitable for lighter papers.

A worktable made of a plywood sheet on horses should be set up near the bathroom.

Most wallpapers are manufactured with selvage, which is a protective band along the sides. It should be removed at the time of purchase.

If the wallpaper has no pattern, I cut as many lengths as needed to 7 feet 11 inches. I mix wheat paste and water in a plastic bucket, using a paint-stirring bit in the electric drill. No lumps should be present in the paste and the consistency should be that of thick potato soup. I lay the paper on the table, brush paste over about half of it, then fold the paper so that the pasted parts are against each other. I complete brushing on the paste and fold the other end. This makes the paper easier to carry and handle and also ensures that the paste covers all of the paper. (For longer lengths of paper, it is more convenient to fold each end of the sheet toward the center—about a quarter of the total length.)

I unfold the top portion and lay the length against the sheetrock so that 1/4 inch lies on the intersecting wall and covers the corner. I unfold the lower portion and with the stiff brush smooth the paper to the sheetrock. My strokes are outward from the center. Unless the paper has a pattern, it is unnecessary to plumb the sheet; the corner itself is an adequate reference.

I hang a second length that laps over the first by at least an inch. I use an 8-foot 1 x 3 as a straightedge, lay it over the lap, and with a matte knife cut through both sheets simultaneously. I remove both cut strips. The sides of both sheets should butt perfectly.

I wipe off excess paste from the joint with a wet sponge.

I use ordinary scissors to cut the paper from all r.o.s. I cut **X**s for all pipes and fit the paper around them. Escutcheon plates will hide the pipes as they enter the wall and no effort need be made to fit the paper perfectly around the pipe.

I use molding at the ceiling and baseboard at the floor so that these fits are also loose.

If bubbles develop behind the wallpaper after the paste has dried, I slit the area with a matte knife, insert paste, and reglue.

Mahogany sells for about 60 cents per foot, about the same as ordinary bathroom tile. It makes a handsome bathroom wall. I used it in a house about fifteen years ago. I sealed the wood with clear shellac and covered this with two coats of varnish. The varnish was Gymseal, an expensive variety. The wood has whitened in spots around the tub but is still in good condition.

If mahogany, teak, or another wood particularly resistant to water is used, it's a good practice to install tub molding. This is a metal band contoured to match the shape of the tub. I lay a thick bead of butyl rubber caulking around the edge of the tub, then nail the tub molding to cats. The molding has a thin metal extension for nailing; this will be hidden by the wood which sits on top of the molding.

The ends of the wood which sit on the molding are often in direct contact with water and particularly absorptive. An extra coat of sealer and varnish on these ends is a good idea.

Marlite, Masonite with a baked-enamel finish, is manufactured in 4 x 8-foot sheets and is a practical bathroom wall covering. It is available in a variety of colors. Grooved metal strips of matching color provide channels into which the sides of the Marlite are laid.

I nail a metal molding in the corner. This piece has two grooves to accommodate sheets of intersecting walls.

I spread Mastic (special adhesive to hold sheet) over sheetrock backing (3/8-inch with *no* joint compound), using a notched trowel. I slip the side of the sheet into the groove of the molding.

I lay a metal divider strip along the length of the other side and press the sheet against the Mastic. I nail the exposed extension of the divider strip.

I lay a scrap of wood on the sheet and tap the sheet to ensure contact throughout.

I cut the Marlite with a plywood blade, cutting from the back of the sheet.

The last piece of Marlite will have to be fitted between two already in position. This is done by "buckling"—bending the Marlite, then allowing it to widen as it is brought into contact with the wall. A good practice is to plan the installation so that the smallest piece is last.

Ceramic tile walls were formerly made exclusively with a masonry backing into which the tiles were embedded. This method is still widely used, but is being replaced by the cheaper and easier use of adhesives to secure the tile to the wall.

At the start of this innovation, the adhesives were relatively poor and tiles often fell off the wall. A special light plastic tile was developed to compensate for the adhesive, but these lighter tiles popped off the walls even more than ordinary ones. The adhesives in use today are quite good and this is no longer a real problem.

At this point the bathroom walls are open and, before the tile is installed, some surface must be provided. The cheapest is sheetrock, which will have to be finished with compound to provide an even surface. The joints needn't be taped, though they do have to be filled.

Sheetrock is not a particularly good material to have around water since it will eventually crumble. Contrary to some notions, ceramic-tile walls are by no means impervious. Water and humidity will be transmitted through the joints between tiles, in corners, around the tub, etc. If the tile is installed over a sheetrock wall, I would expect to have no problems for ten or twelve years, but any further life is problematical.

A superior alternative backing is half-inch exterior plywood, gis.

The best backing is a combination of 3/8-inch plywood and 1/8-inch Flexboard on top of it. Flexboard is a composition asbestos sheet impervious to water.

No matter what type of backing is used, aluminum edging should first be nailed vertically in those corners within the bath or shower area to keep water from reaching wood behind it.

The joint between the tub and tile has long been an eyesore, and despite the many caulking-type products available, I have found none to be satisfactory. Metal tub molding does work and I prefer to install it. It makes a clean and permanent joint. The butyl rubber behind it will stop water from coming through and is out of sight where it should be.

Before I begin the ceramic wall, I install 1/4-inch exterior plywood, gis, over a layer of tar paper on the subfloor. This will provide a surface for the finished floor whether it be ceramic or some form of composition tile. I use aluminum ringed shingle nails spaced 8 to 10 inches apart. I cut out a piece to allow for the brass ring provided for the toilet. The radius of the cut can be an inch or so larger than the ring.

Flexboard backing need not be applied to all the walls in the bathroom; it should be limited to the bath area only.

I use 3/8-inch plywood and 1/8-inch Flexboard here and 1/2-inch elsewhere so that all walls are in the same plane.

Installing Ceramic Tile Wall

Baseboard tile is made in the same color and material as the wall tile, but its **L** shape has been designed to serve as a baseboard. It is produced in a variety of heights and widths. Like the wall tile, it has a baked glaze which repels water. Without the glaze the tile would be porous.

I pop a level chalk line on the walls that is equal to the height of the tile. I align the tops of the baseboard tile with this rather than set them on the floor, which will probably have some varia-

tions in height. If I see that the floor has more than slight variations, I will raise the chalk line correspondingly.

When I buy the tile, I also buy a Mastic adhesive specifically made for ceramic tile *walls* (another type is for floors). The amount of area the adhesive will cover is indicated on the container. I will also buy notched spreaders at the same time. They are cheap and should be thrown away rather than cleaned for reuse. Gasoline is the usual solvent for the adhesive, but this is only for cleaning purposes and shouldn't be used to thin the adhesive. The container should be kept covered when not in

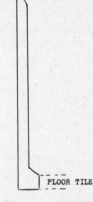

FLOOR TILE

Baseboard tile

use since its solvent is highly volatile and inflammable.

Adhesive that gets on the surface of the tile should be wiped off with gasoline or turpentine within twenty minutes. If allowed to remain longer, it will become much more difficult to remove.

I spread the adhesive on the area to be covered by the baseboard tiles. The adhesive hardens rather quickly and becomes difficult to work and I therefore spread only as much as I can cover in twenty minutes or so. (Whenever I stop work before the tile has been completely installed, I *remove all excess adhesive;* it is a frustrating job to remove it after it has dried. If this does happen, a spinner sander with open coat paper is best to clear it away.)

I start in a corner with a corner baseboard tile. This tile is shaped to a right angle and has a surface on both intersecting walls.

Ordinary wall tiles have slight "pips" on all sides. These extend less than 1/16 inch beyond the tile itself and serve to space the tile with a gap equal to the pip. However, most baseboard tiles aren't made with these spacers and when I set the next tile, I leave a slight gap by eye between the two. The tops of the tiles are on the chalk line. I continue along the wall until I am a foot or so from the next corner. I set a corner tile.

I continue the row until the width between the last tile and the corner tile is less than a tile.

I lay the tile on the sponge-rubber bed so that the line on the surface where the cut is to be made lies directly under a small wheel at the end of the handle. This cutting wheel is similar to the wheel on a glass cutter and operates under the same principle. I slide the handle forward and raise it. This brings the wheel into contact with the tile. I draw the handle back while keeping a firm pressure on the tile. I must *hear* a scratching sound, which is the cutter scoring the tile. I can also see this as a whitish line. (If the cutter slides along the surface of the tile without scoring it, the wheel is either dull and must be replaced or not enough pressure is being used.) I swing the handle down so that the butterfly-shaped extension on the handle strikes the tile. Directly under the tile is a thin metal bar. When the butterfly-shaped piece strikes the scored tile and also the bar underneath, the tile should break along the scored mark.

Because of the cove at the bottom of the tile, the break is often irregular.

If more remains along the cove than desired, the excess is nipped off with this plierlike tool by

Nippers

gripping the excess between the jaws and squeezing. A protruding pin prevents the cutting ends of the jaws from coming together.

My alternative method of cutting baseboard tile is to place a masonry blade in the Skil saw, lift the guard, and keep it in the lifted position by wedging a piece of wood between the outside of the guard and the frame. I then place the saw on the floor with the blade up, which makes a tablesaw arrangment. I press the trigger with my left hand and cut the tile at the curve along the desired line.

I then complete scoring with the tile cutter and break the tile.

This method takes longer than the first, but the probability of breaking the tile along the desired line is excellent. The first method will most likely produce the desired break eight out of ten times.

The edge along the break can be trimmed or smoothed by placing it against the side of the masonry blade with *light* pressure. The blade has little lateral strength and if a strong sideways force is exerted against it, it may shatter.

When using the masonry blade to make a cut, the back of the tile should be up to prevent the surface from chipping. This is particularly true with colored tiles, where the surface glaze is very thin and easily damaged.

If a width is desired that is less than a quarter of the width of the tile, the chances of achieving this with the cutter are dim: it should be sawed with the masonry blade.

I cut about three-quarters of the way through, then start from the opposite side to complete the cut.

If I were to try to make the entire cut from one side, the tile would break before completion and the line of the break would be unpredictable. By starting from the two ends, this element is minimized.

If there was an outside corner in the bathroom, I would set an exterior corner tile first and cut an intermediate tile to butt to it and complete the row.

I gauge gaps between tiles by eye; some people use book matches as spacers.

I complete the baseboard around the perimeter of the room.

Wherever a tile is not resting on the floor, I fill

the gap with wooden shims to keep it from sliding down. The adhesive alone will usually prevent this, but it does happen often enough to justify this additional precaution.

Standard wall tiles are 4-1/4 inches square, though a multitude of other sizes are readily available.

I pop a plumb vertical chalk line 4-1/4 inches from a corner. I will keep all tiles on this line and trim those tiles that may extend beyond this line so that these also lie on it. The trimmed edge will lie in the corner and be hidden by the tile on the intersecting wall.

I spread Mastic in roughly a 2-foot-square area in the corner and lay tiles on the baseboard tiles, butted to each other. Seams are in line but the tiles may also be laid with staggered joints. (The width of the baseboard tile is longer than the wall tile and alignment between them is impossible.)

I am making partial courses and do *not* extend any tile beyond the one below it.

Each tile is set by laying it firmly against the adhesive and butting it to the adjoining ones. Uniform spacing is automatically achieved by the pips on each tile.

I nail a 1-inch batten butted to the ceiling. Its thickness is equal to the thickness of the tile. It will serve as a nailing surface for a molding which will hide the joint between it and the top of the tile.

I continue to build up the wall in the same area until I reach the bottom of the batten. I intend the molding to be 1-3/8 inches wide, and the fit between the top of the tile and bottom of the batten should not be tight. A tolerance of an 1/8 inch or even 1/4 inch is present.

I mark the joints of each successively higher tile at the corner on an 8-foot 1 x 3, then place these marks at the opposite side of the wall to act as a reference and establish these tiles at the same height as the corresponding tiles. By doing this, I ensure that each course will be aligned on all four walls and meet correctly in corners.

The last course on top of the wall will be cut tiles of the same height; I do all of them at the same time by setting this height on the tile cutter with the adjustable fence. I do the same for cutting around the bathtub, etc., and whenever many tiles of the same size are to be cut.

(Some tiles won't break on the cutter. I tap their backs with a hammer after scoring. If the tap is moderate and the tile still won't break, I saw it with the masonry blade or scrap it.)

Under the basin are three pipes. Two are 1/2 inch in diameter and the other 1-1/2 inches. An escutcheon plate will lie over these pipes and against the wall. This makes it unnecessary to cut the tile to fit tightly around the pipe. The plate will cover at least 1/2 inch beyond the circumference of the pipe. (Larger plates are available in case an error is made.)

When the pipe falls between two tiles or on the edges of two, it is easiest to notch it with the composition blade.

When a pipe falls within a single tile, there are several methods of cutting a hole in the tile; none is very satisfactory, and I have broken many tiles before completing the hole.

The best method I've found is to mark the circle on the back of the tile and drill around the circumference with a 1/4-inch carbide-tipped bit. I then place the tile in a felt-lined clamp. This is an adjustable clamp of which two sides are stationary and the other two movable. With the tile securely in the clamp, I tap the hole with the point of an upholsterer's hammer and keep my fingers crossed. I would say that eight out of ten times, it works.

A second method is to omit the drilling and tap with the point of the hammer against the circle where the hole is to be.

The third way is to make one pilot hole and remove bits from the edges to enlarge the hole gradually until it has the desired diameter.

A fourth method is to score the hole with the composition blade within the area to be removed. This works fairly well, but care must be taken that the blade doesn't score beyond the diameter of the hole. The remainder of the hole is cleared with the light pointed hammer by gentle taps along the edges.

There are diamond-pointed drills and saws which will cut the tile and bore holes easily, but they are expensive and are meant for mass commercial work.

Very often, the tile around the area of a pipe is installed in two pieces.

Outside of the bath area, the tile is frequently stopped at a height of 4 to 5 feet. This originated at a time when tile was relatively expensive. It is no longer expensive today, but if this is the intention, the backing is best made of sheetrock and the tile is ended with a convex cap treated similarly to the baseboard. It has its own "coves" to make joints in the interior and exterior corners and doesn't line up with the joints under it.

The two tiles which are set at each end of the top of the tub will have to be shaped into a curve to match the contour of the tub. The curve of the tub is drawn on the back of the tile. A succession of parallel cuts is made with the end of each cut at the line of the curve. The slivers are broken off with the nippers and the cut cleaned and trimmed further by a light sideways motion against the edge of the blade.

The four pipes emerging from the wall for the bath and shower will also have escutcheons as will the supply pipe for the toilet.

The tile around the medicine chest can be cut to sit back 1/4 inch from the r.o. and will be covered by the wider part of the medicine chest, which lies outside of the r.o.

The tile should not be more than 1/4 inch back from the perimeter of all electrical boxes.

If metal soap dishes, toilet-paper holder, etc., are used, the r.o. for these must be cut out before the tile is installed and the tile around these openings should not be set back more than 3/16 inch.

If ceramic fixtures are used, one type is set with adhesive in the desired location and the tile cut around it, leaving a very small gap about the same as between tiles. This installation works all right with soap dishes and paper holders but is unreliable in the tub area, where the recessed soap dish also has a grab bar for assistance in getting in and out of the tub.

To install this particular recessed fixture, I cut out the r.o. first. I mix a large fistful of plaster of Paris and lay it all on the back of the soap dish and along the edges. I place the fixture into the opening, press tightly against the backing, and *do not move* it for at least two minutes while maintaining the pressure. (Before inserting the dish and plaster, I cram newspaper into the opening, which will cause the plaster to spread and form a large key as well as prevent the plaster from falling down the bay.) When plaster is used, the dish should

have holes bored in back to form a key there as well. Most ceramic dishes do have this. Some are only ridged; this type is not as strong as the ones with holes. I wipe off the excess plaster around the edges with a wet sponge.

I allow the tiles to set for at least a day.

All the tiles have a gap between them and I will fill this gap with a material called grout. Grout is very finely ground cement which is ordinarily gray or white but may be colored by adding mineral pigments.

In a clean plastic bucket, I mix the grout with water to a consistency of heavy cream. It is not nearly as stiff as mortar and should be on the runny side.

I spread the grout over the wall with a rubber float and, with moderate pressure, force it into all the joints. The float is a 4-by-6-inch trowel with a sponge-rubber face. After packing all joints, I allow the grout to set for half an hour, then go over the surface of the tiles with a wet sponge which I rinse often. I repeat in another half hour. Toward the end of the day I go over the tile a third time with a damp rag. The next morning a white film will have reappeared; this is removed with a dry rag.

It is important to remove the excess grout before it has had time to dry. Once the grout has dried, it is laborious and time-consuming to remove.

ADDITIONAL INFORMATION

It is especially desirable to keep the bathroom clean while working in it. This means providing a cardboard box for waste pieces of tile, etc.

Chrome recessed soap dishes and toilet-paper holders are sold with metal bars for attachment. These are wider and longer than the r.o. and are held by long machine screws. The screws are inserted in holes in the fixture and threaded partially into the holding bars which form a cross in back of the fixture. The bars are inserted into the r.o. and the screws tightened. The fixture is held in place by the larger cross against the back of the wall covering and the outer lip of the fixture, the wall covering sandwiched between them.

When these fixtures are used with ceramic walls, their r.o.'s (usually 5-1/4 x 5-1/4 inches) are left in the wall and the fixtures installed after the tile has been applied.

In general, washable wallpapers are the cheapest method of covering bathroom walls. The cost of other coverings varies within a small range.

With about half an hour's instruction, most students were able to tile the bathroom walls within a day and do the grouting in two hours or so.

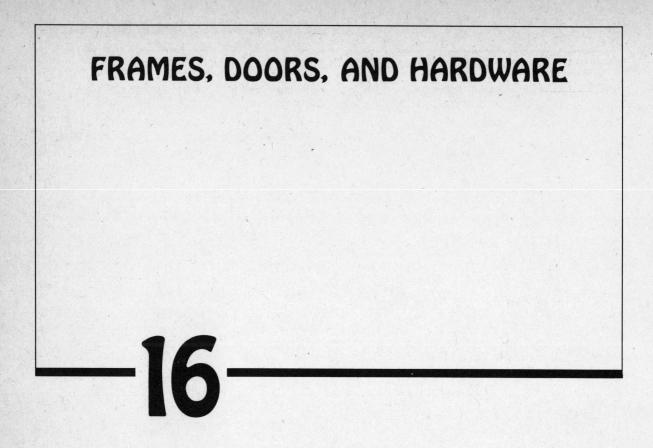

FRAMES, DOORS, AND HARDWARE

16

In the summer of 1971, twelve housebuilding students and I came to an alteration job I had contracted to do in downtown San Francisco. Other students had completed new interior walls and the rough openings were to be finished.
This involved making door frames, hanging doors, installing locks, cutting and nailing stops, and casing.

The owner had given me permission to hold the class. He watched stonily as a young woman with an enormous straw hat and huge sunglasses put down her tool box, which happened to be a shopping bag. A bearded young man wore a Mexican shirt with embroidery that read "There is no gravity, the earth sucks." The owner left abruptly.

None of the students had ever done "finishing" work—work that will remain seen and not be covered by other material. I spoke for a few moments about smaller tolerances in this work and the concentration needed to cut accurately.

At the end of the day the slowest student had almost completed one opening, the fastest two

and a half. A professional carpenter with ordinary proficiency would have completed three with a quality of work no better than that which was done.

The owner had agreed to pay $24 for each completed opening, an amount well below the going rate. This meant that every student had earned a little more than $24. The slowest person offered to buy everyone a beer and also invited the owner.

The owner said that if he wanted a beer he could afford to buy it himself. I asked him if anything was wrong. He said that he wasn't about to pay anyone for learning carpentry and the price was too high. He added that since he'd provided the work and a classroom, the value of these items should be deducted from his cost.

Most of the students felt that the money didn't matter and whatever the owner wanted to pay was cool. Eventually, $15 per opening was paid, which I resented less than the feeling of accomplishment which he had soured.

On the street the young woman with the enor-

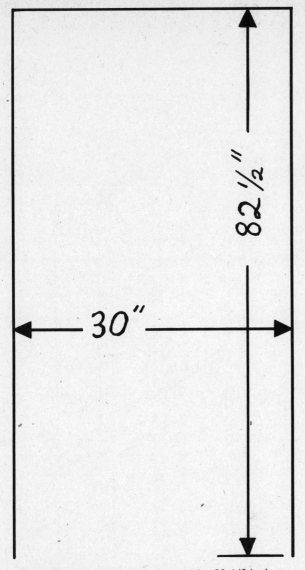

Rough opening for 28-inch door, 30 by 82-1/2 inches

always 80 inches long unless 7 feet is specified. Other heights are custom made.

Lumber yards stock both kinds in 2-inch multiples from 36 inches wide down to 24. Others are available as narrow as 10 inches. Doors wider than 36 inches must be custom made, though this is often avoided by using two doors in the opening.

A 28-inch luan, Philippine mahogany flush door costs $8. The same door covered with birch veneer is a dollar more. Add 40 cents for each 2 inches of width and deduct the same for each 2 inches less. (If a door is to be painted, there is no advantage in getting birch and the cheaper luan should be purchased.)

Panel doors are manufactured in a variety of patterns and the larger millwork companies offer free catalogues, available in lumber companies. Smaller companies sell identical doors from $2 to $5 cheaper. A 28-inch panel door costs about $20 and is also proportionately cheaper or more expensive depending on the width. The same holds true for the louvre type of panel door.

There are also louvre blinds, mistakenly referred to as doors. These are either 7/8 inch or 1-1/16 inches thick, shoddily made, and guaranteed to be warped. A 1-foot x 80-inch blind costs $9.50. A pair at $19 costs about the same as a 24-inch louvre door, which is much the better buy.

Finishing the R.O. for a 28-Inch Door

I check the width and height of the opening, which should be 30 x 82-1/2 inches, since all interior-door framing is 2 inches wider and 2-1/2 inches higher than the door to be used. If the width is between 29-3/4 and 31 inches and the height 82 to 83-1/2 inches, I am within the tolerance for the r.o.

I saw a 14-foot 1 x 12 common pine board in half with a plywood blade in the 6-1/2-inch Skil saw. Each half will provide a jamb (side) for a frame. (I now cut stock for all jambs for all rough openings.)

I cut 30 inches from a 12-foot common pine board for the head (top) of the frame. (I now cut all heads needed. Each length is the same as the width of the r.o. where it will be used.)

The thickness of the wall in the r.o. where I will install the frame is 4-1/2 inches, since the width

mous hat took my arm. "Look, Dan, this morning I didn't even know what you meant by a rough opening. I really don't care about the money. I'm always being ripped off anyway, but this is the first time I came away knowing how to hang a door."

Interior Doors

Almost all interior doors are in two styles, flush or panel. Unlike exterior doors, which are 1-3/4 inches thick, they are 1-3/8 inches. They are

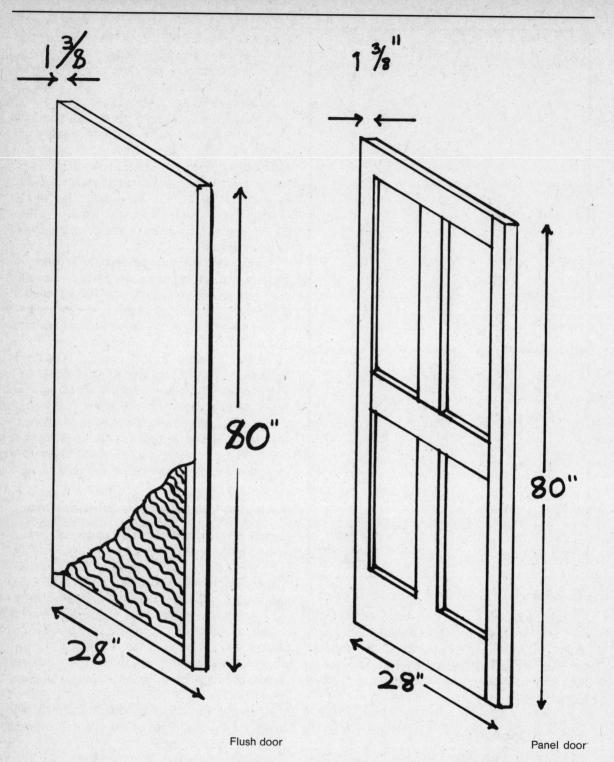

1 ⅜

1 ⅜"

80"

80"

28"

28"

Flush door

Panel door

of the jack is 3-1/2 inches and there is 1/2-inch sheetrock nailed to it on each side.

This thickness will most likely vary a little because of the irregularity of the jack and stud. The amount will rarely be greater than 1/8 inch.

I set the fence of the Rockwell table saw 4-5/8 inches from any of the teeth of the blade that slant toward the fence. I now rip all jambs and heads 4-5/8 inches to compensate for the variations in thickness of 4-1/2-inch walls.

I now rip all other jambs and heads 1/8 inch wider than the thickness of the walls of the rough

Work table

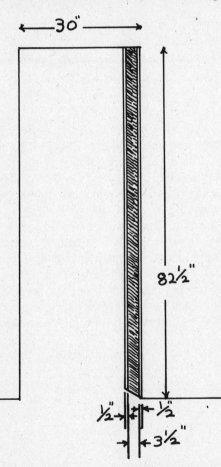

Rough opening with 1/2-inch sheetrock walls

openings where they are to be installed and mark these widths on the back of the members for later identification.

I place horses 8 feet or so apart near the r.o. and nail two 2 x 12s across them to provide a worktable.

I place the better-looking side of the jamb down on the horses, trim one end square, measure up 81-1/2 inches with the Lufkin tape from the squared end, and draw a line across with the protractor set at 0 degrees. With the protractor lying on the jamb and held with my left hand, I start the power saw and ease it forward until the blade nicks the edge of the jamb. I shift the protractor and saw together until the blade nicks the line. I look to the left side of the saw base to make sure it is butting against the protractor and continue to slide along it as I make my cut (by this time one should feel this continuous contact between saw and protractor).

I use light forward pressure until the cut is almost complete (3/4 inch from the end) and push forward more strongly and quickly to complete the cut.

Since I am cutting from the back of the jamb, the nicks that I've made to align the blade with the line won't be seen and the face, which is down, will have the smooth cut.

I trim an end of a head to be square, then cut the other end to leave a piece 28-15/16 inches long.

I lay both jambs good side up on the horses and draw a line 3/4 inch from an end. I draw another line 3-3/8 inches from the same end.

I clamp a straight 1 x 3 scrap along the 3-3/8-inch line.

I insert a 3/4-inch carbide-tipped surface-cutting bit with 1/4-inch shank into the chuck of a Stanley 6-inch router.

I shift the yellow switch to the up and lock position and tighten the chuck by turning the hex nut above the chuck clockwise with a flat open-end wrench provided with the router.

Router bits from left to right

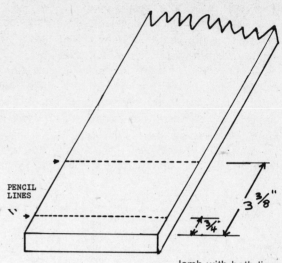

Jamb with both lines

I turn the depth-locking arm counterclockwise, which loosens the body of the router from the frame. The bit can now be raised by turning the yellow threaded ring clockwise. The bit is lowered by turning the ring counterclockwise and pushing the base up against the ring. When the bit is approximately 3/8 inch below the router table, I lock it by turning the locking arm clockwise until it is snug.

I place 1 inch or so of the router table on the 2 x 12 *and look to make sure that the bit is not against the wood and will spin freely.*

I switch on the router, ease it forward *lightly* for 1/4 inch or so into the side of the 2 x 12, and shut it off.

I measure the depth of the cut I have made with the brass extension of the Lufkin folding ruler. Assume that it is 1/2 inch. I want the bit to cut 3/8 inch deep. I therefore raise the bit 1/8 inch.

The wide ring around the router is marked in multiples of 1/64 inch and further subdivided into 1/256 of an inch. I wish to make an adjustment of 1/8 inch or the equivalent, 8/64.

I turn the ring clockwise so that the 1/64-inch mark passes the indicator in front eight times. This raises the bit exactly 1/8 inch and leaves 3/8 inch of the bit below the table. I make another pass and check the depth of the cut. If necessary I will adjust the depth again.

I set an inch or so of the router table on the jamb and against the 1 x 3 fence. I check to see that the bit is free to rotate. I switch on the router and push it forward into the side of the jamb with light pressure. I continue to slide it forward until I have cut most of the way across the jamb. I lift the router straight up and position it on the opposite side of the jamb. I complete the cut, pulling the router toward me with light pressure. Throughout, the router has been butting the fence.

I do not continue across the jamb in one pass, since the bit will tear the far edge as it completes the cut and must be fed into both sides to avoid this.

The cut I have made is called a rabbet.

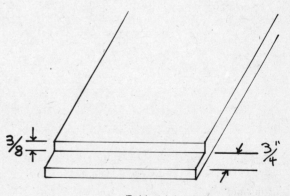

Rabbet joint, 3/8 by 3/4 inches

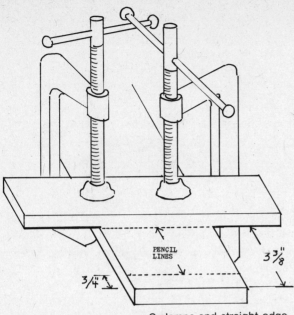

PENCIL LINES

3 3/8"

3/4"

C clamps and straight edge

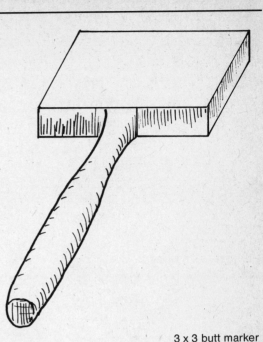

3 x 3 butt marker

I stand in the room into which the door will swing and determine whether the hinges are on my left or right. Since the jamb has now been rabbeted, this end is the top of the frame and the placement of hinges is fixed.

I lay a jamb on the worktable. The rabbet end is on my right and the hinges will go on the right side of the jamb.

I measure 7 inches down from the bottom of the rabbet, mark and place an **X** below the mark. I measure 11 inches up from the opposite end, mark and place an **X** above that mark. I lay a 3 x 3 butt marker over the **X**, its side at the 7-inch mark, its edge flush with the side of the jamb, and hit it sharply with a hammer.

The butt marker has sharply tapered edges and its outline is the outline of the leaf of a hinge. This outline is now scored on the surface of the jamb where the leaf will be located. I mark the leaf at the other end of the jamb.

I adjust the router bit so that the depth of the cut will be exactly the thickness of the hinge. I mortise (cut in depth) as much of the outlined area of the hinge as I can safely do freehand with the router. The bit may easily go beyond the outlined area and must be watched continuously to avoid this.

I place my left middle finger against the end

and back of a 3/4-inch wood chisel and on the jamb. I raise the chisel into a vertical position so that the cutting edge lies on the inside of the scored line outlining the leaf. This is one of the two scored lines that lie cross-grained. I strike the chisel sharply when deepening the cross-grained marks and lightly with the grain. I go around the outline of the leaf. Ideally, the chisel should penetrate into the wood to a depth equal to the thickness of the leaf.

I lay the beveled side of the chisel down on top of the area previously mortised by the router. I place my left hand across the back of the chisel to supply downward pressure while my right hand (which is wrapped around the handle) guides the chisel as I use short jabbing strokes to remove the wood in the unmortised area.

I use pliers to remove the pin that holds the leaves of the hinge together and place a leaf in the mortise. I feel its height in relation to the surrounding wood with my right index finger. If it is more than 1/32 inch below, I cut a piece of thin cardboard and place it behind the leaf. If the leaf is above the wood, I mortise until it lies flush or is slightly below.

If the side of the leaf is beyond the side of the jamb, I tap it in with a hammer until the side of the leaf lies flush with the side of the jamb.

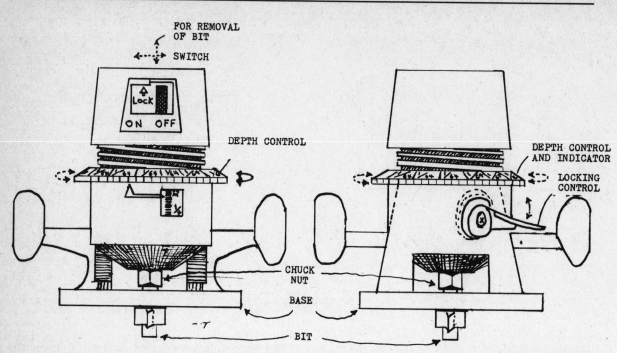

Router—front view   Router—rear view

If I have mortised too far across the jamb and the leaf lies inside the side of the jamb, I will fasten the leaf so its side is flush with the jamb. The gap between the mortised area and the leaf will later be hidden by the doorstop.

I place a leaf in the mortise, lay my left finger across it. I place the shaft of an awl across my finger. This steadies the awl and enables me to aim the point of the awl into the center of the holes in the leaf. I press down lightly on the awl, bring it into a vertical position, and rotate it gently to enlarge the hole. (I've broken many points by

not doing this gently.) The hole I've made is a pilot hole for the screws with which the leaf is attached.

I use a Yankee screwdriver to screw down the leaf in the mortise. No wax or drilling is necessary. I attach the bottom leaf.

If I'm hanging a flush door I check to see if a side is marked "hinge side." If hinges are inadvertently placed on the opposite side of doors stamped this way, when the hole for the lock is bored there will not be solid wood behind the plywood veneer and the lock cannot be installed without

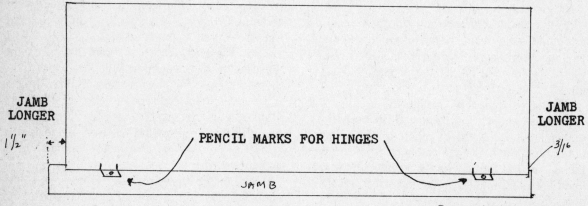

Door on jamb to mark hinges

additional work.

I mark 3/16 inch from the bottom of the rabbet. This will be the gap between the top of the door and the head of the frame.

I lay the door on its side on top of the jamb so that the edge of the door and jamb are flush along the entire length. The top of the door is at the 3/16-inch mark.

I squat, mark the top of the top leaf with an **X** below and then the top of the bottom leaf with an **X** below.

I place a leaf over the **X** with its top at the mark. The side of the leaf is flush with the side of the door. I draw a line across the door at the top and bottom of the leaf and mortise as much of the area as I can safely do freehand with the router. I score the lines with a 3/4-inch wood chisel and mortise the remaining area between the lines. (I have placed the door on the floor, the marked side up. I straddle it and hold it with my legs while mortising.)

The leaves have three holes for the pin in an extension called the knuckle. If the button in the knuckle is on top when the leaf is in place, I put a nail set through the bottom hole and hammer it out. The button is press-fitted and easily hammered into the bottom hole.

I screw the leaves to the door.

The jamb is still lying on the worktable. I place the door on it to check whether the leaves mesh. If they do not, I reposition the leaf of either the jamb or door. My selection is determined by the fact that I must retain the 3/16-inch gap between the top of the door and the head.

I remove the jamb and lay the door flat on the table. The knuckles are up and on the side of the door opposite me. I measure up 36 inches from the bottom of the door (11 inches hinge side) and mark lightly on the face.

The most widely used type of lock is a "key in knob," and I will use a Schlage in this instance. The box in which the lock is packaged contains a paper template (other manufacturers also include this). I fold the template on the dotted line. The wider part of the template lies flat on the face of the door and the narrower part on the side of the

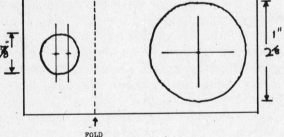

FOLD

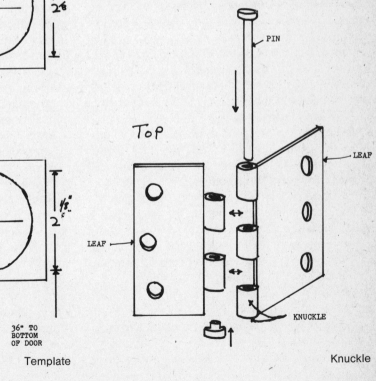

TOP

PIN

LEAF

LEAF

KNUCKLE

36" TO BOTTOM OF DOOR

Template

Knuckle

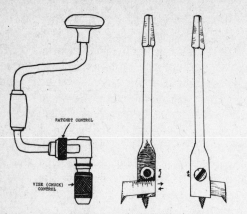

Ratchet control; vise (chuck) control. Erwin expansion bit

door. On the wide part of the template is a large circle with a diameter line. I align the diameter line with the 36-inch mark. A solid dot is at the center of the circle and I pierce the dot with the awl.

A smaller circle is marked on the narrower portion of the template which lies over the side of the door.

Along the diameter line of this smaller circle are another two lines crossing it. The line reading 1-3/4 inches is used for exterior doors, and the other, reading 1-3/8 inches, is used for interior doors. I pierce a hole with the awl where the 1-3/8-inch line crosses the diameter line.

I open the chuck of the brace by turning the forward ring counterclockwise. I insert an Irwin expansion bit between the jaws, slide it up as far as it will go, and lock by turning the ratchet ring clockwise as far as it will go.

I loosen the large screw at the back of the bit. The bit is sold with two cutters, and I slide the longer one in the top groove till it meshes with the semicircular gears at the bottom. I move the cutter so that the stationary scale on the left reads slightly more than 2 inches, then tighten the back screw, which locks the cutter.

I turn the brace and bit clockwise into a scrap of wood until the cutter scores a circle. To remove the brace and bit, I turn the ratchet ring counterclockwise as far as it will go and then turn the brace counterclockwise.

I measure the diameter of the hole with a folding ruler. I want exactly 2-1/8 inches. If necessary, I increase or decrease the diameter of the hole

by loosening the back screw and sliding the cutter in or out. (The scale on the bit is unreliable and the diameter should be measured with a ruler.) I keep adjusting until I have the exact diameter.

I set my Erwin bit ten years ago and haven't changed it since. I use it only for boring 2-1/8-inch holes in doors.

I lay the threaded tip of the bit into the hole at 36 inches which was marked through the template (usually 2-3/8 inches in from the side). The ratchet ring has now been turned *clockwise* as far as it will go. I turn the brace clockwise while keeping the bit perpendicular to the door by eye. When the cutter begins to score the veneer, I turn lightly and slowly and *watch the circle being marked*. Unless the bit is perpendicular, the circumference of the circle will be scored unevenly in depth and I can *see* and *hear* this and make adjustments accordingly much more easily than trying to sight along the bit for a perpendicular attitude.

I make my adjustments at this point by leaning toward the shallower cuts along the circumference, which simultaneously raises the bit from the more deeply cut segments.

As I bore more deeply, differences in depth around the circle should diminish but are a little more difficult to correct. After a quarter-inch or so has been bored, the depth of the hole should be the same throughout.

I've never known anyone who could not do this well enough by eye, but if there is still doubt, the depth can be measured with a ruler and compensation made.

When the depth of the hole is about 3/8 inch and a perpendicular course established, I lay my left palm on top of the brace and increase downward pressure by leaning my chest on the back of my hand, thereby adding the weight of my body.

When it becomes difficult to turn a complete circle, I employ the ratchet device by swinging the handle back and forth in a narrow arc directly in front of me. On the counterclockwise turn, the cutter remains stationary. On every clockwise turn, it moves ahead and continues to cut in a circle. When the handle is near me, it is easiest to turn the brace.

When the hole has been bored about halfway through, I feel the underside of the door for the tip of the bit. As soon as the tip comes through the bottom, I turn the door over and complete boring the hole from that side. If the hole were bored from the same side, the veneer would be splintered as the cutter came through the bottom.

I lay the door on its side on the floor with the mark for the side hole up. I straddle the door and clamp it between my legs. I lay the tip of a 7/8-inch speedbore bit in a 1/4-inch Rockwell variable speed drill into the hole made by the awl through the template. I press the trigger lightly, which produces a slower r.p.m., and watch for differences in depth in the developing hole. These variations can be noticed quickly since the hole is being bored quickly, but at the same time slants develop more rapidly. As a means of control, I drill in short bursts until I can see that the hole is developing in a perpendicular attitude. I then press the trigger back fully for maximum r.p.m. and fastest drilling. I do not increase my light downward pressure. I continue until the bit enters at a right angle to the larger previously drilled hole. (The ideal downward pressure is the maximum which does not place a strain on the drill. When too much pressure is being applied, the drill, like most power tools, will rotate more slowly. This is noted by the change in the sound between a high-pitched whine and a low groaning.)

I insert the cylinder into the 7/8-inch hole with the straight side of the tongue facing the hinges. I trace the outline of the rectangular plate, then score it with a wood chisel to a depth equal to the thickness of the plate. On the long sides, the outline is very near the edge of the door and only very light tapping on the chisel should be done. This is especially true of flush doors where an excessively strong tap will separate the veneer or chip it away.

I mortise the outlined area with a wood chisel to a depth slightly greater than the thickness of the plate. (If the door should ever need planing, placing the metal below the wood surface will avoid a good deal of work.)

I reinsert the cylinder and screw it to the door. (The screws usually have a Phillips head rather than a slot. I have another Yankee screwdriver with a Phillips bit, which eliminates changing bits.)

I insert the knob half with the blank escutcheon plate (round piece of metal directly in front of the knob which hides the gap between the lock and circumference of the hole) on the side of the door opposite the hinges. This part of the lock has three metal extensions. The longest has a semicircular tapered end which slides through the semicircular opening at the rear of the cylinder installed in the 7/8-inch hole.

The other two extensions are small pipes threaded inside. One goes through a round hole in the cylinder, the other through the half hole at the very end.

The second portion of the lock is inserted from the opposite side of the hole. It has two holes in the escutcheon plate. I rotate the escutcheon plate until the holes are aligned with the ends of the threaded pipes. Insert two long machine screws through the holes and into the ends of the pipes and then screw alternately until both knobs and plates are firmly against the door. I turn the knob to make sure the tongue moves freely.

The knob on the outside of the bedroom has a small hole in the center. This is for releasing the lock mechanism on the inside of the room. A key to do this is provided but if this is misplaced, a 6 finishing nail will do the same thing if it is inserted into the hole and pushed forward.

To assemble the frame for the door, I lay a scrap of wood against a wall and set the end of the head against it. Both pieces are on their sides. I place a jamb with the hinge side up so that the head lies in the rabbet. I nail with aluminum shingle nails from both the top and side.

The wall acts as a stop and makes nailing more

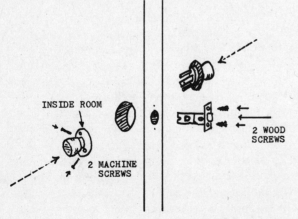

INSIDE ROOM

2 MACHINE SCREWS

2 WOOD SCREWS

Lock components

Assembling frame on floor

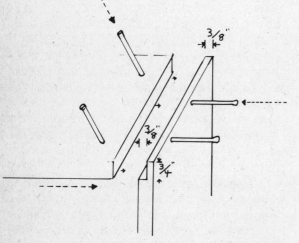

Nailing detail

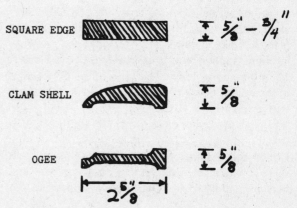

SQUARE EDGE $\frac{5}{8}" - \frac{3}{4}"$

CLAM SHELL $\frac{5}{8}"$

OGEE $\frac{5}{8}"$

$2\frac{5}{8}"$

convenient. By nailing through the top and side of the rabbet, the joint is made more secure against pulling apart (8 finishing nails are an alternative to the shingle nails).

I nail the other end of the rabbet.

I make right-angle marks on both corners 1/8 inch from the inside edges.

These marks are for positioning the casing or trim. Three types are used most frequently.

Clamshell and ogee casing is sold in "sets," which are four 7-foot lengths for the sides and two for the heads. The heads will vary in length depending on the width of the door.

I place a 7-foot length of clamshell casing in a miter box with the face or curved side up.

I trim an end square with an 8-point hand saw (eight teeth to the inch). I place the casing on the left jamb with the trimmed end flush at the bottom and transfer the mark on the jamb to the thin edge of the casing. I add a light diagonal mark on the casing to indicate the miter cut.

I place the trim in the miter box with the mark adjacent to the saw line in the bed and the direction of the angle the same as the light line. When I complete the cut, I want the mark to *remain*. The casing must lie flat in the miter box, which means

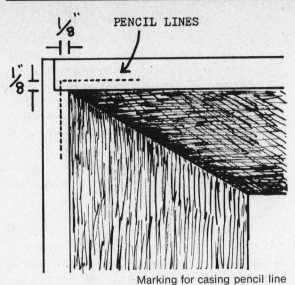

Marking for casing pencil line

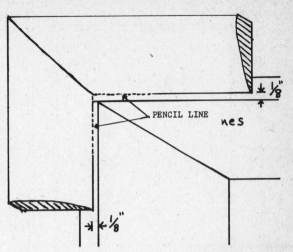

End view casings

that the bed must be clean and that while making the cut I must keep the saw from tilting. (After making a few of these cuts, it's good practice to "undercut," which is tilting the saw slightly so that the top of the casing will be slightly wider than the back. This makes a tighter joint than the straight cut.) I saw the miter.

I nail the thin edge of the casing 1/8 inch back from the inside edge of the jamb with 4d finishing nails. The top thin side where the miter begins is at the right-angle mark and the bottom is flush with the bottom of the jamb. Along the entire length it is uniformly 1/8 inch back from the inside edge of the jamb. This setback is arbitrary and will vary with different carpenters. However, everyone places the casing back some distance and no one nails it flush with the edge of the jamb where variations are more pronounced. I use 1/8 inch because it allows me the maximum nailing surface into the jamb. (I use the same setback for nailing all casing.)

I work from left to right and have made a left miter. I saw another left miter at an end of a head and butt it to the casing I have nailed. (With clamshell or ogee casing, the shorter end of the miter is always at the inside.) I transfer the mark on the jamb to the thin edge of the head, saw a right miter, and nail.

I saw a right miter at the end of a 7-foot length of casing, butt it to the head, mark the bottom end of the jamb on the casing, saw it at a right angle in the miter box, and nail.

The r.o. which I am completing is the doorway to the bedroom and in this area I intend to use oak flooring. It is a standard 25/32 inch thick.

I place a piece on the subfloor on each side of the r.o. (If no flooring is around, I use 3/4-inch scraps and pieces of thin cardborad to get an equivalent height.) I want to install the frame above the subfloor at a height equal to the thickness of the flooring. I do this because it is much easier to slip the flooring under the frame than to cut the flooring to fit around a frame that has been placed directly on the subfloor.

I place the frame on the shims and push forward until the casing is snug against the wall. I start 8 finishing nails a foot from the top and bottom and another at the center. They are about 1/2 inch in from the thick side of the casing, and are on the hinge side of the frame.

I hold a 4-foot level in my left hand against the side of the casing, plumb it, and nail through the wall covering and into the stud behind it.

I lift the door, mesh the top leaves, insert the pin, mesh the botton leaves, and insert the other pin. I do not tap the pins all the way so that it will be easier to remove them later.

The door was hinged so that it would leave a gap of 3/16 inch between its top and the head of the frame. I shift the head casing so that the same gap exists all the way across the top of the door and nail the head casing.

The head of the frame was cut 28-15/16 inches.

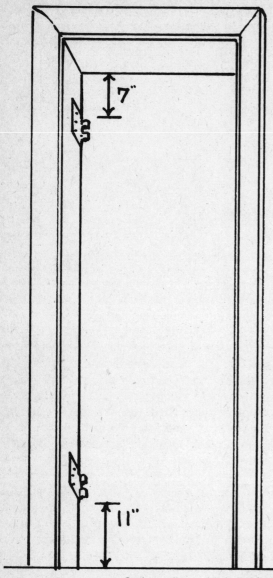

Casing nailed to jamb and head

the jack to flatten it. I then shim between the back of the jamb and jack and drive another nail through the jamb and shim. Both nails are positioned 2 inches from the side of the jamb where the door is hinged and will later be covered by the door-stop.

If the wave is outward, I shim between the back of the frame and jack and nail in the same manner.

The door is 1-1/2 inches above the subfloor, snug against the jamb on the hinge side, with a uniform gap of 3/16 inch along the opposite side and top.

Doors "move." They expand in hot and wet weather and contract in cold and dry weather. I have found a 3/16-inch gap optimum, arriving at it pragmatically. With this gap a door is unlikely to expand enough to stick or to contract enough to press through doorstops. The necessity to plane the door is also eliminated, nor is the gap so wide as to be unsightly. (I haven't planed a new door in fifteen years nor do I know of any that I hung that need to be planed.)

I fit and nail the trim on the opposite side of the frame.

I position the door so that the tongue of the cylinder is against the jamb and mark its top and bottom on the jamb.

I position the striker plate on the jamb so that the rectangle cutout is centered top and bottom between the two lines. The side nearest the door side is exactly 3/4 inch.

I trace the outline of the striker plate and mortise to a depth equal to its thickness. I screw it into

When the depth of the two rabbets are deducted from this, the i.d. of the frame is 28-3/16 inches. Since the door is 28 inches a gap of 3/16 remains between the door and jamb at the head of the frame.

I shift the casing so that the same 3/16-inch gap is maintained down the length of the door on the opposite side and nail the casing.

Occasionally either jamb may go in or out in spots. When there is an inward bulge, I drive a 10 common nail through the bulge in the jamb into

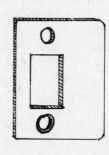

Striker plate   On jamb

the jamb and gouge out the rectangle to the shape of the tongue. It is straight nearest the door side and tapered farther on. (Schlage provides a metal rectangle to house the tongue—it is rarely used.)

Doorstops are milled in the same shapes as casings and also sold in sets.

I place a 7-foot length of stop in the miter box flat side down and trim the end on my left square. This stop will be on the lock side of the door.

I stand the stop on the shim so that the squared end is flush with the bottom of the jamb and mark the thick side to correspond to the inside of the head of the frame. I draw a light line to indicate the direction of the miter.

I lay the stop on its side in the miter box with the mark up, hold the back against the side of the miter box, and saw in the direction of the light line. The mark should be left at the back end or the stop will be short.

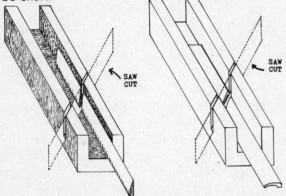

Door stop (left) and casing (right) being mitered.

I start five or six #4 finishing nails along the stop. I close the door. I lay the stop against the jamb on the lock side and push forward *gently* until the tongue lies snug against the back side of the metal rectangle of the striker plate. I tack a few of the nails. I open and close the door to see whether it operates properly.

As the stop is nailed, there is a tendency to drive the stop harder against the door. When this occurs, the door will not close unless it is slammed. To avoid this, after tacking the stop and shifting it if necessary to operate properly, I complete nailing it with the door open. This leaves the work area free and the nails can be driven so that the stop will not be pushed harder against the door.

If the stop isn't snug, the door will rattle. I there-

fore find it a good practice to tack all the nails first and drive them home only when the door is operating properly. Three nails will do for the head.

I complete installing the other two stops in the same manner.

A frequent error is to cut stops with the miter going the wrong way. It's helpful to keep in mind that, since the sides are being mitered and not the face, the back or flat side of the stop is always longest.

The r.o. has been completed.

ADDITIONAL INFORMATION

My father did not use this method to complete door openings, nor have I seen it used by other carpenters except for those that picked it up from me. I formerly used my father's way, which involved assembling the frame first, then nailing it into the opening. The door was then made to fit the frame by planing, and then planed again after being hung.

I found all this to be laborious and time-consuming. During the course of hanging many doors, I evolved the manner of doing it that I have described. It has worked for me and the people to whom I've passed it on. (Incidentally, the student who completed two and a half openings on his first try now does five.)

If the width of the r.o. is between 31 and 31-1/2 inches, I furr a side with wood scraps till it is under 31 inches.

If it is wider than 31 inches, I use 3/4-inch scraps on both sides to bring the opening back to 30 inches.

If the width is less than 29-3/4 inches, I denail the wall covering on both sides of the same jack. I use a cat's claw for this, since the marks will later be hidden by the casing. I remove the jack and replace it with a 1 by 4 to widen the opening. I then set the Skil saw to cut slightly deeper than the thickness of the wall covering and trim that portion of the covering which extends into the r.o. I use a sabre saw in the corners where the Skil won't reach.

If the bottom of the door is at least 7/8 inch

above the subfloor, I am still within the tolerance. If it is less than this but at least 1/2 inch off the subfloor, I would (using the electric block plane) plane the bottom if 1/8 inch or less is to be removed or cut it with a plywood blade if not more than 3/8 inch is to be removed.

If the door is less than 1/2 inch above the subfloor, I would remove the bottom half of the header and use a 1 by 4 in its place to achieve a greater height.

If the height is more than 83-1/4 inches, I would add another header of appropriate thickness and cover with wall covering.

The wall covering should not be set back from the r.o. more than 1-3/4 inches, nor should any of it extend into the r.o.

To make the rabbet joint I will use the router. I consider the router an essential tool and carbide bits so much longer-lasting that I don't use any other kind in spite of their high cost (from $9 to $20 and up).

However, if there is no router, the rabbet joint can also be made by setting the Skil blade to cut at a depth of 3/8 inch and passing over the area a number of times. I clean out the joint with a wood chisel. (I use Stanley chisels with a *solid* metal shaft.)

If a table saw is available, the same rabbet can be made by setting the blade to cut 3/8 inch in height. I would make the rabbet on the head of the frame and adjust further cuts accordingly. The shorter head is easier to handle than the longer jamb. I would also use the miter gauge rather than the fence as a guide since the rabbet is made more accurately this way.

Adjustable dado blades are easiest to use when making a rabbet or dado joint (a joint that is not at the ends). This is a useful tool rather than an essential one.

The rabbet joint for the frame can be omitted and an adequate rather than good frame produced. The head is simply cut to 28-3/16 inches and nailed between the jambs.

If no table saw is available ripping stock for the frames can be done with the portable Skil saw by using the index finger—fence method described earlier. However, this technique does require prac-

tice before it becomes viable.

"Knocked down" or unassembled door frames can be purchased from lumber yards for any standard door. They're usually made of a clear pine and the jambs are dadoed. They will fit into the r.o. dimensions given. The edges are tapered back so that the casing will lie flat on the wall in spite of minor variations in wall thickness. Their cost is about four times as much as making them on the site, and, unless longer heads are ordered and then cut down to leave an i.d. 3/16 inch wider than the door to be used, the door will have to be planed. Door frames can also be bought with the doors prehung and the lock installed but the proportionate cost is very high.

To mortise hinges into the jamb and door, I use a template and router rather than the method I described. Several companies manufacture templates complete with simple operating instructions, but unless housebuilding is to be a profession, I don't recommend the purchase of a template because it's too expensive and better suited to mass production.

The template, or guide, automatically aligns the leaves and the router can mortise the area completely. Standard hinges with rounded rather than square corners are used since the router bit will not cut a square corner.

If only a chisel is used to mortise a hinge, I hold it at a 45-degree angle with the beveled end up to score the area with a series of cuts, striking the end of the chisel with a force I estimate will drive the chisel to a depth equal to the thickness of the hinge. I clear away the wood by lifting the chisel under the cuts.

The key-in-knob lock is the kind normally used with exterior doors. A key fits into the knob and operates the lock. The bedroom set has a button or raised bar on the bedroom side which controls the operability of the knob on the other side of the door. A bathroom set is identical but the lock half on the bath side is chrome. A passage set has blank knobs and cannot be made inoperable from either side. A closet set has a blank knob on the room side and a blank plate on the closet side.

Plated brass or brushed aluminum are widely used finishes. (Any lumber company will have catalogues of other finishes and styles.)

I use Kwikset locks since they are relatively cheap ($7.50 for a key-in-knob, $4.15 for other types), stand up well, and are simple to install. I'm sure other makes are just as good. I found Schlage expensive and no better.

A drop of machine oil in the slot for the key and around the tongue once a year is a good practice to keep locks from "freezing."

For exterior doors, I would use 4-by-4 hot-dipped galvanized hinges with a brass pin which cost about $3.50 a pair. (I use a pair and a half since the door is heavy and more susceptible to warpage.)

I would use only the cheapest hinges, 60 cents a pair, for hanging interior doors. They are plated but present no problems.

The 2-1/8-inch hole may be cut with a Greenlee bit in a 1/2-inch drill. In a production arrangement, the drill would be mounted on a press to ensure a straight hole. However, without a press, the result is problematical. I've tried boring this hole free-hand with a 1/2-inch drill and, although the cut was straight enough, I'm reluctant to use or recommend this method.

There are adjustable hole cutters for ordinary 1/4-inch drills, but I definitely would stay away from them for this type of hole.

The Yankee screwdriver bit is removed by holding the handle against the stomach, pulling the cylindrical ring behind the bit toward one with the left hand and pulling out the bit with the right.

Ogee or clamshell casing costs about $2.50 a set; a square-edge set costs $1.40. The ogee door stop is $1.25 and the square edge 80 cents. Many other types are available at the same cost and only the rarer and older kinds are more expensive.

A maple miter box cost $1.25, a rare good buy. I have an expensive metal one with an expensive back saw, and never use it. These elaborate boxes are totally unnecessary.

There is a manually operated machine for cutting trim. It is similar to a paper cutter but operates laterally. It is by far the best way to cut trim and costs about $45.

If the door swings back by itself, the chances are that the hinges haven't been mortised deeply enough. The offending leaf will have a wider gap between the door and jamb, and must be mortised deeper.

If the door is hard to close as it approaches closure, look at the hinge jamb while closing it. Most probably the jamb will pull toward the door. One or both hinges have been mortised too deeply. Remove the leaf or leaves, place in the mortise a piece of cardboard that is thick enough to bring the face of the leaf flush or slightly below the surrounding wood, then screw the leaf back.

If the tongue of the lock does not extend fully, one of the holes has probably been bored at a slant. The lock must be removed and the hole straightened with a rasp until the tongue moves in and out freely.

If the tongue doesn't extend fully into the striker plate, the gouged area must be deepened or widened or the striker plate itself reset to receive the tongue properly.

If the 2-1/8-inch hole has been bored at a slight slant which will not permit both halves of the lock to fit together, the hole may be enlarged and straightened with a power rasp. The escutcheon plate is 3/16 inch larger than the diameter of the hole and will cover an enlargement up to that amount. (If a portion of the hole is visible after the lock is installed, a bit of the plug that has been cut can be glued back, filled, and sanded to hide that portion.)

Very often people fail to mortise the top leaves deeply enough. Since most of the stress on the door is at this hinge, the error is compounded. The top portion of the door is against the jamb while the bottom of the same side is as much as 1/2 inch away. This error can be overcome by mortising the top leaf slightly deeper than the surrounding wood.

Some people "correct" the sag of the door by racking the frame and compound the error even more.

I would guess that I have transmitted the method described in this chapter to hundreds of people. Some absorbed it within an hour or two, others took much longer, but I never encountered anyone for whom any step was too difficult to perform.

KITCHEN CABINETS

17

The cost of materials for these cabinets is relatively small—under $300. Identical ones built by a supplier would cost between $1400 and $2200. This rather large difference is not unusual; even the same cabinet shop is likely to charge more when busy and less when slow.

It took me three days to build these cabinets. While I have about average speed for most things, I do cabinets more quickly. However, if this is a first attempt, two to three weeks is realistic.

About half the materials used are common pine shelving and 3/4-inch fir plywood.

The stiles or rails, 1 x 2 strips on the face, are frequently hardwood and the doors the same hardwood veneered on 3/4-inch plywood. Birch is widely used.

Since the cost of the rails and doors is relatively small, I would choose wood whose appearance is the most pleasing. Teak, walnut, cherry, mahogany, sedgua, etc., should be considered.

I prefer teak, which shapes easily, stands up well to water, has few problems with warpage, and

is simple to finish. Mahogany has similar qualities and is significantly cheaper.

If economy is the primary factor, ordinary fir plywood or chip board with a factory-applied plastic finish can be used.

If clear cedar has been used for the exterior walls of the house, "scraps" will remain, which will usually provide enough material for the cabinets. (Redwood or plywood scraps can also be used.)

I have selected cedar for reasons of economy and because of its pleasing appearance.

Cedar is very easy to shape and warpage is negligible. It has the disadvantage of splintering in handling and being easily marred. It is also porous and doesn't take finishes well. I have tried finishing cedar with one coat of clear shellac and another of satin varnish. I didn't like the result. I prefer to leave it in its natural state and when it gets grubby to sand it clean again.

If ordinary plywood is used, I would prefer paint to a stain as a means of finishing, although I feel that paint is a parasitic product.

If hardwoods are used, there is an excellent product called Watco which is primarily oil. It is manufactured with different oils for different hardwoods and rubbed on. It leaves a durable finish. The wood should be sanded extremely well before applying the Watco and the sanding done in the final stages with emery cloth on a Rockwell Model 505 heavy-duty orbital sander. For the initial sanding, I use a 3-inch Rockwell belt sander.

The cabinets are all located on the west wall of the kitchen. I have not installed the interior wall covering here and have left the studs exposed.

In colonial times, people were shorter and, as the length of standard beds has grown from 6 feet to 6 feet 4 inches, so have dimensions in cabinetry. They aren't absolute standards and should be altered to suit the people who are going to live in the house.

The standard height from the finished floor to the top of the cabinets is 7 feet, a reasonable dimension, given average heights today. The shelf of the upper cabinet is 8 to 12 inches below the top, accessible to most people and convenient for storage.

Counter and cabinets—side view

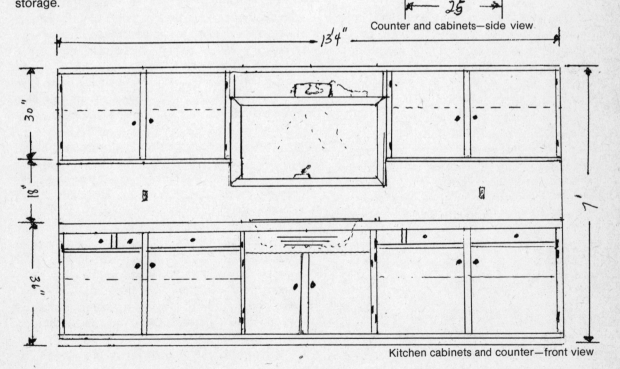

Kitchen cabinets and counter—front view

The standard height of the counter top is 36 inches from the finished floor. The width is between 24 and 25-1/2 inches. It should not be narrower. If an enameled sink is used, it is attached to the counter with a Houdee ring. The metal rim is held by clips, and if the width is less than 24 inches these clips will be difficult to install. The counter can be wider, but a thicker plywood would have to be used to prevent sagging. Greater widths also tend to make it more inconvenient to reach the upper cabinets.

The height of the upper cabinets are 30 to 32 inches.

The area between the top of the counter and the bottom of the upper cabinets is called the splash. This area as well as the counter top is usually finished with formica, a water-repellent material.

Ceramic tile is also widely used, and occasionally maple "butcher block." More expensive material for counter tops and splashes are various plastic sheets. Corion, a DuPont product which has the appearance of marble and is very durable, is an example.

Building the Upper Cabinets

I cut and tack window casing 1/8 inch from the inside edges of the window frame. The cabinets will be constructed around this casing and I want their position fixed.

I measure the distance between the south wall and the outer side of the casing. I deduct 1 inch from this measurement, which will be the o.o. dimension of the width of the upper cabinet on the southerly side of the kitchen.

On the window side of the cabinet I intend to place an additional covering of 3/4-inch-thick cedar for cosmetic purposes. I am also allowing 1/4 inch for variations in the south wall. Together this is 1 inch and accounts for why I am making the o.o. of the cabinet 1 inch less than the actual measurement.

I pop a chalk line across the wall at a height of 84-1/2 inches to mark the top of the cabinets.

Building the Upper Left Cabinet

I cut three pieces of 1 x 12 common pine 2-1/2 inches less than the distance between the south wall and the outer side of the casing.

The reason for this lesser amount is to allow 3/4 inch for each side of the cabinet, an additional 3/4 inch for the cedar face on the window side, and 1/4 inch for wall variation, a total of 2-1/2 inches.

I cut four pieces of 1 x 12 common pine 30 inches long. Two are for the sides of this cabinet and two for the cabinet on the opposite side of the window.

I place a 30-inch piece flat on another, sides and ends flush. I mark 16-3/4 inches up from an end and place an **X** above. This will give me a 16-inch i.d. shelf on the bottom half of the cabinet. I transfer the mark to the second board, then draw squared marks across the faces of both with a framing square. I continue these marks to the edges of each piece as references for positioning the shelf and nailing.

(Before assembling the cabinets it's a good practice to run the belt sander over the 1 x 12 pine to clean and smooth it since this will be more difficult once the cabinet is assembled.)

I tack four shingle nails into the piece 3/8 inch from each end, spacing the nails across the width. I lay the piece on its side, butt the long piece to it with the other end against a wall as a stop. I nail the perimeter of the cabinet in this way. The longer pieces are inside the shorter pieces with all ends flush. I nail a third longer piece between the two 30-inch sides of the 16-3/4-inch marks.

Shelving varies in width. I keep the front flush and variations nearest the wall. If the variation is more than 1/4 inch, I use the electric block plane to remove it.

There is no need to trim the back edges of the 1 x 12s to a perfect plane. The 1/4-inch plywood is flexible enough to curve around the variations; since it lies at the back of the cabinet, these variations will not be seen.

During the assembly of a cabinet, occasionally there is a need to remove a small amount from an end. The electric block plane is particularly useful for this, since it planes edges well and leaves a smooth end. This planing should be done from each side and not across in one pass, since the wood would splinter as the plane passed through the far side.

During assembly it is also particularly useful to

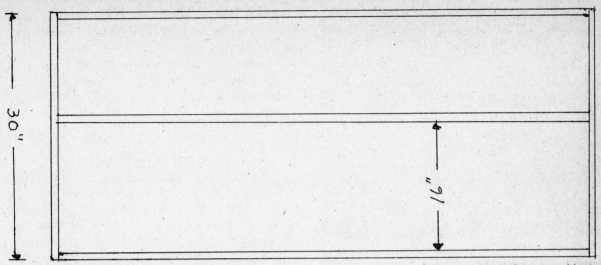

Five members-left upper cabinet

start the nails through the member before positioning the pieces. This eliminates the need for a second person to hold the other end, etc., and avoids the bouncing around that happens when the nails are started after positioning the members.

I examine each member before positioning it and use the better-looking side of each 30-inch piece toward the inside of the cabinet, since both outsides will be hidden. I place the bottom horizontal board with the best side toward the inside, the middle member with the best side down, and the top toward the inside. In these positions, imperfections in the common pine will be least noticeable.

I place the partially assembled cabinet on the floor with the front down. On the back I lay a 1/4-inch sheet of interior plywood, gis. The good side is down and toward the interior.

I shift the sheet so that it is flush at the corner and tack it. I align the long side of the cabinet with the long side of the plywood and nail every 8 inches or so with shingle or lath nails.

I shift the short side of the cabinet so that it is aligned with the 4-foot side of the plywood and nail.

Since the plywood can be assumed to be square, the cabinet will be made square by aligning the cabinet with the plywood.

I pop a chalk line 30 inches from the 8-foot side along the length of the plywood and cut it off with a plywood blade in the Skil saw.

I draw a line on top of the plywood between the ends of the cabinet and cut the plywood that extends beyond it.

If plywood still remains beyond the cabinet, I trim it off with the power plane.

I pop a chalk line across the back of the plywood at 17-1/8 inches, which corresponds to the center of the middle shelf, and nail through the plywood into it.

Plywood backing aligns the members and keeps them from sagging at the back when weight is placed on them. Their fronts will be supported later by vertical stiles.

On the side of the cabinet nearest the window, I nail tongue and groove **V**-jointed cedar with bottoms flush. The tops may be irregular but should not be above the top of the cabinet.

I tack a cleat on the wall 30 inches below the 84-1/2-inch chalk line and parallel to it.

I place the cabinet on the cleat and shift so that the cedar side butts the outer side of the casing. This should leave a gap of 1/4 inch or so along the south wall which will later be covered by a vertical stile.

I attach the cabinet to the wall by driving 8 common nails through the plywood backing into every other stud 1 inch above the middle shelf where the nails are least noticeable. These nails should be driven at a slightly downward angle for better holding power. They are more than strong enough to hold the cabinet when the shelves are full.

Cabinet with 1/4-inch plywood back before trimming

Cabinet on wall before doors and trim are installed

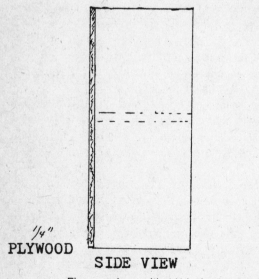

1/4"
PLYWOOD

SIDE VIEW

Five members with 1/4-inch plywood back

I build a second cabinet in an identical manner and mount it on the right side of the window in the same relative position.

The area above the window and between the two cabinets may be dealt with in several ways. It's too small and high to be practical for storage, though this is possible. Since it is also located directly over the sink, I prefer to install a recessed light in this area. I run a #14 wire there, leaving a foot or so extending beyond the studs.

I cut a 1 x 12 clear cedar board to a length equal to the width between the two cabinets. I place the housing of the recessed fixture on the board and trace its outline. By convention, it is centered on the board. I remove the outline with a sabre saw.

I nail the cedar between the two cabinets so that its bottom side is butted against the upper side of the head piece of casing.

I cut a 1 x 12 pine board the same length as the cedar and nail it so that it is flush with the tops of the cabinets. After I have installed the recessed fixture, I will nail 1 x 6 pieces of cedar over the front of this area, using the sides of these two pieces as a nailing surface.

A foot or so remains between the tops of the cabinets and ceiling along the entire length of the wall. If this area is to remain open, I cover the wall with the same material used in the rest of the kitchen. This makes another shelf but not a very practical one since it is at 7 feet and less than 1 foot in usable height. It is also a dustcatcher. Unless some decorative touch is intended, I close off this space with a dummy wall.

I nail 1 x 2 strips to the ceiling set back 3/4 inch from the front of the cabinets along the entire length between the walls. I nail 1 x 2s to the tops of the cabinets, set back 3/4 inch. These provide a nailing surface.

I cut cedar to a length 1/2 inch less than the distance between the top of the cabinets and ceiling. I do this on the table saw and cut enough pieces to fit from wall to wall. I face-nail these to the 1 x 2 strips. The joints and nails at the top and bottom will later be hidden by trim.

I begin the lower cabinets by popping a chalk line on the subfloor at 21-1/2 inches from the west wall. This is to mark the line of the kick space, a recessed area at the floor which provides toe room when standing at the cabinets. There is no standard for this; I use 3-1/2 x 3-1/2 inches since these dimensions work for the intended purpose and a 2 x 4 on edge gives me the desired height.

I nail a 2 x 4 on edge on the inside of the chalk line along the entire length between the walls. I complete a rectangle of 2 x 4s on edge on the subfloor.

I set the fence on the table saw at 23-15/16 inches from any tooth of the blade slanted toward the fence. I place a 4 x 8 sheet of 3/4-inch exterior plywood, gis, with the good side up on the table. I lift it from the opposite end and shift so that the 8-foot side butts the fence. A helper starts the saw. I am positioned on a diagonal opposite the fence, maintaining firm pressure against it by pushing forward and sideways at the same time. I feed the sheet into the blade, my right hand used to raise the sheet and keep it level with the table. My helper makes sure that the side of the sheet is against the fence as cutting begins. He then goes to the back of the saw and holds up both cut pieces, moving backward as I continue the cut at moderate speed. His responsibility is to keep the sheet from falling and mine is to keep the side butted to the fence. As I near completion, I move from the diagonal corner to the center of the sheet. I place my left and right hands toward the outer sides of the sheet and well away from the blade. My thumbs are along the edges for additional forward pressure. As the cut is completed, I continue to push both pieces beyond the blade, move the one on my left outward, and walk around to pick it up. The helper takes the other piece. Both should have identical widths, or within 1/16 inch. If they vary more than this, I will trim the wider one on the table saw so that they are identical.

Four-by-8 sheets of 3/4-inch plywood are unwieldy and it is a good practice to have the help of a second person when ripping them. If this isn't possible, I place a horse at the back of the saw slightly below the height of the table saw so that the ripped pieces will have a surface to rest on.

I repeat this with another 4 x 8 sheet.

I place a ripped 3/4-inch piece of plywood on the 2 x 4 rectangle and butt an end to the wall. I mark the opposite end of the plywood on both long 2 x 4s, then nail a cleat on edge on the floor, cen-

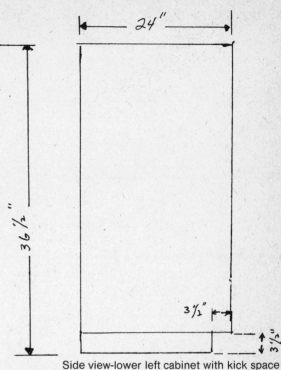

Side view-lower left cabinet with kick space

tered on these marks. The cleat serves as a nailing surface and support under the joint between the two 3/4-inch ripped pieces. I nail the first ripped piece to the 2 x 4s under it with aluminum shingle nails spaced 8 to 10 inches apart.

I measure the distance between the end of the first piece of 3/4-inch plywood and cross-cut the second piece of 3/4-inch plywood 1/8 inch shorter. I butt the end of the second piece to the first, place the 1/8-inch gap against the wall, and nail. The gap will be hidden by the side of the cabinet. I cut it 1/8 inch shorter so that it will fit easily. This is the bottom of the lower cabinets.

In order to achieve a height of 36 inches from the finished floor to the counter top, I first pop a level line at 35-3/4 inches along the wall and sides of the cabinet. This allows for the 1/2-inch thickness of the finished floor and the thickness of the counter top, which will be 3/4 inch.

The finished floor will be quarry tile, 1/4 inch thick. The underlayment for it on top of the subfloor will be 1/4-inch exterior plywood; the two will make the finished floor 1/2 inch above the subfloor. I am allowing 1/2-inch thickness for the kitchen floor.

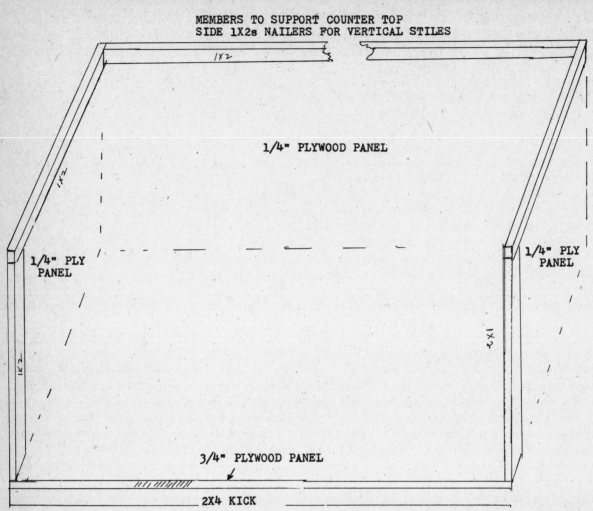

MEMBERS TO SUPPORT COUNTER TOP
SIDE 1X2s NAILERS FOR VERTICAL STILES

1X2

1/4" PLYWOOD PANEL

1/4" PLY PANEL

1/4" PLY PANEL

1X2

1X2

3/4" PLYWOOD PANEL

2X4 KICK

1x2s nailed together

The height from the base of the cabinet to the chalk line is 35-3/4 inches minus 3-1/2 inches for the 2 x 4 and 3/4 inch for the plywood on it, for a total of 4-1/2 inches. Subtracting this from 35-3/4 inches leaves 31-1/4 inches. I rip two pieces of 1/4-inch exterior plywood 31-1/8 inches. I place one ripped piece with the factory edge down on the base of the plywood and the side butted to the wall. I mark the position of the 1-1/2-inch sink-drain pipe, the two 1/2-inch water lines, cut the holes for them from the back, then place into position and nail to the wall.

The ripped length of the 1/4-inch plywood lies 1/8 inch or less below the chalk line and may vary so that there is no need to have ripped it perfectly straight. It is easiest to do this with the Skil saw.

The intersection of the factory sides at the bottom should make a tight fit.

I pop plumb lines up from front edge of the 3/4-inch plywood at cabinet bottom on each wall.

I cut two side panels from the ripped 1/4-inch plywood 1/8 inch less than the intersecting chalk lines and nail to the north and south walls. The gap of 1/8 inch or so is at the top of the panel and the front and will be hidden.

I nail 1 x 2s to the west wall so that their tops lie at the 35-3/4-inch chalk line and hide the 1/8 inch gap. They extend to the vertical chalk line at the front of the cabinet.

I place a 1 x 2 on the plumb line at the front of the cabinet, mark it at the intersection of the horizontal line, cut it there, and nail. This hides the 1/8-

inch gap between the 1/4-inch plywood and the plumb chalk line. I do the same on the opposite side. The front edge of this 1 x 2 is on the plumb chalk line.

On the south and north walls, I nail pieces of 1 x 2 so that the top edge of each piece lies on the 35-3/4-inch level chalk line and hides the 1/8-inch gap between the 1/4-inch plywood and the level chalk line.

I start a nail in a 1 x 2 at 36-1/8 inches, which is the center of the counter top side as measured from the subfloor. I will use this as a temporary prop.

I place a ripped piece of 3/4-inch plywood on top of the 1 x 2 cleats, an end butted to the side wall and the long ripped side butted to the back wall. I place the 4-foot level across the counter and tack the prop to the front edge so that the ripped

Counter top with 5/4 x 2 edging

piece is level. I now make a fine adjustment to achieve a perfect level by shifting the 1 x 2 prop to lower the front side of the counter or shimming the prop to raise it.

I cut the second ripped piece of 3/4-inch plywood 1/8 inch shorter than the remaining distance between the north and south walls, butt the 24-inch sides, and leave the 1/8-inch gap at the opposite wall. I prop and level this piece in the same way as the first piece.

The counter top has been made of two butted pieces of 3/4-inch plywood. It is essential that neither should be higher or lower than the other. The possibility of this can be reduced by inserting a carbide-tipped splining bit in the router and cutting a 1/8-inch groove on the sides of the plywood where the butt exists. The groove is 3/4 inch deep. A slightly narrower strip of 1/8-inch plywood is cut, glue brushed on, and inserted into the groove of both pieces. This will align them and ensure the same plane for both pieces. A scrap is placed over the butted joint and clamped.

From this point, whenever I nail a new member, unless otherwise stated, I will first brush casein (white) glue on the back to make a stronger bond.

The sink will be a double-bowl stainless. It is available in various sizes: 36 x 18 inches is common. The water lines, waste, and trap are directly under the tank. A shelf in this area isn't practical. For convenience while doing the plumbing a 4-foot opening is usually allowed. After the plumbing has been installed, it is divided in half since a 4-foot door would be cumbersome.

The west wall is 13 feet 4 inches i.d., which places its center at 6 feet 8-1/2 inches. I mark this on the plywood base, plumb the 4-foot level on the mark, and mark the counter.

From these center marks, I measure back 2 feet on each side and mark both counter top and base.

I hold a 1 x 2 clear cedar piece against the edges of the 3/4-inch plywood base and counter, its side on the marks. The bottom of the 1 x 2 is flush with the bottom of the base. I mark the top of the counter on the 1 x 2 and cut it there on the table saw. I apply glue to the back of the top and bottom of the 1 x 2 and nail with #8 small head ring nails to the edges of the bottom plywood and counter top. These nails are available in a tan color similar to cedar.

I repeat this at the marks which are 4 feet away.

These stiles will keep the counter level and the temporary props can now be removed.

I mark the position of all the vertical stiles on the bottom of the cabinet, plumb up from them, and make corresponding marks on the sides of the counter top. I install all the vertical stiles except the center one.

I measure the i.d. dimension between stiles and cut 1 x 2 cedar a hair longer. I position this piece

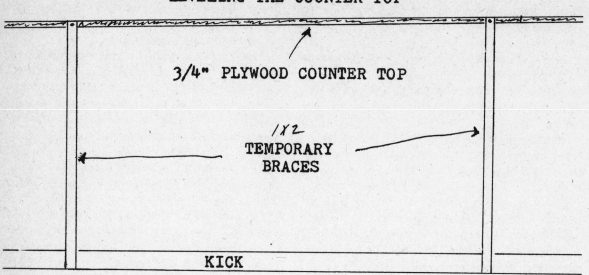

LEVELING THE COUNTER TOP

3/4" PLYWOOD COUNTER TOP

1x2
TEMPORARY
BRACES

KICK

Leveling counter top with temporary 1x2 braces

against the edge of the plywood at the bottom so that its down side is flush with the bottom of the plywood, and nail.

I install all the lower horizontal stiles in the same manner.

The cabinets on both sides of the sink have drawers and a shelf. They are uniform only for simplification of construction and should be divided in a manner to suit the intended user. The sequence of operations is the same no matter how wide or deep the drawers or at what height the shelf is placed.

I cut a 3/4-inch piece of plywood to a height that is equal to the i.d. between the top of the plywood base and the underside of the counter. It may be a trifle shorter but not longer, since this will raise the counter and push it up out of level.

The width is the i.d. between the back wall and the back of the stile, which has been nailed 2 feet from center or slightly less. If the member is wider it will cause the stile to be pushed out.

The i.d. between the bottom and counter is 31-1/4 inches. I am going to make the drawers 6 inches deep, though these should vary between deeper ones for bread, etc., and shallower ones for silverware, etc. This leaves a utilizable height of 25-1/4 inches. I will place the height of the shelf on each side of the sink area at 12 inches i.d. above the bottom.

On the 3/4-inch plywood member I have last cut, I measure up 12 inches and place an **X** above. I start four finishing nails 3/8 inch above the 12-inch line to attach the shelf later. (The area inside the cabinet is restricted, and a good policy is to do as much of the work as possible outside of it.)

On the side wall I mark a level line at 12 inches above the bottom and nail a 1 x 2 pine cleat with its top edge at the line. (The length is 2 inches shorter than the width of the shelf.)

I position the 3/4-inch member so that it is centered behind the stile at 2 feet from the sink. I tack two ring nails through the face of the stile to hold it in that position.

I place a framing square inside the cabinet, the tongue lying against the bottom stile. I shift the 3/4-inch member so that it lies against the blade. I draw a line on the back wall to mark the squared position. The line is on the sink side. I nail a vertical cleat at the rear and nail the panel to the cleat.

The panel is tight against the back of the stile, and any gap that exists is between the panel and rear wall. This is on the side opposite the sink, where it will not be seen.

I install a panel in the same manner against the stile 2 feet from center on the opposite side of the sink and a cleat on the side wall at 12 inches from the bottom of the cabinet.

I rip 3/4-inch plywood to the i.d. depth of the

cabinet or slightly narrower and to the i.d. length between the panel and side wall or slightly shorter. I place the piece with an end on the side-wall cleat, the other end butted to the panel. The long side of the shelf is butted to the vertical stiles and if there is a gap, it is placed at the back. If it is shorter, the gap is placed at the side wall. I nail the shelf to the cleat and through the panel with the nails started at 12-3/8 inches.

I repeat this to install the shelf on the cabinets on the opposite side.

Between the tops of the vertical stiles, I nail 1 x 3 cedar horizontal stiles to the side of the counter, omitting the stile in the sink area. The top of the 1 x 3s is flush with the top of the counter.

Between the vertical stiles in the sink area, I install a 1 x 6 horizontal stile. This 1 x 6 stile hides the side of the sink that lies below the counter top. I make decorative saw marks or holes for ventilating.

I install a plumb 1 x 2 cedar stile below the 1 x 6 cedar which is centered in the 4-foot area below the sink.

Drawers

I cut two pieces of 1 x 2 common pine to a length 1/4 inch less than the i.d. depth of the cabinet. I nail these together on edge to form a right angle. The bottom sides of the drawer will rest on it and it will act as a runner.

I mark 6 inches down from the 1 x 3 horizontal stile on the 1 x 2 stile butted to the south wall. I place the mark on the inside edge of the 1 x 2.

I place the angled 1 x 2 against the south wall,

the narrower side vertical. I shift so that the horizontal and wider part lies a hair above the 6-inch mark. I nail through the narrower part into the wall with one nail at the forward end.

I measure the distance between the bottom of the counter and the bottom of the angled piece, shift the rear to the same distance, and nail there to the wall. The angled piece can be assumed level since it is equidistant from the bottom of the level counter.

I mark this same distance near the intersection of the back wall and 3/4-inch side panel, then draw a line between them. This line from the bottom of the angled piece is also equidistant and level. I nail a 1 x 2 cleat to the rear wall between the side wall and panel. The top of the cleat lies along the bottom side of the line.

I cut a 1 x 2 and a 1 x 6 to a length 1/4 inch less than the i.d. depth of the cabinet. I mark the center of the 1 x 6 on each end, center the 1 x 2 on the marks, and nail.

I measure down 6 inches from the 1 x 3 cedar stile and mark the inside edge of the first vertical stile from the south wall. I position the above T-shaped piece so that an end rests on the rear-wall cleat and the other end is butted to the back of the stile and centered. I nail through the vertical stile into the end of the 1 x 6 so that the top of the 1 x 6 lies a hair above the 6-inch mark.

I measure the width between the 1 x 2 angled pieces at the front of the cabinet, shift the T in the back to the same width, and nail.

The vertical parts of the angled pieces are primarily for attachment.

The horizontal pieces form the surface on which the drawer will slide.

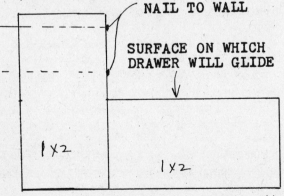

Drawer runner and side guide

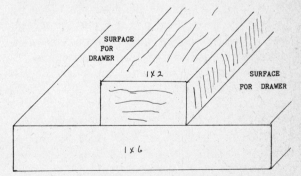

Runner and side guide for adjoining drawers

I duplicate the first right-angled piece and install it in on the 3/4-inch side panel in the same relative position.

I repeat this for the drawers on the opposite side of sink.

With this arrangement, the drawer will move in and out in a horizontal plane. The vertical members of the angled pieces will prevent excessive lateral movement but not eliminate it.

In order to reduce the lateral movement of the drawer, I first mark the center of the drawer opening on each 1 x 3 cedar stile attached to the front edge of the counter.

I draw a corresponding line on the rear wall of the cabinet.

I measure the distance from the underside of the counter to the bottom of the 1 x 3 stile and place the corresponding distance across the vertical line drawn at the back. I measure down 1/2 inch and place a second horizontal mark.

I cut a 1 x 2 common pine to a length equal to

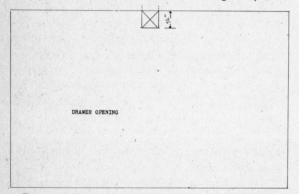

DRAWER OPENING

Drawer upper guide extending 1/2 inch into opening

the i.d. depth of the cabinet. On an end of this piece, I measure 1/2 inch up and mark.

I position the piece so that it is centered on the center line at the front and rear and is 1/2 inch below the 1 x 3 stile in front and the corresponding mark on the back wall. I nail it in this position.

This piece will serve as a top guide for the drawer; I install one in the same relative position at each drawer opening.

I install 1 x 2 horizontal cedar stiles at the 6-inch marks between vertical stiles to complete the drawer openings.

I have used the table saw to cut stiles to length. I have set the miter gauge at zero and held the side

of the stile against it while cutting, which produces a right angle across the width of the stile. For ease in making exact cuts, I mark the desired length on the side and bottom of the stile nearest the saw blade. The blade will make contact first at this point and if the mark is there, the stile can be shifted laterally for an exact cut before a significant amount of wood is removed. Any nicks will be at the rear and not visible.

For reasons of simplification, I have selected a length of 16 inches for all drawers.

For the sides of the drawer, I cut two pieces of 1/2 x 6-inch mahogany 16-1/2 inches long, both ends squared on the table saw.

For the back of the drawer, I cut a piece of 1/2 x 6-inch mahogany a hair shorter than the width of the drawer opening.

For the front of the drawer, I rip 1 x 8 cedar a hair less than the height of the drawer opening. I cut the ripped cedar a hair less than the width of the drawer opening, the same length as the back.

I examine both sides of these four pieces and place the better-looking one toward the inside of the drawer.

I insert a 1/2-inch carbide-tipped rabbeting bit into the router and lock. I adjust the bit to cut at a depth of 1/4 inch.

I set up horses and a 2 x 12 as a worktable.

I place the drawer side on the worktable and hold it to the 2 x 12 with C clamps. A piece of cardboard between the clamps and wood keeps the wood from being marked by the metal jaws. The good side is up and I rabbet the bottom along the length.

I repeat for the other side of the drawer.

I rabbet the sides and bottom of the piece to be used at the back of the drawer and the same for the front.

I assemble the four sides of the drawer with glue and ring nails.

I cut a piece of 1/4-inch plywood for the drawer bottom to fit within the rabbets at the bottom of the four sides, glue, and nail with 1-inch ring nails. The good side of the plywood faces the interior of the drawer.

Since I have used a 1/2-inch bit, the sides of the drawer extend 1/4 inch below the bottom of the plywood. The drawer will slide better if contact is made on the sides only and I therefore remove a slight amount from the front and back of the bottom of the drawer with the electric plane.

I place the drawer into the opening. The top guide which I have installed extends downward 1/2 inch into the opening. On the top edge of the back of the drawer, I mark the **U** shape of the guide.

By hand or with sabre saw I notch the back of the drawer to correspond to the guide.

I insert the drawer into the opening and slide it forward until the front of the drawer is flush with the surrounding stiles.

I mark the rear of the drawer on the horizontal right member of the angled piece. I glue and clamp with **C** clamps a scrap of wood at the rear of the line which will act as a stop and prevent the drawer from sliding in beyond the stiles.

In order to prevent the drawer from sliding out completely when pulled open and dumping the contents, I place two finishing nails in the top of the back of the drawer with the heads 1/4 inch above the height of the opening.

In order to insert the drawer, it is now necessary to raise the front end up. When the drawer is pulled out, the nails will stop it from going out completely, but the drawer can still be removed by tilting the front up and sliding it out.

I install the stiles for the upper cabinets in the same manner as for the lower.

Cabinet Doors

I rip the **V** and groove off a length of 1 x 6 cedar. I measure the height of the door opening and cut the ripped cedar 1-1/2 inches or so longer than the height. I measure the width of the opening and cut as many pieces of 1 x 6 as necessary to cover this and extend 3/4 inches or so beyond.

I place a sheet of plyscore on the horses as a work surface.

The **V**-joint side of the cedar is to be the face of the cabinet door and the door itself will fit inside the opening and be flush with the stiles.

I lay the ripped piece on its face, brush glue on the tongue, insert the next board, and repeat until all the pieces are assembled. I use a damp sponge to remove excess glue.

I cut two 1 x 3 pieces of cedar 1-1/2 inches less than the width of the opening. I spread glue over the "bad" side of a piece and position it 3/4 inch in from the ripped piece and 3 inches or so down from the top. I lay the framing square with a side against the ripped piece and the other side at the 1 x 3. I shift the 1 x 3 to the square so that the 1 x 3 lies at a right angle to the ripped end piece.

I tack the 1 x 3 to the back of the 1 x 6s.

I measure up 1-1/4 inches from the tip of the 3/16-inch drill bit and wrap electrician's tape around it at this point to act as a depth indicator. I drill two holes through the 1 x 3 and into the 1 x 6 beneath, stopping at the tape. I repeat this for every 1 x 6.

I insert 1-1/4-inch #8 galvanized screws into the pilot holes in the 1 x 3 cleat or batten and screw it to the 1 x 6.

I screw the second batten in the same relative position at the bottom of the door.

Using the framing square and the ripped end piece as a reference, I mark out the opening for the door on the face.

I trim with the miter gauge and table saw, removing the lines which will make the door slightly smaller than the opening.

With the electric plane, I bevel slightly the back side of the door which will close at the stile. This is necessary since the gap between the stile and door at this point is very small and the back of the door would strike the stile and prevent closure.

The ripped 1 x 6 is to be the hinge side of the door. I measure up 2 inches from the bottom and place an **X** above. I measure down 2 inches from the top and place an **X** below.

The door is to be flush-mounted, which means that it will lie in the same plane as the stiles. I will use cabinet hinges that have the advantage of containing a spring device, so that the door will shut itself and stay closed without the need for additional hardware.

I place the top hinge on the top **X** and at the mark. Half the hinge which will be attached to the stile will extend beyond the side of the door. I screw to the door, using an awl to provide the pilot hole. I screw half of the second hinge in the corresponding position.

I place a piece of thin cardboard, 1/32 inch or so thick, on the edge of the bottom stile of the opening.

I position the door on the cardboard. The cardboard separates the bottom of the door from the stile and the gap guarantees the door won't stick.

I screw the other halves of the hinges to the stile.

All the remaining doors are assembled and installed in the same way.

To work on the splash, I first remove the sides and bottom pieces of casing around the window. I place these pieces in the cabinet for later installation.

I rip two lengths of 3/4-inch plywood to a width slightly less than the height between the counter top and the bottom of the upper cabinets.

I place a ripped piece on the counter top against the wall. The ripped side is up and I draw marks on it that correspond to the outside of the window frame and cut this away from the splash so that it will lie against the wall and around the outside of the window frame. Since casing will later cover the gap, these cuts should not be tight-fitting.

I place blue powdered chalk over the edges of the electrical boxes, set the splash against them to mark their location, then cut them out with the same method used earlier. I nail the piece to the studs with 8 finishing galvanized nails. I want a smooth surface on which to glue the formica later.

I do the same with the second piece, cut it to length, and nail to complete the splash backing.

I take two long pieces of rippings, say about 10 feet and 5 feet. I place them on the counter and spread each outward until their ends are at the opposite walls. I place a pencil mark at their lap. This gives me the exact length between walls.

I lay the rippings on a 14-foot length of 5/4 x 2 clear pine, One end lies at the end of the pine. I shift the other ripping to the lap mark and then mark its end on the pine.

I cut the 5/4 x 2 piece to length. I brush glue over its back and nail it on the 1 x 3 stile and flush with the counter top.

Formica

I lay a 4 x 8 sheet of formica face down on the sheet of plyscore and pop a chalk line 2-1/2 inches in along an 8-foot side. I pop a second line at 5 feet.

With a plywood blade in the Skil saw I cut these two strips.

I place a formica strip on a length of 5/4 x 2 with both sides extending beyond the the width of the pine. The face is up. I hold the formica in position by placing **C** clamps intermittently along the length.

I insert a straight-cutting carbide-tipped formica bit in the router and adjust the height so that the roller at the end of the bit lies about halfway down the side of the pine.

I feed the bit into the formica until the roller guide stops further inward movement since it is being held by the side of the pine.

I move the router along the side of the pine and formica. The bit removes the excess formica and leaves it flush with the side of the pine.

The **C** clamps obstruct the router and I change their position as needed but hold the formica tightly to the pine wherever I am trimming it.

I trim the formica on the opposite side and produce a ribbon the exact width of the 5/4 x 2-inch pine.

On the 5/4 pine edging, which I have attached to the counter, I brush on a glue called contact cement. The glue should completely cover the surface.

I brush contact cement on the back of the trimmed piece of formica.

I allow about twenty minutes for the contact cement to set up. I test whether this has happened by placing a finger on it. It should *not* be sticky to the touch.

It should be realized that once the two glued surfaces have made contact, it will be very difficult if not impossible to shift the formica without breaking it or splintering the wood on which it has been placed. Occasionally a very narrow piece can be shifted slightly if not more than 1 inch or so has made contact.

I hold the ribbon between my fingers at the pine, the glued back facing it. My right hand is 1 inch from the end, my left hand several feet away.

I place the tip of the end of the ribbon on the pine at the wall. Only 1/8 inch or so is making contact with the pine. I raise or lower the formica so that it is flush on top and bottom with the pine. (If the formica has been ripped slightly wider than the pine, the top should be made flush and the bottom lower than the pine.) My right thumb and index finger at the top and bottom do this shifting. When I position the formica correctly, feeling this with thumb and index finger, I relax slightly the outward pressure from my left hand, which has been keeping the ribbon from making further contact, and slowly guide the ribbon with my right thumb and index finger against the pine. In this manner, I position the 8-foot ribbon.

To complete the ribbon to the opposite wall, I trim and cut it to the length already established on the two marking strips. I do *not* apply the glue until after I have cut the ribbon and checked its fit on the pine. I butt the factory edges and place the end I have cut against the opposite wall.

At this stage the depth of the counter is about 25 inches. I cut two pieces of formica about 25-1/4 inches x 8 feet to use for surfacing the counter top.

I place one piece on the counter top, a side butted against a wall. I lay the second sheet with its side against the opposite wall and the end on top of the first sheet. I measure the amount of the overlap and mark this on the end that will lie against the wall.

I remove all but 1/4 inch of this with the Skil saw.

I clamp the formica to a straight piece of scrap. The scrap is on the down side of the formica and lies right on the line. I trim with the router. I butt this piece to the first and check the fit. (If needed, the formica can be trimmed again to remove any excess.)

I brush contact cement on the counter top and on the back of the formica, and allow to set.

My left hand holds up a piece of the formica and keeps it from making contact while my right hand positions an end against the splash and wall. Only 1/8 inch or so is actually making contact with the counter top. In a manner similar to positioning the ribbon, I keep the back of the formica tight against the splash and lower it slowly onto the counter top.

Once the side of the formica has been butted to the wall and splash, it is only necessary to keep it hard against the splash; this is done with firm pressure from my right hand. The front side hangs over the 2-inch pine and will be trimmed later. I install the second piece of formica, previously fitted in the same way.

I cut formica for the splash. The tops of these two pieces will be covered by trim under the upper cabinets and casing around the window and needn't fit tightly except on the counter surface.

I cut out the formica for the electrical boxes with a metal-cutting blade in the sabre saw. This blade has very fine closely spaced teeth. I cut and fit the two pieces for the splash before brushing on the contact cement.

In applying the formica for the splash, once it has been aligned with a wall, it is only necessary to press down to ensure that the bottom is lying against the formica previously glued to the counter. Again, I butt the factory sides and place the end I have cut against the wall.

The formica on the counter top extends 1/4 inch or so beyond the 2-inch ribbon edge. It can be trimmed with the straight cutting bit, but I prefer another carbide-tipped bit which will leave a rounded-over edge, a very small arc. I replace the straight cutting bit in the router with another that does this and trim off the excess.

The walls do not permit the router to remove all of the excess, and about 3 inches will remain at each end. I remove most of this with the sabre saw and the balance with a hacksaw blade. I use a metal file to complete the trimming and rounding over.

By convention, the carpenter is responsible for cutting the hole in the counter top for the sink.

I place the stainless sink top down on the counter and center it with the window and counter depth. I draw the outline of the sink on the formica, remove the sink, and draw a second outline 1/4 to 3/8 inch inside the first.

I bore a 1/2-inch hole inside the smaller outline, insert the blade of the sabre saw, and cut out the smaller outline. The sink will be supported on the plywood by 1/4 inch all the way around its perimeter.

Handles for Doors and Drawers

There are literally thousands of handles and knobs to choose from. Lumber companies carry some types, hardware stores usually have a greater variety, and in some places that specialize in them the choice seems endless.

Most types have a threaded hole in back of the handle or knob. A hole is drilled through the door or drawer and the knobs or handle attached with a machine screw.

Another type is a wooden knob to which a wood screw has been attached; this type simply screws into the face of the door or drawer.

In determining the position of knobs or handles, it is more convenient to place them in the lower third of the upper cabinets and upper third of the lower cabinets.

Unless a drawer is more than 2 feet wide, the knob or handle is usually centered. Wider and deeper drawers should have two handles or knobs spaced inward a few inches from both ends.

With these particular cabinets, I made my own handles from scraps of cedar, glued, and screwed them to the drawers and doors. The handles were 3 inches high, 1-1/2 inches wide, 3/4 inch thick, and tapered to 1/2 inch toward the rear. I cut the top and bottom at a 20-degree angle sloping to a smaller height against the door and drawer.

ADDITIONAL INFORMATION

1 x 12 shelves with 1/4-inch plywood backing are appropriate for bookshelves, etc. An alternative to the fir plywood backing may be 1/4-inch mahogany plywood or Masonite. The same sequence is followed.

If a shelf has a span of more than 3 feet, it will probably sag if weight is placed on it; vertical stiles to prevent this should be considered. An alternative to stiles is vertical blocking within the shelf area and supported at the bottom.

The common pine shelving can be expected to have nicks and gouges. The knots will be tight, but pieces of them will probably have fallen out. Most likely they will be covered later by contact paper or some such covering. I fill in these imperfections with a powdered crack filler that has been mixed with water. It doesn't shrink during drying and holds to the wood. It is much better than plastic wood and cheaper.

The 1 x 6 horizontal member directly in front of the sink is a vestige of earlier cabinetry, though it is still universally used. Since the sink trap is located here, presumably there will be odors, and this member will be the "breather" and permit these odors to be dispelled. It is also a touch of gentility, hiding the unsightly side of the sink which extends below the counter top. I consider it purely optional.

The drawer installation I've used is the cheapest, since it eliminates the use of hardware but it functions only adequately.

Of the many types of drawer hardware, I would avoid the side-mounted ones, which have practically no tolerance, are difficult to install, and incidentally are the most expensive.

The type which uses an overhead guide and nylon rollers works quite well and is easiest to install. It costs about $3.50 per drawer.

I have made all the doors flush with the stiles. The joints between the doors and the surrounding stiles are visible and any error is also noticeable. With a table saw, fitting the doors properly isn't at all time-consuming but it does require concentration and care.

An alternative is to build the door 1/2 inch greater than the opening. I then rabbet the back of the door with a 3/8-inch rabbeting bit set to a depth of 3/8-inch. The same type of magnetic self-locking hinges are available with a 3/8 inch offset. The door itself will extend beyond the outer edges and cover the opening.

When I do this, I usually round over the face edges of the door with a 3/8-inch rounding-over bit in the router. (A similar arrangement can be made with the drawers.)

A dovetail template is available for use with the router (this joint is similar to interlocking fingers), and makes a very strong joint holding intersecting members. It looks nice, but the joint I've described is perfectly satisfactory.

I have used white casein glue throughout except for the formica. When clamps are applied or the joint nailed, a half hour or so should be allowed for the glued joint to set. If no pressure is applied to the glued joint, it will have very little or no holding power. Using annular nails with glue is a quicker substitute for clamps, though not as good.

Occasionally blisters of trapped air develop under the formica after contact glue has been applied. They can be removed by placing a moist cloth over the formica, then running a hot iron over the cloth. It may sometimes be necessary to pierce the formica with a pinhole before the formica will adhere.

Contact glue is an excellent product (it is also useful to glue materials like leather and canvas in making patches for tarpaulins).

FLOORS

18

In dwellings, wood remains the most widely used material for floors. Long-leaf yellow pine, maple, and other hardwoods were formerly significant sources of flooring but today the "red" or "white" variety of oak is most often the material used. It has the advantage of being durable, relatively resilient, and easy to install. Being a poor conductor, it has excellent insulating qualities. It has the drawback of requiring periodic refinishing.

Standard oak flooring is milled in random lengths. The sides are tongue-and-grooved and the ends "matched," which is to say that they are also tongue-and-grooved. Two and a quarter inches remain exposed on the finished floor. Standard thickness is 25/32 inch.

Unfinished oak sells at 55 cents per square foot. The amount of flooring ordered should be 30 percent greater than the area to be covered—thus making up for loss of area covered by the tongue-and-groove milling. Even so, oak is competitive with other types of flooring and lies in the moderate-priced range.

Oak flooring is also sold in a prefinished state. It sells for 63 cents a foot. Its finish is frequently some stain like walnut which hides imperfections and provides uniformity, then a coating of factory-applied varnish and sometimes wax on that.

The sides are slightly rounded over. This is done to mask variations in height between adjacent boards. (These would be removed through sanding if the floor were unfinished.) The rounding over creates a slight gap, 1/16 inch or so in depth and width. A good practice is to fill this gap with molten wax for ease in cleaning and maintenance.

Unless some cosmetic effect is intended, prefinished flooring is far cheaper than finishing the floor on the site and most probably much better.

Nationally advertised prefinished floors should be avoided, since their cost is likely to be 25 percent more than the equivalent product sold by smaller companies.

When ordering the flooring, provisions for obtaining a manually operated floor-nailing machine should also be made. The supplier will usually make the machine available free of charge. Other sources may rent it at a cost of anywhere from $2 to $5 per day. A new nailing machine sells for about $35.

Special nails must be used with the machine. A box which costs $15 will be sufficient for 1000 square feet. These nails are joined into clips, have an overall length of slightly less than 2 inches and the head is turned at a right angle to form an **L**.

The machine is operated by loading clips of nails into a slot, positioning the bed on the tongue of the oak and against the raised portion directly above it. A mallet is struck against a rubber-capped cylinder. This drives a nail at a toenail angle through the oak and into the subfloor and joist below. The head of the nail lies in the angle of oak directly above the top of the tongue and flush with the wood. It will be hidden by the next piece of flooring.

Using this machine, flooring can be done in this house in two and a half days—assuming that oak would be used everywhere but in the kitchen and bathroom.

The design of the machine doesn't permit its use near walls parallel to the flooring and three courses must be laid by other means.

Installing 1 x 3 Prefinished Oak Flooring

I sweep and vacuum the room. I lightly staple 30-pound tar paper over the subfloor. The purpose of the tar paper is to prevent the underside of the flooring from rubbing against the subfloor and creating squeaks. It also acts as a vapor barrier and has a slight insulating quality.

On the tar paper I pop chalk lines that represent the positions of the floor joists, which I determine from the nails driven into them from the subfloor. The flooring is laid at right angles to these joists and nails applied at each of them. (Occasionally an intermediate nail is necessary to drive a piece of flooring more tightly against the one previously nailed or to remove a curve.)

I clip the head off a 6 finishing nail with wire-cutting pliers and use this as a drill bit. I select several pieces of straight flooring and bore holes 1/2 inch in from the grooved side. I space the holes

16 inches or so on center.

I place a piece of drilled flooring in the corner made by the intersection of the west and north walls. The lengthwise groove of the board lies against the north wall and the grooved end is against the west wall. I use 8 finishing nails through the drilled holes to fasten the piece. (Oak is much too hard to hammer a finishing nail through and is also likely to split unless the holes are drilled. The baseboard will later hide the nails.)

I butt a second piece to the first and use the rubber mallet to position it. (With this mallet, I avoid scarring the oak while it is being positioned prior to nailing. On the next course it will also be used to fit the groove into the tongue of the previously nailed piece. The fit is usually tight and the mallet often has to be used forcefully.)

I continue down the north wall in this manner until I must cross-cut to length a piece of flooring which will fit to the intersecting wall. I mark the length to be cut, then cut it 1/4 inch less, since the gap at the intersecting wall will also be covered by the baseboard.

In cutting the last piece for this first course and all successive ones, I use the part with the grooved end and start the next course with the tongued part.

I drill holes at a toenail angle in the first course at each of the chalk lines and nail with 8 finishing nails.

If another person is available, I have that person lay out courses behind me, while I nail. The second person should try to minimize wastage and stagger joints between ends of flooring so that they do not accumulate in the same area. He should also select straight pieces to avoid the hassle of removing warps before the machine's power can be employed.

I begin the second course with the tongued piece that remains after cutting the last piece of the first course. I can fasten it by drilling toenail-angled holes at the joists and driving 8 finishing nails, or avoid the drilling and use standard flooring nails. These are not round but square-edged, case-hardened, wide at the top then tapered, and have no head. The nail is started directly above the tongue and at a toenail angle. Its wider side is parallel to the flooring. I use the two-pound hammer to drive it. If the nail twists out of the parallel position while this is being done, I remove it since the twisting action will cause the tongue to split and prevent the groove of the next piece from fitting into it. When the head of the nail is near the tongue, I drive it with additional force so that the head will lie flush with the wood. (I do not recommend doing this without adequate previous practice, since it is very easy to scar the flooring.) The nail may be completely driven by using a nail set.

I complete the second course and then the third, either using flooring nails or predrilling.

I lay the successive courses with the nailing machine.

Generally oak flooring is fairly straight since the lengths are rather short. If a gap of 1/8 inch or less exists after they are driven into position with the rubber mallet, it will be closed as the machine drives the next piece against the one previously nailed.

If the gap is not more than 1/4 inch at any point, I can usually close this by using intermediate nails. If this doesn't happen, I use the wedge device (the same as used for closing gaps in paneling) for closing it, then renail.

If the gap is greater than 1/4 inch, I cut the oak at the point of greatest curvature and use the pieces to start and finish a course.

When I have laid the floor to within three courses of the hallway partition, I have the same problem of not being able to use the machine and again have the choice of predrilling and nailing with 8 finishing nails or using flooring nails.

If 5/8 inch or less remains between the finished floor and the hallway partition, the 3/4-inch thickness of the baseboard will cover it and no further work has to be done here.

If more than 5/8 inch remains, I rip pieces of flooring on the table saw 1/4 inch narrower than the remaining gap and drill 16-inch o.c. holes, 1/4 inch in from the ripped side. I nail with 8s.

I continue the flooring until it extends into the hallway.

I repeat the process in the second and third bedrooms and stop as soon as I have entered the hallway.

I stretch string between the east and west walls directly over the forward edge of the flooring that I have laid in the three bedrooms.

I rip pieces of flooring 1/4 inch narrower than the distance between the string and hallway wall. I have removed the grooved portion and am using the tongue portion. I drill these pieces 16 inches or so o.c. and 1/4 inch in from the ripped side. I nail these pieces so that their forward edges are aligned under the string and with the flooring previously laid. I now have a continuous line of flooring from the east to west walls, the pieces aligned since they are aligned to the string.

The balance of the floor is laid in the same manner previously done.

Exterior Saddle

The ends of the oak flooring will have been butted against the inner side of the front door sill and a saddle is used to cover the joint between them.

Two main types are used. One is aluminum with a raised rubber piece. The bottom of the door is beveled, high in front, low in back to lie against the rubber. The fit is difficult to make exactly. In addition, the door itself "moves," so this saddle is really worthless.

A better type is the aluminum interlocking kind. The saddle is butted to the door and a line drawn on the door that is the height of the saddle. The bottom of the door is then trimmed. The saddle is screwed into place and the door hung.

Facing the inside of the house is a slot in the saddle. A right-angle piece of metal the width of the door is screwed to the bottom of the door, a leg of the angle fitted into the slot.

Composition Tile

I personally would use quarry tile as the finished kitchen floor, but most people use some type of composition tile. Among these synthetic floor coverings are vinyl, vinyl asbestos, and rubber. An ordinary dimension for a tile is 9 inches square though 12-inch squares are standard also.

Vinyl tile, the most expensive of the three, scratches easily and wears least well.

The cheapest, vinyl asbestos, is most durable.

Rubber tile (which has fallen into disfavor for reasons unknown to me) is the composition tile I prefer, though personally I don't like any of them. Rubber maintains itself quite well and is flexible enough that cracking or buckling is rare, and it adheres satisfactorily. (Some floors are still in good shape after more than twenty years.) It is much more easily cleaned and maintained than vinyl, and costs approximately 35 cents a square foot.

Costs range between 20 cents per square foot for the cheapest asbestos types to a dollar or more for the vinyl. The cost of the underlayment must be added to this. I use 1/4-inch exterior plywood, gis.

All the composition tiles are installed in a similar manner.

Installing 9 x 9 Rubber Tile in Bathroom

I cover the subfloor with tar paper, then 1/4-inch exterior plywood. I use small-headed annular nails and space them 8 to 10 inches apart.

In cutting out the hole for the toilet drain, I can make the diameter of the hole 1 inch or so larger than the brass ring over the 4-inch waste line since the toilet will cover it.

I mark the centers of the four walls and pop chalk lines between them. This divides the bathroom into four quadrants.

I spread *waterproof Mastic* in one quadrant, starting from the intersection of the chalk lines. I use a notched trowel to do the spreading.

I lay the first tile at the intersection of the chalk lines, its sides at the right angle formed by the crossing lines. I butt succesive tiles to each other, working outward. I continue to lay tiles in the quadrant until less than the width of the tile remains to the wall.

I lay tiles into the second quadrant, working toward the exterior wall, and stop when less than the width of a tile remains.

I clean all excess glue from the underlayment and tiles. (Gasoline, turpentine, or woodlife can be used as a solvent.)

I complete the remaining two quadrants, omitting all tiles which have to be cut. I am working backward out of the room and into the hallway.

I allow the composition tile to set overnight. What remains now are the tiles to be installed around the perimeter of the room and at the tub.

First I place a full tile directly on top of a tile adjacent to the wall.

I place a second tile on top of the first, with one of its sides butting the wall.

Using a sheetrock knife, I score the first tile by running the knife along the side of the second tile, the side opposite the wall.

I bend the first tile along the score mark. The pieces will usually separate along the scored line, but if necessary I bend it again to do this.

The portion of the lower tile that was exposed will fit into the remaining gap between the wall and the tile previously glued.

I check the width between tiles and wall at various places in the bathroom. They should all be identical.

I count up the number of cut tiles I'll need and, using the first as a model, score and cut them.

I spread Mastic and set the tiles.

Around the tub, I use the same method for marking and cutting those tiles.

Around the brass ring I cut by eye, since the tolerance is large.

Composition baseboard is available in the same materials as the floor, with the exception of vinyl asbestos. It is molded into a curve at the bottom edge and is flat for the remainder. It comes in strips often 3 feet long. It is cut with a sheetrock knife.

I spread Mastic on the back of the baseboard strip. I lay it against the wall and on the tile. I butt lengths and go around the bathroom in this way.

Over large areas a heavy roller is rolled over the floor before the tile has set, but this is unnecessary in a small area such as the bathroom.

I cover the joint between the composition tile and the oak in the hallway with a chrome saddle that has a 1/2-inch bend.

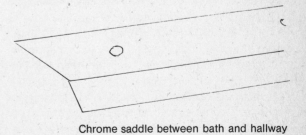

Chrome saddle between bath and hallway

167

I cut the saddle to length with a metal-cutting blade in the sabre saw.

The flat portion of the saddle lies on the oak. Holes have been drilled in it and twist nails provided for attachment. I nail through the holes into the oak. The tapered side lies on the tiles.

Ceramic Tile Floor

Ceramic tile is by far a better material for the bathroom floor. It is likely to cost about 60 cents per square foot. Since the area to be covered is small, the use of better and more expensive tiles should be considered.

There are two methods of installation.

One is to prepare the floor in the same way as was done for the composition tile, with tar paper and 1/4-inch exterior plywood.

If the tiles are 2 inches or larger, I divide the room into quadrants and work outward.

If the tile is less than 2 inches, I begin in a corner of the exterior wall.

In both cases, I use a notched trowel to spread ceramic tile *floor* adhesive.

The smaller-sized tiles are usually made with a backing of paper and mesh which holds individual tiles together to form a sheet 1 foot square. The mesh allows the glue to make contact with the underside of the tile.

In laying the sheet on the Mastic, I move entire rows rather than individual tiles, since this avoids creating excessive waviness of each row. I use the side of a long square-edged trowel to straighten the individual tiles.

I leave gaps between sheets equivalent to the gaps between individual tiles.

When less than the width of a tile remains to the baseboard tile previously installed when doing the walls, I cut the tiles to the necessary width by means of nippers. The tile is placed between the jaws at the desired width and then the handles are squeezed. The sharp ends of the jaws break the tile at the point where they have clamped it.

I allow the Mastic to dry overnight and the tiles to set.

I mix three pounds of grout, a handful of fine sand, and water to form a loose runny mixture. I spread this and press it between tiles with a rubber float. The joints between tiles are quite small and the runny, watery mixture is necessary in order to ensure that it flows down between the tiles and that enough of it is present to form a stable joint.

I allow the grout to set for half an hour or so, then wipe off the excess with a large sponge, rinsing it in clear water frequently to remove the excess. I repeat a half hour or so later.

The next morning I remove the film of grout that lies over the tile with a damp cloth.

I prefer ordinary cement and fine sand as the fill between tiles to grout. It is cheaper and tougher and stands up better.

When it is necessary to remove portions of the sheet of tiles, I do so by cutting the backing with a sheetrock knife.

The backing itself can be removed if need be by soaking the tile sheet in water.

A superior method of installing the same ceramic tile, requiring a bit more skill and labor, involves a masonry underlayment.

I cover the subfloor with tar paper.

I nail wire lath to the subfloor. The lath will not lie perfectly flat, nor do I want it to.

I prepare a mixture of one part Portland cement and three parts of fine sand. I add *only* enough water to dampen it thoroughly. It is important that the sand, cement, and water be thoroughly mixed.

I make a bed of the mixture on the lath that is 1-1/4 inches thick. I screed the bed to establish a level.

I use a very long (3-foot) wooden float to pack and smooth the surface, starting in a band at the exterior wall.

I lay a sheet of tile in a corner, pressing the entire sheet into the concrete so that the mixture rises between the tiles. Only light pressure is needed for this.

I lay a course of sheets at the exterior wall.

I lay the screed board flat on the tiles and tap high spots until I have achieved a flat plane. Again, the pressure of the taps is only light.

In the same manner, I continue to lay parallel sheets, then establish a level plane with the screed board.

I kneel on a 2 x 2-foot square of plywood as I lay the tile and level it. I am working backward toward the door.

I cut tiles at the perimeter and around the tub, etc., with the nippers as I go along.

When I move the square of plyscore back, I fill the depression caused by my weight on it.

I remove the excess concrete that has oozed up in the joints with a sponge as I go along.

I am setting the tiles and grouting in the same operation.

I allow the floor to set for at least twenty-four hours.

I use a chrome saddle to cover the joint between the tile and oak in the hallway.

I place the saddle with the tapered side on the oak, mark the predrilled holes on the tile, and use a 1/8-inch carbide-tipped bit to bore through the tile to the subfloor. I then use aluminum, brass, or chrome screws to fasten down the saddle.

The key to this type of installation is the consistency of the bed. If it is too loose, tiles will sink unevenly and dips and rises in the floor that are impossible to control will result.

If the bed is not properly mixed, adherence of particles will be weak and a solid underlayment will not be achieved. This will of course result in sections of tile giving way, and the concrete will crumble after some use.

The bed must be thoroughly damp and completely mixed. All holes in the bed should be filled and tamped with the float. A smooth surface isn't desirable or necessary, but a level and packed one is essential. This work is all done by eye, and I recommend that it be done only when the possibility that the finished floor may be irregular is accepted.

I do not mean to imply that this method requires some mysterious skill beyond the ability of anyone who has not had vast experience with it. On the contrary, what is needed most of all is an "eye," and if anyone knows that they have this "eye"— the ability to *see* variations in height—this type of installation will not present problems.

A variation of this installation is to prepare the bed in a normal consistency rather than a "dry" one, screed, and use a metal trowel to leave a smooth surface. I allow the concrete to harden at least twenty-four hours.

I then divide the floor into quadrants, spread Mastic, and lay the sheets of tile in the same manner as if the floor had a 1/4-inch exterior-plywood underlayment.

It should be remembered that grouted joints are not at all impervious to water. If an interior plywood is used as an underlayment, the chances are that it will rot out within five years. Exterior plywood should last much longer, although there are many variables, the most important being the quality of the glue that binds the layers of plywood together. Marine plywood is the best and most expensive and can be relied on to last indefinitely as an underlayment. Tempered Masonite is also used. The best underlayment, however, is masonry.

Sanding and Finishing Oak Floors

If unfinished oak is used, the variations in height between boards are removed by sanding.

A floor sander with a coarse closed-coated paper is run first at right angles to the flooring. (This closed face is sufficient for a new floor, but if an old one is being done the first sanding should be done with open-coated paper.)

It is essential that the sander be in forward motion when the drum is lowered to make contact with the floor or gouges will be created. The same thing is true when the drum is raised. The machine should be moving forward until the sandpaper is no longer making contact with the flooring. Most of the scarring done to floors occurs at these times.

The second step is to use medium-closed grit paper and run the sander parallel to the flooring.

The third and final step is to run the sander parallel to the flooring with fine paper.

(Clarke sanders are best and can be rented at a nominal cost. Sanding this house should take a day.)

While operating the sander, the excess cord should be draped around the shoulders and behind the neck to remove it from the work area.

The better sanders operate on 220 volts; a temporary hook-up can be made at the electric-stove circuit breaker.

The floor sander cannot come close enough to the walls to do this area and an "edger" is employed. This machine sands in a circular motion. It has wheels on the base which help move it along the boards at the walls.

The edger cannot reach into corners; these areas are done by hand with a hook scraper. This hand tool is used by laying the blade on the flooring to be scraped, pressing down with the left hand, and drawing the blade back with the right (which is wrapped around the handle). The blade becomes dull fairly quickly but can be resharpened in a few seconds with a flat file.

Once the floor is sanded and scraped, I vacuum it thoroughly. I mix epoxy glue and sawdust and fill cracks, etc., as needed.

Using a roller and extension handle, I apply a coat of shellac thinned with 10 percent denatured alcohol. On a hot day this will dry in half an hour. If the day is cold and damp I will allow it to dry overnight.

I apply a coat of Gymseal varnish with a roller, allow it to dry for twenty-four hours, then apply a second coat after removing the nap with steel-wool pads on a rotary waxer. Unless the gym seal is high gloss and a dull finish is desired, I do not use wax.

An alternative to this rather old method is to apply a polyurethane coating to the raw oak.

Any cosmetic treatment should be done directly to the raw wood.

Other Methods of Finishing Oak Floors

An old method of treating floors is to wash them with a mop, using a strong solution of lye. If this is done frequently, a gray driftwoodlike patina develops. It makes a particularly attractive floor and of course doesn't require polyurethane or varnish, and the only maintenance is the mopping.

This treatment has the disadvantage of not sealing the surface of the wood and there is consequently no protection against staining. Ship decks were formerly treated in a similar manner.

The unfinished oak floor can also be stained with a whitener such as Firzite, then polyurethaned.

ADDITIONAL INFORMATION

Flooring may be obtained in the plank form in widths greater than 4 inches and at times even as wide as 18 inches, though 7 and 8 inches are most common.

The problem with these wide planks is that cupping (becoming concave) cannot be prevented unless there is some means of securing the planks across their relatively wide width. This is done by drilling holes, screwing down the plank to the subfloor, then covering the screws with plugs cut from the same wood or from another for contrast.

Because of the greater width, it is also more difficult to align the sides of successive boards, and even slight curvatures are difficult to eliminate. The wedge device works best for this but it is time-consuming to set up the wedge at every variation and draw the plank to the one previously installed.

The planks may be face-nailed at 16 inches o.c. If this is done, in order to avoid rust and staining when the floor is later cleaned, it is advisable to use aluminum nails of the flooring or horseshoe type.

I would not suggest that face-nailing be done when using expensive hardwood plank flooring but would limit this installation to the harder variety of pine planks and some special types of fir flooring.

Although vinyl tile is available in a staggering variety of shapes, colors, and designs, I do not recommend its use for any purpose, especially as a floor covering. It is outrageously priced, scratches easily, absorbs dirt and stains, and is simply not an adequate surface for a floor because of its susceptibility to surface damage.

If economy and the ability to withstand hard use are the prime considerations, vinyl asbestos has to be the choice. Unfortunately the colors, designs, and shapes of these tiles are rather unattractive and choices are most limited.

Vinyl asbestos tiles are brittle, especially in cold weather. If they are being installed in a cold room, they should be warmed by passing them across the flame of a butane torch before setting.

They are also difficult to score with a sheet rock knife. A manually operated cutting machine similar to the asbestos shingle-cutter should be used. The supplier of the tile will most likely make this tool available.

Vinyl asbestos tiles are most appropriate over concrete floors.

Larger ceramic floor tiles come as individual pieces rather than on backed sheets. Floor adhesive is used instead of wall adhesive. Their installation is essentially the same as wall tile. They are cut in the same manner, either with the tile cutter or a composition blade on the Skil saw.

Some tiles are produced with a glaze that makes them waterproof and stain-proof. However, many are unglazed and porous. These will absorb foreign material and stain easily. Unfortunately, some of the most attractive tiles such as the French provincial type, clay-colored hexagonals, suffer from this disadvantage. Many "sealer" products which assert their ability to provide a protective coating are on the market. These are clear liquids which are brushed onto the tiles and grout and presumably create an impenetrable film. My experience with them has been that with ordinary use they whiten and flake off within a few weeks or a month and leave an ugly surface. If unglazed tile is used, I recommend it be left as is.

The width of the joints between floor tiles is arbitrary. If hexagonal shapes are used, I would make these joints at least 3/16 inch, since the tiles themselves are not uniform in size and if the joints are made very narrow there is a likelihood that some of the tiles will be too large for their respective areas and trimming them can be time-consuming.

This variation in size is particularly true of the Italian and Mexican floor tiles. American tiles are much more uniform on the whole, with smaller tolerances.

Like all wood products, flooring has risen sharply in price and is likely to go even higher. Tile, on the other hand, while having risen, has not gone up as steeply—nor is it likely to do so, since the basic cost involved in producing it is incredibly small compared to its retail price.

Ceramic tile, at 50 cents to the square foot (cheapest), is certainly an alternative to wood in areas other than the bathroom and kitchen and should be considered for other rooms.

There are a variety of floor coverings such as 9 x 9-inch walnut-faced tiles which are glued to the subfloor much as composition tiles are. They are available in many hardwoods and can be laid in a parquet style, etc. They make an attractive floor.

They have the disadvantage of being 3/8 inch or so thin, which leaves little allowance for possible sanding and refinishing. They are also incredibly overpriced, so much so that very often standard flooring in the same hardwood as the tile can be bought for less money.

Slate is an excellent floor covering. It is of course durable and requires no more maintenance than an occasional mopping for cleanliness. It costs about 60 cents per square foot and up and is installed in the same manner as ceramic tile in a concrete bed. (I make the consistency of the bed somewhat looser than the sheet-tile underlayment.)

I would avoid the use of wax on wooden floors. It creates a perpetual maintenance problem and does nothing for the wood despite all the assertions to the contrary by wax manufacturers. This is particularly true with the polyurethane finishes.

The original purpose of the wax was to reduce the shine of high-gloss varnish, which was esthetically displeasing to many people. With the advent of satin varnishes, even this reason is no longer valid. (Incidentally, the same holds true for furniture.)

If the surface of the floor is scratched, I rub in a bit of lemon oil, which will hide it.

19

The purpose of trim is to hide joints between adjoining surfaces and avoid the time-consuming work which would be necessary if these surfaces were fitted to each other. Houses have been built without trim, or a minimum of it and the labor costs of these houses are many times an ordinary one. If one doesn't like the appearance of trim (there is a huge variety) and is prepared for more work than is required to build the rest of the house, trim may be eliminated.

At the intersection of the ceiling and walls, a joint is created. The molding to cover it is often referred to as a crown, but this is confusing since crown molding is a specific type rather than a category. This particular trim is better called ceiling molding. These are two simple, inexpensive types in addition to clamshell.

Installing Lattice Ceiling Molding

In order to establish the i.d of the walls at the ceiling, I select two scrap rippings whose length when butted is about half again as long as the room. I stand on a ladder at the center of the room and hold both rippings in my left hand. I extend both outward until their ends butt opposite walls. I then make a pencil mark on either of the rippings at the point where they overlap. This pencil mark now indicates the position of the rippings when they correspond to the i.d.

I square the end of a length of lattice in the miter box with an 8-point hand saw.

I lay the rippings on the lattice so that the end of one is flush with the end of the lattice. I shift the other ripping so that it lies on the pencil mark. I then mark its other end on the lattice and this is the exact length between the walls and at the ceiling.

I saw the lattice in the miter box at the mark.

I start half a dozen 3 finishing nails in the lattice, lay it against the wall and pressed up against the ceiling, and nail.

I use the same technique for all the ceiling molding.

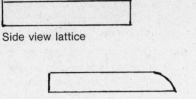

Side view lattice

Side view—clam shell, 3/8x1 3/8-inch

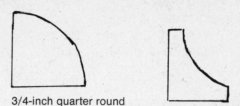

3/4-inch quarter round

End view 3/4x3/4-inch cove molding

Installing Clamshell Trim

I have used clamshell doorstop for ceiling molding fairly often. I establish the overall length in the same manner. However, in the corners, after cutting the first length square at each end, I miter the intersecting trim which gives me the profile of the stop, then cope out this profile with a coping saw.

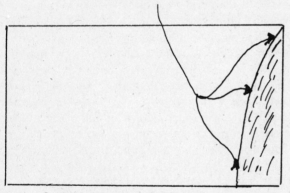

COPE ALONG THIS LINE

Coping profile of clamshell cope along this line

This will usually result in a cleaner joint between the intersecting clamshell molding.

Installing Interior Window Casing

There are of course many types of casing. It is conventional to use the same trim design throughout the house, though this is by no means an absolute law. All serve equally well and the selection should be based on appearance.

The standard width of a window jamb is 4 inches. This allows 3-1/2 inches for the stud behind it and the thickness of the sheathing, which is 1/2 inch. When the window is ordered, unless specified, the width of the jamb will not allow for the thickness of the interior wall covering. It is therefore necessary to extend the width of the jamb an amount which is at least equal to the thickness of the interior wall. The Anderson windows come equipped with extensions for the jambs. These are simply rippings whose width is greater than the thickness of any likely wall covering.

I rip these jamb extensions 1/8 inch wider than the thickness of the wall covering and nail them to the edges of the window jambs. The additional 1/8 inch is to allow for variations in the wall adjacent to the jamb and on which the casing will rest. If the edge of the jamb extends into the room slightly beyond the plane of the wall, there will be no problem of seating the casing. If the jamb is behind the plane of the wall, a gap will be created between the casing and edge of the jamb; if the gap were removed by nailing the casing to the edge of the jamb, the casing would not lie flat on the wall.

The windows we have been using are trimmed out in picture-frame style, simply by nailing four mitered pieces to the edge of the jamb and the wall around the perimeter of the window. Double-hung windows have a "stool" or interior sill and an "apron" directly beneath them (and therefore cannot be trimmed in picture-frame style).

The sides of the four pieces of casing are set back from the inner edge of the jamb 1/8 inch or so, since nailing them flush to the inner edge would cause variations and imperfections in the jamb and casing to be more apparent.

If square-edged casing is used, mitering may be optional and a square cut the simpler alternative.

In either case, I drive 4 finishing nails into the edge of the jamb and 8 finishing nails through the outer face of the casing into the wall and stud behind it.

A good practice is to position the lower casing

member directly under the crank housing of the window in order to give support to it.

I use the same method for positioning the casing as described in the chapter on doors (see pp. 132ff.) and the same method for cutting and installing (see page 142).

Baseboard

The same technique used for installing the ceiling molding is used for the baseboard. The interior corners are coped joints, the exterior corners mitered. I establish lengths with two rippings and use the miter box for cuts. I use 8 finishing nails through the lower half of the baseboard and angle them down to be sure of entering the shoe. Where needed, I drive 3 or 4 finishing nails through the upper half of the baseboard into studs if there are gaps between the wall and top of the baseboard.

I have often used 3/4 x 3/4-inch quarter round as the baseboard. It is of course much cheaper.

The quarter round may be used alone or with clamshell or other baseboards to close the gap between the bottom of the baseboard and the flooring. The main purpose of this additional member is to present an upper rounded surface for ease in cleaning and to avoid dust-catching areas.

The ends of baseboards are butted into the casing around the doors.

The joints at intersections of quarter round are coped as was the clamshell. (This is optional; a simple mitered joint is the alternative.)

ADDITIONAL INFORMATION

Ceiling moldings and baseboards are milled from pine and a variety of hardwoods but not from redwood or cedar, because of their softness. However, redwood and cedar are very common coverings for interior walls and the use of moldings made of the same wood may be desirable. These can be produced on the site at about the same cost as the milled trim. Carbide-tipped bits for the

router which will produce a variety of designs are available. Among these is the rounding-over bit with a 3/4-inch radius. If 1-by-3 or- 4-inch clear cedar or redwood stock is bought, an edge can be milled with the router to produce a profile whose upper portion is in the shape of a quarter round.

1 x 4 cedar milled with 3/4-inch rounding over bit in router

The rounding over may be done by nailing a 2 x 2-foot square of plywood to horses. A 1-inch hole is bored in the center of the plywood, then the router is screwed to the underside of the plywood with the router bit extending upward through the hole. The bit is raised or lowered as needed to produce the rounding over. The stock is then simply fed into the router bit. This arrangement is a quick way of simulating a milling machine. I have milled baseboard for an entire house in this way in less than an hour.

It should be kept in mind that the Stanley router which I have been using, while being adequate for work previously described, is not a milling machine and should not be used as such except when handling softwoods and then not in very great volume. There are more powerful routers which are more appropriate for production work.

An alternative to milling trim of the same wood used for the walls is to buy standard trim and stain it the color of the walls. An oil stain is best for this, but my own luck with this has been poor and other jobs I have seen haven't been much better, though occasionally I have seen excellent results.

When installing the stiles of the kitchen cabinets, molding, etc., I have been using small-headed or finishing nails and many of these remain exposed. My own judgment is that they should be left this way.

An alternative is to drive them below the surface of the wood with the use of a nail set, then fill the hole, wood putty is an adequate filling; it is available in colors similar to the wood used. If painting is projected, this is of course redundant.

AUTHOR'S NOTE

The total cost of materials for this house is around $12,600. This includes $1600 for electrical and plumbing supplies. If more expensive alternative materials are used, the figure could go up quite a bit very quickly. Ten or fifteen costlier items can easily run into thousands of dollars. If less expensive materials were used, a savings of perhaps a thousand dollars could be achieved. On the average, for a moderately priced house, a cost of $10 to $11 per square foot is a realistic figure for materials.

In addition to using inexpensive materials consistently, a significant savings can be achieved through the use of a noncontinuous foundation and similar cost-saving approaches at each step of the process. I have indicated some but a complete discussion of these alternatives is beyond the scope of this book.

This particular house, using the same materials or the equivalents that I have indicated, would have a sale price of between $30,000 and $40,000.

A crew of three experienced people should complete it in eight to ten weeks.

In addition to the materials cost, about $500 must be allocated for essential tools, with about another $300 for necessary ones. A good number of the tools I have described are not truly essential; however, the time and effort involved in doing work without them is so great that the tools pay for themselves in the end.

I have omitted items such as a screen door since I felt that a screen door was much easier to hang than ordinary ones and these had been covered in detail. I omitted closets and several other items for similar reasons.

I have done everything presented in this book many times and have often taught these operations to others. Rarely have I encountered anyone so inept he could not execute a particular piece of work or so dense he could not understand what he was trying to achieve. On the contrary, I have been impressed by the speed and dexterity of people who were fairly distant from the building trades, and I offer this fact as encouragement to those who want to build.

I can appreciate the doubts and hesitations of people who would like to build a house themselves and have little or no experience. It is my hope that this book will help resolve those doubts and that it will become a useful tool in the work that follows.

INDEX